PLANNING
The Irish Experience

By the same author

The Emergence of Irish Planning, 1880-1920
Edited by Michael J. Bannon. (Copies of this volume are available from Wolfhound Press)

PLANNING

The Irish Experience
1920 — 1988

Edited by
MICHAEL J. BANNON

WOLFHOUND PRESS

© 1989 M. J. Bannon and individual contributors

First published 1989 by
WOLFHOUND PRESS,
68 Mountjoy Square,
Dublin 1.

All rights reserved. No part of this book may be reproduced or utilised in any form or by any means, electronic or mechanical, including photography, filming, recording, video recording, photocopying or by any information storage and retrieval system, or otherwise circulated in any form of binding or cover other than that in which it is published, without prior permission in writing from the publisher.

British Library Cataloguing in Publication Data

Planning: the Irish experience
   1. Ireland. Environment.
   I. Bannon, Michael J. (Michael Joseph)
   1940 -
   363.7'3'09145

ISBN 0-86327-211 8 hb
ISBN 0-86327-212-6 pb

Cover design: Jan de Fouw
Typesetting: Redsetter Ltd., Dublin.
Printed by Billings and Sons Ltd.

CONTENTS

	Illustrations	6
	Acknowledgements	7
	Contributors	8
	Introduction	9
Chapter One	Irish Planning from 1921 to 1945: An Overview *Michael J. Bannon*	13
Chapter Two	The Evolution of Irish Planning, 1934-1964 *Kevin I. Nowlan*	71
Chapter Three	Environmental Conservation: Concern and Action, 1920-1970 *Ken Mawhinney*	86
Chapter Four	The Control of Development and the Origins of Planning in Northern Ireland *John Hendry*	105
Chapter Five	Development Planning and the Neglect of the Critical Regional Dimension *Michael J. Bannon*	122
Chapter Six	Epilogue: Environmental and Planning Policies in the 1980s *Michael J. Bannon*	158
	Notes and References	174
	Index	192

LIST OF ILLUSTRATIONS

1.1	Reconstruction Proposals for N.E. Central Dublin	17
1.2	General Scheme of Central Dublin Re-organisation	18/19
1.3	Dublin Civic Survey Map of Bad Housing and Decayed Areas	24
1.4	Cork and the Surrounding Region	27
1.5	Inter-War Housing Layouts: (a) Gurranabraher; (b) Crumlin	30
1.6	Sub-National Units: (a) The Circuit Court Areas); (b) The Emergency (Planning) Regions	37
1.7	Local Dublin Developments: (a) The Blue Lagoon Scheme; (b) Redevelopment Proposals for Gloucester St Area	45
1.8	Regional Scheme for Cork Area	50
1.9	Abercrombie's Sketch Proposals	55
1.10	Corporation Scheme of Peripheral Expansion	56
2.1	Planning Authorities which passed resolutions to adopt the Town and Regional Planning Act (1934) up to 1959	80
2.2	Dublin Sketch Development Plan: Metropolitan Area	81
3.1	Sites of Scientific Interest in Ireland	101
4.1	Northern Ireland Development Proposals: (a) The Belfast Regional Survey, 1964; (b) Development Programme 1970-75; (c) The District Towns: Development Strategy, 1975-95.	116
4.2	Road Proposals for Central Belfast: (a) Belfast Urban Motorway Proposals (after B.D.P. 1969) (b) Belfast Road Proposals (Review of Transportation Strategy 1977)	118
5.1	Settlement Hierarchy for Limerick Region	142
5.2	National Development Strategy: (a) Buchanan's Proposed Growth Centres; (b) Industrial Locations	146 / 147
5.3	Proposals for Ministry of Regional Development	149
5.4	Development Strategy for the Dublin Area: (a) Myles Wright 1967; (b) Dublin Co. Council Development Plan Strategy	151
5.5	Regional Strategies: Urban Structure; (a) Development Startegy for the Midlands Region, 1981, (b) Donegal — Leitrim — Sligo Regional Strategy, 1987	153
5.6	Regions for Programmes for E.C. Funding	156
6.1	The Proposed Wicklow Mountains National Park	161
6.2	Dublin's Inner City	167
6.3	The Custom House Docks Development	169
6.4	Recommended Settlement Strategy to 2001, Dublin Sub-Region	172

ACKNOWLEDGEMENTS

The contributors to this volume have been engaged in the study and practice of Irish planning over a great many years. During that time they have received the assistance and support of many individuals and organisations, too numerous to mention.

Publication of this book, together with the earlier volume on *The Emergence of Irish Planning, 1880-1920*, has been made possible through the generous support of the following individuals and institutions:

Environment Awareness Bureau
Foras Forbartha Teo
Commission of the European Communities (Irish Office)
Institute of Irish Studies
Irish Planning Institute
Fergal MacCabe, Planning Consultant
Planning History Group
Resource and Environmental Policy Centre, U.C.D.
Royal Town Planning Institute, Irish Branch
Society of Chartered Surveyors in the Republic of
   Ireland (Planning and Development Division)
University College Dublin, Publications Committee

On behalf of the contributors and on his own behalf the editor acknowledges the assistance received from Mary Clark, the Dublin City Archivist, from the staff of the National Library and from Paula Howard of Pearse Street Public Library during the researching of this volume. To the staff of the U.C.D. library at Richview, especially Mrs. Kelly, a very special thank you. The editor is particularly grateful for the help received from Gordon Aston, Mrs. Rita Childers, Mrs. Patricia Gibney, Mrs. Pamela Durdin-Robertson and Commander Peter Young of the Department of Defence. The maps in the text have been reproduced with the kind permission of the Ordnance Survey and the assistance of the National Library of Ireland in the preparation of many of the illustrations is gratefully acknowledged. To Eddie Buckmaster who drew a number of the maps and to Gerry Hayden who prepared many of the illustrations a special word of thanks. The assistance of these and all who helped the contributors is gratefully acknowledged.

CONTRIBUTORS

MICHAEL J. BANNON was educated at University College, Dublin, the University of Alberta (Edmonton) and Dublin University, where he was awarded a Ph.D. in 1972. He has been engaged in Irish planning research, education and practice since 1967; he was a member of the team which produced *Regional Studies in Ireland*. While working with An Foras Forbartha he initiated a major research programme on the development of office activities in Ireland. He joined the staff of the Planning School in U.C.D. in 1974 where he offers courses in Planning History and Regional Development. He has also acted as consultant to a large number of Irish and international public agencies engaged in development and planning.

KEVIN NOWLAN, an Engineer, Barrister and a Fellow of the Royal Town Planning Institute, has worked in numerous Local Authorities including Dublin County and Dublin Corporation, where he served as Deputy Planning Officer. He was a member of staff of the Department of Local Government in the early 1960s and was closely involved in the formulation of the Local Government (Planning and Development) Bill, 1962. He joined University College in 1966 as a Lecturer in Town Planning where under his guidance a Department of Town Planning was established and he became the first Professor of Regional and Urban Planninng. He is author of *A Guide to the Planning Acts*, and *A Guide to Planning Legislation in the Republic of Ireland*.

JOHN HENDRY, an architect and planner, has had many years experience working in Sweden, Canada, Southern Rhodesia, Britain and Northern Ireland. He joined the Department of Town and Country Planning in Queen's University in 1966 and has been Professor and Head of Department since 1983. He has been involved in a wide ranging research programme into Northern Ireland's housing and planning development and he has produced a number of articles on the evolution of physical planning policy for Belfast and Northern Ireland.

KEN MAWHINNEY, graduated in geography from Queen's University, Belfast, and after post-graduate study in Canada, worked as a planner with the Government of Northern Ireland. In 1966 he joined An Foras Forbartha where he has undertaken research and advisory work in aspects of planning relating to recreation, amenity and conservation. He was General Editor of the National Heritage Inventory and Manager of the Conservation and Amenity Advisory Service to local authorities. In 1987-88 he was Director of the Environment Awareness Bureau and organised Ireland's contribution to the European Year of the Environment. He is a past chairman of the Royal Town Planning Institute, Irish Branch – Southern Section.

INTRODUCTION

This book examines the gradual evolution of Irish environmental planning from 1920 up to the 1980s. As in the case of *The Emergence of Irish Planning*, this book is based upon a wide use of original material and, for the first time, presents a detailed record of the achievements and the difficulties associated with Irish planning experience.

The vibrant and internationally led town planning movement which flowered in Dublin from 1911 to 1914, and which has been documented in *The Emergence of Irish Planning*, was to have a continuing but limited influence in the 1920s and 1930s. The early town planning movement was essentially a Dublin phenomenon, highly dependent upon a political élite which was soon to be rejected. Following the establishment of a Dublin government and a Northern Ireland administration, planning had to relate to more modest civic objectives and it also had to adopt an approach applicable to areas and to towns outside Dublin. Against a backdrop of a war of independence followed by political subdivision of the island and a bloody civil war, politicians were more concerned with problems of survival than with issues of long-term national planning. Particularly in the case of the Irish Free State, an inherited legacy of social problems, limited resources and changing economic policies made it difficult to adhere to any long term strategy or to contemplate taking such a strategy on board. In both the Free State and Northern Ireland, power largely rested in the hands of rural politicians, many of whom had little commmitment to the solution of urban issues and problems.

The study of Irish planning history before 1960 illustrates the close parallels in the experiences of both parts of the island and the sharp contrast of these approaches with the British commitment to a detailed form of planning regulation and control. Neither in Stormont nor in Dublin was there evidence of a strong commitment to planning at central government level. In so far as planning existed it was largely permissive and all too often illustrates the folly of seeking to solve Irish problems through the replication of schemes and policies formulated in an entirely different political milieu. This is especially true in respect of attempts to formulate relevant planning law; repeatedly, throughout the years 1910 to

1960, Irish legislators were advised by domestic and foreign advisers to formulate 'legislation . . . of a kind to suit our particular needs' and not to slavishly copy English legislation. Yet the record, North and South, has been of a failure to formulate planning law and practice relevant to the needs of a relatively underdeveloped, strongly rural and highly individualistic society. The outstanding exception to this generalisation was the formulation of the National Planning Conference in 1942 — an island-wide group of committed representatives from rural and urban backgrounds and including both professional and voluntary interests.

In both parts of Ireland environmental planning remained a non-issue until the 1960s when, suddenly, commitment to planned development became an integral part of public policy. The 1960s political commitment to a new role for planning was dependent upon the recognised intimate interrelationship between economic and physical planning; planning flourished within a context of administrations characterised by new and dynamic leaderships pursuing vigorous policies of economic and industrial expansion and growth. In a few years Ireland appeared to offer a model of integrated physical and economic planning which could have relevance to Third World and other less developed and post-colonial societies.

Unfortunately the 1960s renaissance in commitment to environmental planning was based on insecure foundations with an over-dependence on the success of economic planning, the implementation of an agreed national development strategy and the introduction of a succession of reforms in local administrations enabling them to function as development corporations. There was also a potential source of conflict between the political commitment to physical planning as an aid to economic expansion and the planning profession, charged with implementing planning legislation, which derived much of its inspiration from the design professions and which all too often saw planning as a regulator. In any case, the dream of an integrated approach to economic and physical planning was short-lived and the 1970s witnessed both a political disenchantment with planning and an increased emphasis on control functions with a corresponding abandonment of its developmental role.

The Irish planning experience since 1920 has relevance both for the future of Irish planning and for planning advances in other less developed societies. A study of this period shows that planning must prove sensitive to the political tempo of the era; it must also prove relevant to the solution of the major economic and social ills of the society if it is to have a significant role in public policy. But above all else, planning thought, legislation or procedures cannot be successfully imported; they must be developed indigenously, drawing widely on the best available international experience. Finally, as Ireland and most other countries face periods of slow growth and as the planning profession turns its attention to problem areas, such as the inner city, the philosophy of Irish planning can have a continuing relevance both at home and abroad.

The six chapters in this volume deal with the Irish planning experience in largely chronological order. Thus, Michael Bannon, with the use of official records and published material, provides an outline of the evolution of planning from 1920 to 1945. While this chapter highlights the 'inevitability of gradualness', a good deal was achieved and the basis for a 1960s style of 'development planning' was emerging. Kevin Nowlan looks in detail at the legal basis of planning, in particular the Town and Regional Planning Acts of 1934 and 1939. He suggests that in some ways the 1934 Act was superior to the 1960s legislation and that the 1934 Act could have served Ireland well, if there had been the requisite political will to implement it. Ken Mawhinney in Chapter Three reminds the reader of the necessity to adopt a broad view of planning. In this chapter he traces the gradual build-up of para planning and environmental conservation legislation and policies from 1920 to 1970. This chapter also documents the growth of an Irish tourism policy and its relationship to national development policies and planning issues.

In Chapter Four on 'The Control of development and The Origins of Planning in Northern Ireland' John Hendry provides an outline of the evolution of planning in Northern Ireland from 1930 to the 1980s. This fifty-year experience is rather reminiscent of that south of the border, and his conclusion that the form and function of planning must be tailored to the local political system and context has a relevance for all of Ireland, North and South. Chapter Five by Michael Bannon documents the story of 'Development Planning and the Neglect of the Critical Regional Dimension', and seeks to evluate both its successes and the reasons why the high expectations of the early 1960s proved unrealistic. In the absence of either a grand strategy for development or a National Plan, Chapter Six documents the shift of emphasis towards local scale developments, including urban renewal, rehabilitation and community development.

Finally, this book should be read in conjunction with *The Emergence of Irish Planning, 1880-1920*; in particular Arnold Horner's chapter in that volume dealing with the continued growth of

Dublin, alongside a repeated failure to modernize institutions or reform local government, is in many respects a microcosm of the wider failure to grasp at opportunities and to maximise Ireland's resources. In many respects *Planning: The Irish Experience*, should be regarded as an introductory exploration of an important domain of public policy. The findings of these chapters show the extent to which dimensions of physical planning policy impinge upon almost all facets of public policy and in turn affect many aspects of the private domain. As such, planning might usefully be viewed as a Cabinet rather than a departmental issue.

This book highlights the wealth of largely untapped records relating to all aspects of development policy. Almost all of the issues touched upon in this book merit further in-depth research, research that can only proceed if greater attention is given to compiling official records, especially in the case of the Department of the Environment. In addition, private firms must be encouraged either to retain their records or to ensure that valuable historical material is lodged with the Irish Architectural Archive, the universities or other relevant national institutions and made available to researchers. Only through such research can Ireland formulate the type of public policy relevant to its own needs.

CHAPTER ONE

IRISH PLANNING FROM 1921 TO 1945 AN OVERVIEW

Michael J. Bannon

In as much as physical planning implies a commitment to the orderly, long-term development of the physical landscape, Ireland, in the years between the two World Wars, provided a difficult and often hostile environment for the success of any such ideal. The trauma and destruction of a war of independence, resulting in the political division of the country, followed by a civil war in the Irish Free State, all concentrated the minds of political leaders primarily on the immediate questions of survival. In the case of the Free State, an inherited legacy of chronic unemployment and serious urban housing problems was to tax the energies and drain the limited resources of the state for half a century. In both parts of the island, many of the new political élite came from a rural background and had little sympathy with a movement committed to any form of urban development. In addition, the dramatic variations in economic policy experienced in the 1920s and 1930s — from free trade to limited quotas to intense protectionism — provided an unsuitable framework for consistent or national physical planning.

Nevertheless, there existed many and persistent voices championing the cause of planning. The activities of Patrick Geddes in Dublin prior to 1916 were to inspire the members of the Civics Institute of Ireland and to bear fruit through the Civic Surveys and other activities in the 1920s. Ironically, the destruction of Dublin in 1916-1922 was to prove a catalyst for the advancement of planning as the Dublin Reconstruction Movement sought the orderly redevelopment of the city. It was widely recognised that the solution of Dublin's working-class housing problems called for social approaches to site and location planning; in turn, the administrative reform of the Dublin area called for a regional planning approach. The cause of planning, social reform and the protection of the heritage was championed by the small Labour Party and especially by its leader, Thomas Johnson. Irish planning continued to benefit from external planning influences. Raymond Unwin and Patrick Abercrombie had a continuing association with Dublin, while W. Davidge was deeply involved in formulating proposals for Belfast and Northern Ireland. Inevitably, these influences inspired the reproduction in Ireland of planning theories and solutions translated from foreign and very different situations. On a more positive note, just as Geddes had inspired Horace O'Rourke, Unwin and Abercrombie were to stimulate Manning Robertson, who worked unceasingly for the advancement of Irish planning from 1927 until his untimely death in 1945.

The study of the tortuous evolution of Irish planning in this period is of considerable relevance in the present era of limited growth and scarce public resources. Study of this period is also an object lesson in the futility of importing theories from abroad and seeking to impose solutions which are not tailored either to local resources, requirements or realities. While few if any major plans were to be adopted, the absorption of planning standards, principles and proposals in new developments did have a direct benefit in terms of both urban arrangements and housing layouts. Likewise, planning theories were to influence strongly the strategic deliberations of those concerned with local government and housing reform. Above all, there was a desire to create a widely based planning movement commanding the support of all sections of both urban and rural society.

The Redevelopment of Central Dublin

As has been documented in *The Emergence of Irish Planning*, central Dublin presented in the early 20th century an unsavoury mixture of social and physical problems: a large impoverished and unemployed population living in overcrowded tenements, a city with an obsolete building stock, widespread dereliction and serious problems of traffic congestion. To these was added the war-time destruction of many of the public buildings and much of the area around O'Connell Street. Although such destruction offered an unexpected opportunity to replan Dublin, it posed additional problems for a new government requiring accommodation for its parliament and offices and desirous of making Dublin a fitting capital of the new state, while ensuring that priority was given to the urban working class housing problems. Dublin once again became the primary focus of planning debate and activity.

While there was universal condemnation of the destruction of central Dublin during the Rising in 1916, the *Irish Builder and Engineer* believed that through the destruction 'a unique and unexpected opportunity is afforded for putting into practice the true principles of town planning'.[1] In any event, the reconstruction required the enactment of special legislation — The Dublin Reconstruction (Emergency Provisions) Act, 1916 – and Mervyn Miller has detailed the role of Raymond Unwin in obtaining the co-operation of the various interests in support of this legislation.[2] The 1916 Act[3] had three main objectives:

(a) Design control of rebuilding by means of a requirement whereby the City Architect was empowered to examine, modify or if necessary reject redevelopment proposals,

(b) To enable the acquisition of land for street widening and the acquisition of derelict sites when building had not commenced within two years of the passage of legislation,

(c) To enable the making of loans towards rebuilding by the Local Government Board.

A broadly similar piece of legislation was promoted in 1922 by Dublin Corporation to cover areas devastated by the Civil War and to improve the powers in the original Act relating to the acquisition of derelict property which had proved unworkable.[4] The Dublin Reconstruction (Emergency Provisions) Act, 1924, enabled the Corporation to deal with derelict sites through a process of acquisition and sale of interests in a site with the provision for the erection of suitable buildings within two years. The special Reconstruction Committee of Dublin Corporation assumed responsibility for the rebuilding and from 1916 onwards they had the support and assistance of an advisory committee of Dublin architects and of Raymond Unwin.[5] There is considerable evidence to show that the Corporation Committee wished to adopt a more confined remit than their advisors[6] and in the end the Corporation confined itself to the widening of part of North Earl Street, the laying out of Sean MacDermott Street Upper and the control of building design, particularly in O'Connell Street. Influenced by Unwin and Abercrombie, O'Rourke produced composite designs for O'Connell Street and avoided the type of uniform imposed frontages suggested by the Royal Irish Academy and sketched by Professor Scott in 1916.[7] The Corporation availed of the design expertise of many prominent architects and planners, including Abercrombie,[8] whose views were readily adopted by Horace O'Rourke. By December 1923 the Corporation had made advances of almost £60,000 in respect of rebuilding, but reconstruction was to continue at a slow pace throughout the 1920s.

In addition to the devastated streets, the destruction of Butt Bridge was to aggravate further a serious traffic circulation problem.[9] At the same time, virtually all the major public buildings were in a ruinous state, creating an acute accommodation problem for the new Irish Government and making Dublin a quite unattractive environment for the new national administration. On top of this there was a legacy of unfit housing, tenements and derelict sites.

Taking advantage of the opportunities and possibilities offered by these challenges, the Greater Dublin Reconstruction Movement set to work on a comprehensive solution, believing that:

> Young Dublin — Young Ireland — literally overflows today with energy and ambition. You can then take your part in directing that energy and that ambition from violence and destruction to the noble conception of building up a greater and a better city — at once the symbol and the centre of the new Ireland.[10]

The Movement included E. A. Aston, Wm. Purcell O'Neill, Lady Aberdeen and Frank Mears who was employed on a number of schemes in Dublin in the early 1920s.[11] But its motive force was Aston who had 'a very strong committee of all sorts, including Senators and Deputies'.[12] The principal proposals of the Movement were announced in a lecture by Aston to the Engineering and Scientific Association of Ireland in December 1922 and published as *Greater Dublin: Reconstruction Scheme Described and Illustrated*. The proposals were exhibited in the Mansion House from January 1 to 12 and they received 'the general approval of the Government' from the Governor General, Mr Healy and the Minister for Local Government and Public Health, Ernest Blythe.[13] Some months later detailed proposals were produced for the improvement of the north-eastern part of the central area.[14] These publications outlined the general nature of the reforms and improvements which were required, including local government, housing, circulation, use of public buildings and the strengthening of the financial base of the city. The Movement's report repeated the calls for the amalgamation of the various existing local councils — 'one problem! one authority'.[15] The necessity of municipal reform was viewed as inevitable since 'the forces of municipal progress must find an opening in one direction or the other'.[16]

The report stressed the continued necessity of massive effort in the field of working class housing: 'the need is desperate; the money is available,' as Aston argued to the press.[17] Aston had also floated a notion of continuing relevance when he called for the 'abolition of the existing railway line from Harcourt Street to Bray and its use as an extension of the electric tramway system, so providing a means to develop the magnificent building sites which lie along the route from Dundrum to Shankill'.[18]

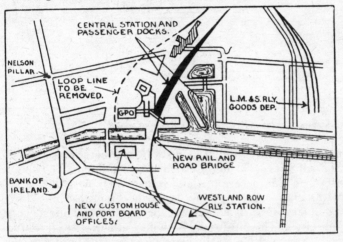

Fig. 1.1 Reconstruction Proposals for N.E. Central Dublin. (Source: *Illustrated Review*).

In relation to transport improvements, the most important was the suggestion to remove the loop line and to replace it with a new road and rail bridge just east of the renovated Custom House (Fig. 1.1). Amiens Street Station would be extended southwards and enlarged into a central railway station adjacent to new docks to be used for cross-channel passenger traffic. Complementing this, the Custom House would become the new GPO, and plans were prepared showing a majestic neo-classical Central Station building alongside the Custom House and terminating the view along Abbey Street from O'Connell Street[19] (Fig. 1.2).

The change of use of the Custom House was one of the many changes proposed. Thus the legal functions would remain in the Castle where they had moved following the destruction of the Four Courts, and with which move the legal profession was said to be well satisfied.[20] In turn, the restored Four Courts would be used as

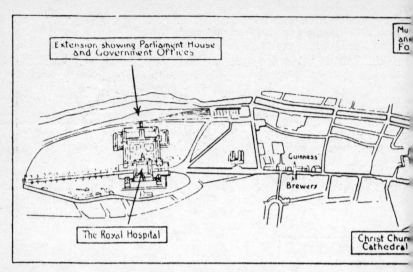

Fig. 1.2 General Scheme of Central Dublin Re-organisation.

an art gallery and the City Hall would be housed in the former GPO on O'Connell Street. The new Catholic Cathedral remained under discussion; on this occasion a site immediately east of Christchurch was chosen for a gothic design by Frank Mears, which would complement Christchurch and 'be visible from almost every part of the city'.[21] This site for the Catholic Cathedral was favoured by Lady Aberdeen although she had a more practical proposal for the handing over of Christchurch to the Catholics before the Episcopalians 'have to sell it from poverty'.[22]

But the greatest interest focused upon the location, temporary or permanent, of a home for the houses of the Oireachtas. There was a strong lobby which favoured, on historical grounds, the use of the old Parliament Buildings in College Green. Cosgrave, the President of the Executive, countered that he doubted 'whether the old Parliament House, College Green, would be found convenient for the needs of a modern parliament'.[23] Cosgrave also feared that a move to College Green would take five years and cost up to £2 million. The Greater Dublin Reconstruction Movement favoured housing the Oireachtas in an enlarged Royal Hospital at Kilmainham, both for the civic and national reasons. The Chairman of the Movement, Senator James Moran, put the case for Kilmainham forcefully:

From the civic point of view the argument for Kilmainham is over-

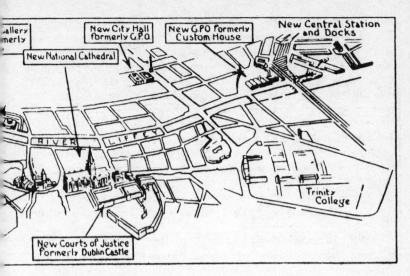

(Source: *Illustrated Review*).

whelming. During the last century Dublin has grown eastwards towards the deepwater harbour and south-eastwards to the sea. The 'west end' with all its natural beauties, has consequently fallen into decay. With the Parliament and Government offices at Kilmainham the social and commercial life of Dublin would quickly and naturally revive.[24]

In addition, an improved route through the historic city would make the site accessible and improve access to the city from the west. Cosgrave strongly favoured the Kilmainham site, for which plans had been prepared, and on 24 January 1924 he proposed that immediate steps be taken to have the buildings of the Royal Hospital, Kilmainham, made available for the temporary accommodation of the Oireachtas.[25]

In the event, doubts had been raised about the distance of Kilmainham from the city[26] and a joint Committee of the Dáil and Senate rejected Kilmainham on grounds of its poor access and the high costs of refurbishment.[27] Instead they recommended that the Oireachtas should continue in Leinster House on a temporary basis.[28] Leinster House, initially loaned by the Royal Dublin Society for use by the Government, was purchased in 1924 for £68,000,[29] thus cancelling out an essential ingredient in the rearrangement of a new city structure.

The other major component in the Reconstruction Movement's

plans for Dublin was the enlargement of the port and the translation of the Cattle Market to the harbour area.[30] The Movement's plans, which represented a bold approach to the replanning of the capital city, were presented to Dublin Corporation in 1923[31] and the Movement's work was described in the *Irish Builder and Engineer* as being 'of very great interest and importance'.[32] Nevertheless, the publication of these proposals revealed a sharp conflict with Professor Abercrombie, whose competition designs of 1916 were about to be published.[33] Unlike Abercrombie, the Reconstruction Movement believed that 'the real Civic Centre of Dublin is ready made at O'Connell Bridge and 20 Abercrombies cannot move it'.[34] Abercrombie's proposals had been criticised as prohibitively expensive; he was referred to as 'a very fine chap for the commercial industrial Midlands of England but he doesn't understand Dublin a little bit'.[35]

Somewhat ironically, Abercrombie rounded on the Reconstruction Movement for having attempted to make proposals in advance of a Civic Survey.[36] While praising the initiative of the Movement, and in particular the industry of Aston, the *Irish Builder* alluded to the fact 'that movement has drawn considerable criticism upon some of its methods and proposals. As, for instance, in relation to the question of a Civic Survey and the future use of certain public buildings'.[37] This note of caution was echoed by President Cosgrave who, while praising the work of the movement, spoke of the 'many points of difference on some subjects and matters....'[38] The President concluded his letter on a positive but vague note:

> The existence of your movement and of similar bodies is proof that many are alive to the need for definition of some at least of our Capital's problems, and the findings of such associations when duly recorded, must surely prove advantageous to the community of this city and to the nation.[39]

In making particular proposals in advance of a Civic Survey, the Movement exposed itself to criticism. In relation to the location of public functions, the same conservatism that supported the reconstruction was likely to also favour a return to the previous use as well. In the case of a home for the Oireachtas, Leinster House was available and relatively inexpensive. Being near the city centre, the location was convenient and it was adjacent to the Government Buildings begun in Merrion Street in 1913. Although the Railway Commission had heard proposals from the Board of Works favouring a central station and was sympathetic to the idea, the Commission concluded that 'we have not sufficient materials before us to judge whether such a plan is advisable or feasible at present or in the near future'.⁴⁰

In the end, little of the proposals of the Reconstruction Movement was implemented. But by the discussion of such large-scale changes in the Dublin environment they rekindled in the public consciousness a recognition that development proposals should conform to a plan which was derived from a thorough Civic Survey.

The Civic Surveys

As early as 1909 Unwin's classic textbook, *Town Planning in Practice,* had highlighted the duality of approaches to the preparation of planning proposals. Unwin contrasted the value of the two:

> The fancies of the man who can only work when his mind is free from consideration of conditions are likely to be of little value, while the work of the one, who lacking in flights of genius, is yet able to grasp and provide for the needs of the case, will at least be safe and serviceable.⁴¹

The importance of basing a town plan upon a comprehensive survey was quickly recognised as professionals and practitioners accepted the logic of the Geddesian paradigm: Survey to Analysis to Plan. From his first arrival in Dublin Geddes emphasised the necessity of embarking uon the task of compiling a Civic Survey.⁴² In his evidence to the Housing Inquiry in 1913 Geddes stressed the importance of having adequate survey material, particularly along the lines of Charles Booth's 'Survey of London' and Roantree's 'Survey of York'.⁴³ The Geddesian emphasis upon the importance of a Civic Survey for Dublin was quickly accepted. Thus, the memorandum added by J. F. McCabe of the Local Government Board to the Report of the Housing Inquiry went so far as to state that 'if even the areas which have already been acquired are built upon before a Civic Survey is completed, I shall look upon it as a grave misfortune'.⁴⁴ The Housing and Town Planning Association encouraged the preparation of civic surveys for all Irish towns preparatory to the making of town plans and in 1914 the Dublin Summer School of Civics had included a symposium on 'The Dublin Survey'.⁴⁵ The mass of proposals elicited by the Dublin Town Planning Competition, and the adjudicators' praise for the Report submitted by Ashbee and Chettle with 'its appeal for Civic Survey, and its lucid indications towards this', served to highlight the importance of basing any plan upon a thorough survey.⁴⁶ In calling for a Dublin Town Planning Commission, Brady, in 1917, saw 'the establishment of a permanent Civic Survey' as one of its most important tasks.[47]

But it was not until a return to peaceful conditions in 1923, and in the face of precipitate proposals, that the idea of a comprehensive Dublin Survey took firm root. The idea was formally proposed by George F. Beckett of the Civics Institute of Ireland on 15 December 1922,[48] and Abercrombie was invited to lecture on 'Civic Studies' to the Dublin Rotary Club in February 1923.[49] A twenty-two member Civic Survey Committee, drawn from the professions, the Civics Institute of Ireland, the voluntary associations and the local authorities was set up on 5 March 1923, although it is repeatedly evident that the driving force behind the whole enterprise was the Committee's Chairman, Horace T. O'Rourke, 'the keen and earnest City Architect of Dublin'.[50]

As well as obtaining the joint support of a large number of civic-minded organisations, O'Rourke sought a wide measure of popular support and public commitment for the Survey. Thus, in a letter to the *Irish Builder and Engineer* he outlined the contents and purpose of the Survey. For him 'a Civic Survey is the representation of things as they are in a community, and the resultant Town Plan is the representation of what they should be'.[51] O'Rourke went on to point out that the success of such a venture was dependent upon the assistance rendered by the public in assembling information. O'Rourke also prepared an explanatory booklet in which he defined the purpose of the Survey, outlining the major problems of Dublin, and in which he pointed to the educational role of such surveys as 'the best education a local community could have'.[52] Throughout 1923 and 1924 O'Rourke kept up a barrage of publicity encouraging support for the Civic Survey and stressing its vital practicability to the development of Dublin. Speaking to the Architectural Association in February 1924, he stated:

> If our capital is to resuscitate itself we must resolve to shake off the unhappy desolation of the present and the past. If we continue the log-rolling methods of to-day, within a short period of time an address such as this will not deal with the body that is ailing, but with the corpse that is dead.[53]

However, the Civic Survey of Dublin, completed in 1924 and published in 1925, adopted a more positive view of Dublin's potential, since 'there is probably no city of any antiquity with which so much could profitably be done to bring it into line with all the requirements of a modern community, and there is none more favourably suited'.[54] In his 'Introductory Statement' O'Rourke dealt at some length with the role of the city as an indicator of the population's character and the relationship of the 'physical aspects of a town upon the spiritual and moral life of its community'.[55] The report emphasised the national importance of Dublin as a capital city, whose reconstruction would require state involvement. The naieve optimism of the people about the potential of the new state was reflected in O'Rourke's introduction:

> Following the establishment of legislative independence, there can be little doubt that a tremendous industrial and commercial development will take place in the near future. The exploitation of the mineral wealth of the Free State, coupled with the natural adaptability for enlargement and extension of its industries, will call for the greatest care to ensure that these developments are carried out on modern lines, and associated with scientific civic planning.[56]

The Civic Survey was repeatedly seen as the necessary precursor of a town plan. 'With a civic survey before the town planner no serious mistake is likely to occur, as it educates both the expert and the citizen in the factors and conditions governing his town life'.[57] In turn, the published survey would stimulate legislative action for a Dublin town plan for which the British model 'may not prove suitable, as conditions are fundamentally different. In any event a measure should be drafted for the capital by itself; there is ample justification for such a step.'[58]

The results of the surveys, based in part upon questionnaire responses, airphotography and traffic counts, and extending over Dublin city and nine adjacent existing council areas, were presented under seven headings:

1. *Archaeology:* dealing with the prehistoric and historic artefacts of the city — roads, bridges, railways, canals and public buildings. The findings pointed to the contradiction wherein 'No country in Europe possesses remains of greater interest to the antiquary than Ireland, and in no country are they so much neglected.'[59] The report welcomed the moves by the Royal Irish Academy and the Royal Society of Antiquaries to draft a Bill to protect monuments.

2. *Recreation:* dealing with indoor and outdoor facilities and activities. As Geddes had shown in 1913, the existence of the large Phoenix Park obscured the reality that Dublin had only 227 acres of green space elsewhere, with the result that in many parts of the city 'bad and congested housing causes the

Fig. 1.3 Dublin Civic Survey Map of Bad Housing and Decayed Areas. (Source: *Civic Survey, 1925*). The black areas indicate tenements and unfit housing. The grey shading indicates decayed areas.

children to convert the streets into playgrounds'.[60] The Report foresaw the possibility of converting institutional lands to recreational use and of opening up the Phoenix Park with tram services. The report provided a comprehensive inventory of open spaces, their locations, size, principal uses and amenities.

3. *Education:* this chapter revealed the almost total overcrowding and the inadequate provision of schools at all levels from primary to university. The report highlighted the difficulty of extending educational institutions because of 'the unwillingness of private property owners to let or sell sites for school purposes'.[61]

4. *Hygiene:* a chapter which demonstrated that Dublin was well served with water and sewage systems, but the city continued to have excessively high levels of infant mortality. The chapter concluded that 'a largely contributing factor to the high deathrates is the presence of insanitary areas, or areas of special poverty'.[62]

5. *Housing:* the relationship of bad hygiene to poor housing areas had long been observed. O'Rourke had earlier highlighted the severity of Dublin's housing issue: 'Housing in Dublin today is more than a question and more than a problem — it is a tragedy! Its condition causes either a rapid or a slow death — rapid when the houses fall on the tenants, as has already happened — slow when they remain standing dens of insanitation'.[63]

The chapter emphasised the extent to which migration from rural Ireland was compounding the housing question. The Report showed the very high extent to which people lived in overcrowded conditions to be close to their places of work. The Civic Survey decidedly favoured the enlargement of the tramway system to open suburban sites to house the majority of the population. The Report lists a series of suburban sites on which to provide 23,653 houses over the years 1924-27. These areas should be developed within the framework of a statutory town plan. The objective was to eliminate the tenement problem by building sufficient suburban dwellings. But the Report cautioned that it 'is an illusion to base a housing programme on the idea that by a brief and intense application of collective activity, the housing shortage can be eliminated. The elimination of the problem is nothing short of perpetual construction at the required rate'.[64]

6. *Industry and Commerce:* This chapter provided an inventory and map of all major sources of industry and commerce. The chapter also proceeded on the basis that 'the next couple of generations will, it is hoped, see Dublin a throbbing hive of industry, and a centre of great commercial importance'.[65] The chapter also recommended that steps be taken to control advertising, which was then a major concern to the architectural institutes.

7. *Traffic:* By the use of traffic surveys and maps of Dublin's decreasing accessibility the Report showed the crisis of congestion facing Dublin as the use of the motor car increased. O'Connell Street represented the major source of vehicular congestion and, while the Report saw the temporary value of traffic management innovations — e.g. One-way streets — 'Dublin is in immediate need of a new traffic centre, which should be situated at the focus of the existing arterial routes, and by which all through traffic might be carried as well as the developed traffic of the inner circumferential routes'.[66]

The published report was universally acclaimed. The 'Leader' in the *Irish Builder* on 26 December 1925 proclaimed that the Report 'should be in the hands of every person interested in the future of the city of Dublin'.[67] The *Irish Builder* saw this survey as the essential bedrock for a Dublin Town Plan which would put an end to piecemeal, unconsidered and irresponsible proposals. Manning Robertson reviewed the Survey report for *The Builder,* stressing its local and practical relevance. He described the Report as a monument of patience and research which could serve 'as a model of what a systematic survey of existing conditions in a town ought to be'.[68] But the general hope was that this 'vast volume of voluntary labour'[69] could provide Dublin with the basis for 'a thoroughly practical and complete town plan to guide future developments'.[70]

As in the case of the Dublin Survey, *Cork: A Civic Survey*[71] was also in large part the product of one man, D. J. Coakley, who by his unrelenting efforts, and particularly through his 1917 lecture on 'General Principles of Housing and Town Planning', had kept alive the flickering flame of planning in Cork.[72] The Cork Town Planning Association, with an executive committee of ten members and Coakley as Hon. Secretary, was set up in March 1922 to undertake a Civic Survey of Cork and District. Professor Abercrombie and Sydney A. Kelly were appointed as advisers.

Like the Dublin Survey, the Cork Civic Survey Report reflects the **post-colonial** optimism of the authors with respect to the role of

Cork in the new state 'with its impulse towards devolution'. Cork would become a major regional centre, Cork harbour was being planned as a national port for Ireland with a trans-shipment harbour at Cuskinny, and it was envisaged that sites would have to be provided for major public buildings, including government offices, a City Hall, public libraries, concert hall, art gallery and museum. The initial chapters dealt with Cork's physical setting, its historical legacy and its regional context (Fig. 1.4). As to the physical growth of Cork, the Report was to foreshadow proposals which were to receive statutory effect over fifty years later in respect of satellite town expansion. Thus the Report envisaged that

> It is unlikely that the City as a town will extend continuously over this region, but satellite growth especially along the waterfront .... is inevitable, as indeed has already occurred. This growth will be of three sorts: residential, industrial and recreational in addition of course to the actual growth of the Port, whether near the City or at Queenstown.[73]

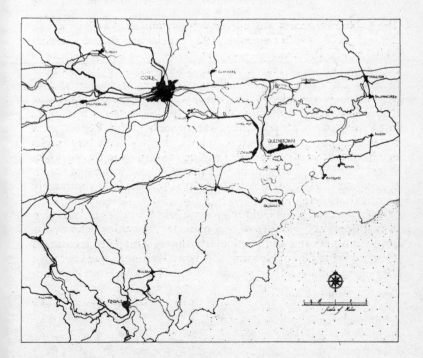

Fig. 1.4 Cork and Surrounding Region. (Source: *Civic Survey, 1926*).

Much of the Report was devoted to Cork's three principal problems: bad and insufficient housing, inadequate open space and poor accessibility. Maps illustrated the correlation between high death rates and insanitary districts, and the Survey estimated that 18,645 persons, out of a total population of 80,000 were residing in unsatisfactory housing conditions. The authors were perceptive enough to add that 'the redistribution of so large a proportion of the population will naturally take years to accomplish' and should be carried out 'as part of a general scheme of Town Planning and redistribution of the population'.[74]

The authors carried out a comparative analysis of the levels of open space provision in Cork and twenty-three other cities, including Belfast and Dublin. Whereas Edinburgh had 7.7 acres of open space per 1000 population and Dublin had 5.7 acres, Cork possessed a mere 0.54 acres per 1000 persons, having recently allowed Ford's to take over one of the city's major amenities for its car assembly plant. An analysis of the city's communications patterns revealed the high degree of traffic congestion, resulting principally from the converging nature of the road system and the lack of river crossings down stream. Other topics covered in the Survey included the urban design character of the city and the siting of public buildings. Thus, the Survey provided a comprehensive basis for the making of a town plan which would help to guide the 'multitude of smaller forces at work whose resultant influence, while it has not been progressive in the recent past, if rightly directed, should bring about a slow and steady growth in future years'.[75]

The Report received an enthusiastic reception upon publication. The *Irish Builder and Engineer* provided a summary of the main parts of the Survey and above all, supported the view that any future development should take place within the context of a town plan: 'Cork we repeat, has beautiful surroundings, streets on the whole pleasing, no extraordinary pressing need for hasty, ill-considered buildings and every reason for well-thought-out development. Festina lente should be the motto?[76]

The collective achievements of the Civic Surveys were assembled by the Civics Institute of Ireland for its 1927 Dublin Civic Exhibition. As part of the programme of events of the 1927 Dublin Civic Week, a Housing and Town Planning Exhibition was put on at the Engineer's Hall, Dawson Street.[77] The exhibition included a number of exhibits from Ireland, England and the Continent. The Dublin Civic Survey, the Abercrombie Plan, the Shannon Scheme (Ardnacrusha), the Cork Civic Survey and a model map of Dublin prepared by the architectural department of University College were the home-produced highlights. From Britain, there was the South Wales Survey and the Regional Planning Diagram of England and Wales, plans from Welwyn Garden City, the Thames Valley and an exhibit from Mid-Surrey. London County Council sent a model of improved housing areas while from Germany came the plans for the Ruhr Region including Essen and Dusseldorf. The exhibition also included a plan of the Copenhagen Region. This first exhibition provided added stimulus for planning progress, as did a similar exhibition in 1929. These exhibitions were largely due to the initiative of Manning Robertson, who for twenty years operated as the principal planner in the country.

Planning and the Urban Housing Problem

It has been repeatedly shown in *The Emergence of Irish Planning* that the atrocious urban housing conditions were to persist until well after World War II. Throughout the life of the Irish Free State, the alleviation of the urban housing crisis remained a continuing priority. Many advisers championed the case for planning in the belief that good and proper planning would accelerate the pace of housing reform. Equally, major housing developments undertaken in the absence of a planning framework could prove both wasteful in themselves and disruptive of long-term urban development. Finally, the need for decent housing necessitated the introduction of reasonable development standards both in respect of estate development and the layout and construction of individual houses or groups of dwellings. The major agent of urban change in the inter-war years was to be suburbanisation, and the planning and development of suburban workingclass housing estates was to be the major focus of planning interest (Figs. 1.5a and 1.5b).

There had been strong and persistent opposition to the suburbanisation of the working-class population of Irish cities. This resistance was due in part to a recognition that many of the low-income workers needed to live close by their work; the local authorities did not have control over the tram systems and, thus, they could not operate cheap fares for workers.[78] There was also a strong desire on the part of housing applicants to receive new accommodation in their own area. In addition, suburban housing development entailed a move away from the traditional bye-law housing approach, implied a scale of development which was unprecedented and often involved land acquisitions either outside or transcending the municipal boundary.

Discussion of suburbanisation had continued for the first twenty years of the century; the 1903 Housing Conference had proposed a

30 *Planning: The Irish Experience*

Fig. 1.5 Inter-War Housing Layouts. *Source*: Ordnance Survey, Revisions 1943-50.

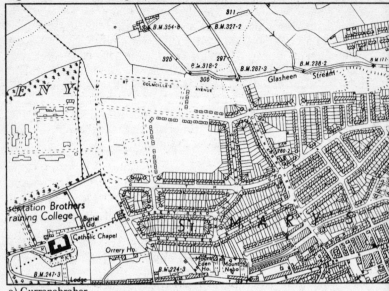

a) Gurranabraher.

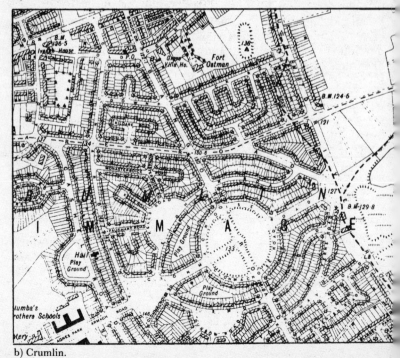

b) Crumlin.

strategy of suburban housing related to the tramway system.[79] Similar arguments had been made repeatedly, especially during the 1913 Housing Inquiry, where Aston developed a system of suburban housing rings.[80] This line of reasoning was reinforced by the expert opinion of Geddes and Unwin recommending that the Corporation 'acquire lands on the outskirts of the City area, and build there working class houses of reasonable accommodation provided with gardens or allotment gardens, and having ample open space to secure fresh air, sunlight, and possibilities of recreation both for children and adults'.[81] In the succeeding years many public officials came to accept the necessity of suburbanisation as the major solution to the problem of unfit housing. Thus, P. C. Cowan, Chief Engineer of the Local Government Board, recommended that 'at least 12,000 out of the total of 16,500 new houses can and should be secured in approximately equal proportions in the Clontarf, Drumcondra, Cabra and Crumlin districts'.[82] But he cautioned that 'it would be most unwise to attempt to provide them until most carefully considered plans with respect to them, and all that they entail, have been prepared by men of foresight and broad views'.[83]

But urban authorities, particularly Dublin and Cork, desired 'to accommodate the greatest possible number of working-class tenants under city conditions in a hygienic manner without overcrowding', i.e. conforming to bye-law housing standards.[84] This approach was most forcefully supported by nationalist councillors, including W. T. Cosgrave, who argued the necessity of providing houses near to where people worked, pointing to the record that 'there has been usually five times the number of applicants for the number of cottages we have to let, and the waiting lists are always well filled'.[85] Later, Cosgrave was to argue that less than one in five of the housing applicants wanted a suburban location,[86] a view that led McKenna to point out that 'if one in five, or even one in ten, of the slum dwellers were moved out to the suburbs, would not the congestion of the slums be immensely relieved?'[87]

In favouring the solution of the housing problem through the construction of cottages in city areas, Cosgrave also vehemently opposed the idea of rehabilitating first class tenements as had been proposed by Geddes and Unwin. Such dwellings would, he argued, lack privacy, prove difficult to maintain, generate a variety of nuisances, prove expensive to run and require a large number of sanitary inspectors.[88] The standard corporation terraced house, often on a cleared site, remained the acceptable norm with most politicians, especially the nationalist group, until around 1920.

But since land was not available in the centres of urban districts to accommodate more than a small fraction of the required housing, suburbanisation had to be considered. Thus, in the case of Dublin, the Marino site had been discussed for almost a decade prior to the first Corporation plans for its development,[89] often with stress being laid upon the area's proximity to the docks. By 1918 the Housing Committee of the Corporation had accepted the inevitability of finding a solution to the housing question largely through suburbanisation. A report of the Housing Committee which found that sites were available for 2000 dwellings on central areas to the north of the Liffey also raised 'the question of finding space on virgin sites within the City for the 8,100 dwellings to complete the new accommodation for the number of families requiring to be re-housed on the North side of the City'.[90] In the case of Dublin, houses had to be found for those of the indigenous population who were in poor accommodation. In addition, many saw Dublin's problems compounded by immigration from other parts of Ireland. As Cowan put it: 'Dublin is the rest house or alms house to which people broken in health, character or fortune come from all over Ireland to shelter or hide themselves or to take advantage of its numerous hospitals and almost innumerable overlapping charities.[91] As a result, the number of urban working-class houses needed to meet the housing emergency was increasing rather than decreasing, and was estimated to be approaching 50,000 dwellings.[92]

Not surprisingly, the expansion of the housing industry was a top priority after 1921. The Provisional Government made available, in 1922, a sum of £1 million as a grant for urban housing schemes to be divided amongst municipal authorities in the ratio of £2 for every £1 provided by the local authority. The Housing (Building Facilities) Act, 1924, and the Housing Act, 1925, enabled the government and local authorities to make grants to private individuals or groups wishing to erect new dwellings or to reconstruct dwellings in town areas. The 1925 Act sought to encourage the activities of public utility societies and other forms of co-operative housing action.

Whereas only 8750 dwellings had been erected by urban authorities in the forty years up to 1922, the five years from 1922 to 1927 saw the erection or planning of schemes for 6441 local authority dwellings, with a further 6000 private dwellings initiated. Over this period £1,900,000 was made available in housing grants by the government, with over half of the money going to Dublin, where almost 4000 local authority dwellings were erected or being planned.[93]

Since 'the majority of these houses are on virgin sites convenient to the city ... care is being taken to ensure that the planning of the area will interfere as little as may be with the future of the surrounding lands'.[94] The new housing developments increasingly conformed to the relatively low density garden suburb ideal with a growing recognition of the need for enlightened site planning and the necessity of seeing each development in its wider urban context. Thus the architect Ruthen stressed the importance of well-planned layouts which ensured

> the retention to the greatest possible extent of the amenities of nature; the broad outlook in regard to future needs and requirements, the consideration of one district in relation to neighbouring districts; the correlation of districts with each other, and the interplay of rural and urban interests, as well as the interdependence and linking up of all in the proper scheme of national development; are all matters which, unfortunately for national life, have not in the past received proper and due consideration.[95]

The regulations issued by the Local Government Board under the Irish Housing Act of 1919 accepted the Tudor Walters standard of housing densities of not more than twelve houses to the acre outside central urban areas. In conformity with these standards, O'Rourke's 1919 plans for a 50-acre suburb at Marino shows small terraces of two storey houses, set in ample open space with an overall density of eleven houses to the acre, with a generous allocation of land for open space, schools, shops and public buildings.[96] The final scheme for the enlarged Marino site allowed for a density of 9.5 houses to the acre,[97] while war homes at Killester laid out by Frank Mears had a density of only four houses to the acre.[98] Other Dublin suburban schemes, such as Drumcondra, Glasnevin and Cabra adopted the Garden city norms, whereas schemes such as those at Capwell and Turners Cross in Cork were erected at substantially higher densities.

At least in the field of public housing, developments increasingly adopted the planning standards in vogue in Britain, while the overall layout of estates was increasingly seen in its wider metropolitan context. Thus 'Marino Road', the first mention of Griffith Avenue, was not only a connector between two new housing areas but the first stage of a major metropolitan ring road.[99]

On the other hand the quality of many of the private suburbs and the spoilation of the countryside by new housing was a constant cause for concern and a prime example of how town planning might have improved the environment. *The Irish Builder and Engineer* repeatedly criticised the lack of any zoning ordinance for Dublin — a city which now provided an 'object lesson of the evils that flow from the lack of zoning regulations in respect of the type of buildings that may be erected in certain localities'.[100] Later the journal was even more forceful: 'Around our cities and even into the heart of the country, the new bungalow is becoming a menace to beauty. Usually ill-designed and glaring in colour, it is an eyesore, bad when alone but hideous when in groups.'[101] The comment that 'it is painful to contemplate what may be the appearance of the greater part of County Dublin in another quarter century'[102] was unfortunately too prophetic. The writer and journalist P. L. Dickinson predicted that unless some 'restrictions are imposed the beauty of our countryside will soon be a thing of the past. Our good villages will have vanished.'[103] For Dickinson the reason why so many villages were 'spoilt by vile jerry cottages' resulted from the apathy of the architectural societies which were failing to give a lead to public opinion.[104] The upsurge in building activity had given rise to a rapid expansion of urban areas, particularly Dublin. As J. F. McCabe saw it, 'The centrifugal tendency in Dublin has been apparent for years. Every motor car or 'bus is a stimulus thereto and the progress towards the mountains and the sea should be thought out and orderly, rather than haphazard as heretofore.'[105] This view was re-enforced by Professor Butler who regretted the deterioration of Dublin's environs and saw the only hope as being through 'the early enactment of some measure of control over building design, and the provision of a well thought-out town plan.'[106] O'Rourke, as City Architect, lent his support in favour of some form of aesthetic control of building. O'Rourke pointed to the continental and American experience in this field and that 'it has been proved to the satisfaction of the Commissioners that enlightened city development cannot take place without town-planning powers applicable to built-up areas, and, as the English Acts do not cover these areas, their enactment here would be practically useless'.[107] Rather than the British approach, Dickinson encouraged Irish readers to examine the possible suitability of a Fine Arts Commission similar to that set up in the USA in 1910.[108]

In any case the major question of housing, its adequate layout, its use of resources and its impact on the environment, all gave urgency to the enactment of some measure of town planning. It was with some relief therefore that E. P. McCarron, Secretary of the Department of Local Government, let it be known officially that 'in association with the officers of the Department and with the assistance of high specialist advice, the City Commissioners are discussing the lines on which a Town Planning Bill might appropriately be laid'.[109] In effect many of the principles and standards of what was regarded as good planning were being implemented in the absence of any city plans or any planning legislation,[110] but, formally, planning machinery was essential if there were to be proper co-ordination.

Regionalism and Planning

In addition to housing and civic improvements, planning was seen as an important tool in fulfilling government objectives with respect of countering the growth of Dublin, boosting the development of rural areas and ensuring the rational development of the Greater Dublin area. Reflecting the rural dominance of the Irish independence movement, there existed a strong anti-urban bias in the philosophy of many of the country's founding fathers, most notably P. H. Pearse. Writing in April 1916, just days before the Easter Rising, Pearse outlined his vision of a new and independent Ireland:

> In a free Ireland there will be work for all the men and women of the nation. Gracious and rural industries will supplement an improved agriculture. The population will expand in a century to twenty millions, it may even in time go up to thirty million. Towns will be spacious and beautiful ... but since the country will chiefly rely for its wealth on agriculture and rural industry there will be no Glasgows or Pittsburghs.[111]

In many ways such views of a rural utopia were largely an anti-Dublin philosophy — antipathy towards the seat of colonial rule and its institutions. The new government initiated a programme of legislative reform aimed at removing the worst excesses of the inherited system and promoting the role of public institutions throughout the country.

The first legislative manifestation of the government's professed commitment to devolution came in the Terms of Reference to the Glenavy Committee, established to advise on how best to give effect to the Constitution and to devise a system of law and justice 'according to the dictations of our own needs'.[112] The Glenavy Committee was specifically instructed by the President that 'Questions such as those of the centralisation or decentralisation of the Courts ... will be amongst the many subjects which must anxiously engage your attention.'[113]

The findings of the Glenavy Committee were adopted into the Courts of Justice Bill, which followed the court procedure under the Dáil from 1919-22, and proposed a devolved system of regionalised circuit courts to replace the county courts and aspects of the work of the high court. The Bill adopted the Glenavy Committee proposal for eight 'circuits' or regions; each circuit was devised so as to have an approximately equivalent range of population, the largest being Dublin City and County with 476,000 persons, and the smallest the Southern Circuit with 348,000[114] (Fig. 1.6a).

The commitment to devolution and decentralisation was evident also in the Government's decision to abolish the Rural District authorities in favour of the strong County Councils. While the Government argued that the Local Government Bill, 1924, would further the cause of devolution, Thomas Johnson, leader of the Labour Party expressed concern that the Bill would in fact reverse the process that

> government has been following and which I think is desirable
> . . . to devolve upon local authorities the control and power and the responsibility for the administration of their areas.
> . . . we have to make up our minds whether we want a centralised administration, or whether we are to encourage local authorities to bear responsibility and take an interest in the good government of their own neighbourhood.[115]

In retrospect, such reservations were to prove particularly relevant as local authorities (the newly empowered counties) saw power shift to the Central Government as Johnson had so forcefully predicted.

The drive for regional development was also evident in the Government's efforts to restructure the Land Commission, in its support for the work of the Industrial Development Association[116] and its endorsement of many recommendations of the *Commission of Inquiry into the Resources and Industries of Ireland*.[117] The report dealt with all the country's basic resources and intensified the debate about the importance of water power as a source of ample and cheap energy. Indeed, the Government decision in 1925 to proceed with the Shannon electrification scheme was undoubtedly the most important action of national development in the 1920s.[118] The widespread availability of ample power supplies was to lay the foundations for regional development, but the conditions for workers at the Shannon works also demonstrated the social costs of a lack of adequate town planning. But national decisions about energy, roads and transport or individual municipal decisions on infrastructure were taken on an ad hoc basis without reference to an

Irish Planning from 1921 to 1945   37

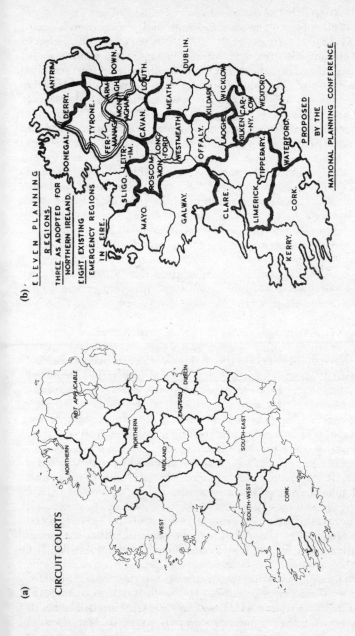

Fig. 1.6 Sub-National Units: (a) The Circuit Court Areas (Source: *Atlas of Ireland*); (b) The Emergency (Planning) Regions (Source: *National Planning Handbook, 1944.*).

overall national, regional or local plan.

Questions of town planning and regionalism remained largely a Dublin issue. The report of *The Greater Dublin Commission of Inquiry* was to provide a badly needed official boost for the introduction of town planning. The rationalisation and extension of the municipal boundary of the Corporation had been under periodic discussion for upwards of fifty years and the recommendations of 1880 had never been given effect.[119] On 4 July 1924 the Government appointed a twelve-member parliamentary committee under the chairmanship of Professor William Magennis to examine and report on local government reform in the Dublin area.[120] The report, published in 1926, proposed the establishment of a Greater Dublin Council with an elected Council to administer the whole contiguous urbanised area around Dublin; subsidiary to the Great Council would be the local councils of Dublin and the southern coastal borough. The Committee recommended the adaptation of the County Manager system 'to the special conditions of Greater Dublin'.[121]

The Commission paid particular attention to the role of town planning in solving Dublin's problems. Speaking of the service known as town planning the Commission stated:

> Properly understood it is a service which makes for the conservation of human energy and the preservation of human life, particularly of child-life. It does not aim at mere beautification; it aims at creating first a good city rather than an ornate city.... It reduces the cost of Civic development and improvements by applying business methods to Civic business determining beforehand a definite plan of orderly arrangement into which later constructions will fit as they become needed: this is simply to substitute the reign of wise foresight for the abandonment of development to Chance, with all the dislocation, ruinous expense, and Civic debt, which haphazard procedure entails.[122]

Many aspects of the report reflected the social concern of Dr Oliver St J. Gogarty, who added a minority statement calling for a grand town plan to order the low-density housing extension which he desired.[123]

After four years of what the *Irish Builder and Engineer* termed 'Hesitation! Procrastination! Patchwork,'[124] the Government in 1930 proceeded with the Local Government (Dublin) Bill. The Bill largely rejected the Commission's report, particularly in respect of a Greater Dublin Council. Instead, a single Borough Council of

Dun Laoghaire was established, while Dublin Corporation was extended to include the townships of Rathmines and Rathgar and Pembroke as well as some thirty-four adjoining townlands in County Dublin, together with parts of some other townlands. The measure was a bitter disappointment to the many advocates of reform for two reasons: firstly, the extension to the Dublin Corporation area did not include all the contiguous urbanised parts of the County, (e.g. Dun laoghaire and Sutton-Howth) and it was feared that urban areas in the County would be left 'at the tender mercies of a body of backwoods farmers'[125] while the failure to create a northern coastal borough was seen as endangering the orderly development of the 'Blue Lagoon'[126] while the isolation of Howth was also regretted.[127]

Secondly, the measure was roundly condemned for the exclusion of any reference to town planning even though Dublin's Chief Commissioner had pointed to the need for 'a town planning body'.[128] In an editorial in March 1930 the *Irish Builder and Engineer* condemned the exclusion of town planning issues and went on to say that 'without the accompaniment of town-planning provisions irreparable damage may be done, damage that will only be apparent when it is too late to remedy'.[129] The *Irish Builder* had earlier pronounced that 'Town Planning is of the very essence of ordered civic development. Without it we shall see all the beauty spots from the Dodder to the Vico Road destroyed or obliterated as if they never existed.'[130]

Within the Dáil and Senate the Bill received a critical reception and in the face of repeated criticisms the Minister for Local Government conceded the importance of planning, especially at the regional scale, which 'outside the city and into the country should be for the purpose of serving the interests of a growing city'.[131] But it was Sean Lemass who voiced the strongest opposition, both to the inadequate extent of the administrative changes and the absence of a planning content. Referring to planning, he said:

> There has been consultation about this question for twenty years, but nothing has been done. What is required is legislative power in the hands of some executive authority, so that the question can be properly dealt with.[132] . . . If we want to secure that the growth of the city of Dublin will be properly regulated, we must have not merely a town planning authority, but around the city a belt of virgin land on which building has not yet begun and over which any development that takes place can be properly controlled.[133]

The Local Government (Dublin) Bill passed into law without any reference in it to town planning. But the issues behind the Bill had generated an intense debate on the need for planning. Amongst other things this debate forced the Minister, Mulcahy, to do an abrupt about turn in respect of planning. It was reported that on 1 March, 1930, upon return from an International Town-Planning Conference in Rome, Mulcahy had publicly declared his belief that this country 'could not afford to indulge in town-planning undertakings'.[134] Two weeks later, under pressure from Thomas Johnson and the Labour Party, he committed himself to a departmental town planning bill[135] in place of the measure introduced to the Seanad in 1929.

In any event, the case for town planning legislation and the coordination of development within a planning context had been consistently argued throughout the 1920s in relation to the rebuilding of devastated city areas, to ensure orderly municipal improvements, to ensure the proper control of urban and suburban housing developments and as a necessary corollary of local government reorganisation and municipal reform. The combined pressures from these various viewpoints led to the introduction of Ireland's first comprehensive Town Planning Bill on 2 May 1929.

The Town Planning Bill, 1929

Reacting to a paper delivered by Manning Robertson to the Architectural Association of Ireland on 'Town Planning in Ireland',[136] the leader writer to the *Irish Builder and Engineer* summed up the evident frustration at the continued procrastination by the government with respect to the enactment of a town planning measure. Commenting on the existence of a draft Bill, the leader stated that 'It is certainly high time that the Government took some belated steps to introduce and pass a town planning measure to control building development in city, suburbs and countryside.'[137] At the behest of the Civics Institute of Ireland, Thomas Johnson, leader of the Labour Party, agreed to introduce a town planning Bill in the Senate. The Town Planning Bill was based upon an earlier draft bill prepared by the Royal Institute of the Architects of Ireland in 1923[138] as amended in the light of the English legislation of 1925.

According to its long title, this was 'An Act to authorise and direct the preparation of Civic Surveys of certain areas in Saorstát Éireann, and to provide for the making of town planning schemes and for other matters affecting the preservation of public amenities.'[139] The main provisions of the Bill were to enable local authorities to prepare Civic Surveys and to take the steps necessary for the preparation and implementation of planning schemes. Under the Bill, a town planning scheme could contain provisions for dealing with any of the matters set out in the first schedule, which were as follows:

1. Streets, roads and other ways, and stopping up or diversion of existing highways.
2. Buildings, structures and erections.
3. Open spaces, private and public.
4. The preservation of objects of historical or artistic interest or natural beauty, and control of advertisements.
5. Sewerage, drainage and sewage disposal.
6. Lighting.
7. Water supply.
8. Ancillary or consequential works.
9. Extinction or variation of private rights of way and other easements.
10. Dealing with or disposal of land acquired by the responsible authority, or by a local authority.
11. Power of entry and inspection.
12. Power of the responsible authority to remove, alter or demolish any obstructive work.
13. Power of the responsible authority to make agreements with owners and of owners to make agreements with one another.
14. Power to add to the matters in respect of which a local authority may make bye-laws.
15. Power of the responsible authority or a local authority to accept any money or property for the furtherance of the objects of any town planning scheme, and provision for regulating the administration of any such money or property.
16. Application with the necessary modifications and adaptations of statutory enactments.
17. Carrying out and supplementing the provisions of this Act for enforcing schemes.
18. Limitation of time for operation of scheme.
19. Providing for periodic revision of the Civic Survey and the making of necessary modifications in a town planning scheme.
20. Co-operation of the responsible authority with the owners of land included in the scheme or other persons interested.
21. Charging on the inheritance of any land the value of which is increased by the operation of a town planning scheme the sum required to be paid in respect of that increase, and for that purpose applying, with the necessary adaptations, the provi-

sions of any enactments dealing with charges for improvement of land.

The Bill also contained measures to control advertising and had limited provisions in respect of compensation. Perhaps the most interesting aspect of the Bill was the power which was bestowed upon the Minister for Local Government and Public Health to direct local authorities to carry out Civic Surveys [140] or to make and implement planning schemes. The professional enthusiasm for a planning act was in contrast to the conspicuous lack of political interest in the subject as evidenced by the abandonment of the Bill's second reading on 16 May in the absence of a quorum. When the second reading was resumed on 5 June Johnson emphasised that he wished this Bill to be viewed as a non-party issue, stressing that preservation of amenities and the development of industry were compatible objectives. The Bill's second reading was supported by Senator Gogarty, who saw the urgent need for a town planning act to deal with questions of utility, health and aesthetics, especially in the case of Dublin — a city with 'the most varied architectural experiments and the most unvaried failures'.[141] The Bill received a generally positive reception and was referred to a Committee of the Senate. The retitled 'Town Planning and Rural Amenities Bill' received its final reading in the Senate on 12 March 1930. The Minister for Local Government and Public Health sought the approval of the Senate for a six-months postponement of the Bill to enable his officials to examine the measure and to introduce suitable amendments or a new Bill in the Dáil.

The *Irish Builder and Engineer*, which had expressed the view that 'the Bill appears to possess all the essentials of a good measure,'[142] was concerned with the Minister's apparent lack of enthusiasm for planning and questioned the need for any delay, especially in the case of Dublin where it was felt that the Local Government (Dublin) Bill should have contained town planning provisions.[143] Manning Robertson, however, saw in this delay an opportunity to update the Bill in the light of developments outside England since the 1925 Act was introduced. He cited the case of Western Australia where new planning legislation existed to prevent 'the erection of ugly buildings' and to ensure 'harmony in the exterior design of buildings'.[144] Robertson was particularly conscious of the inherent danger of seeking to apply to Ireland the types of procedures relevant to urbanised England. 'Our legislation must be of a kind to suit our peculiar needs,' he stressed.[145] 'In Town Planning we are not pioneers, and for this very reason we are in a position to take and to improve upon what has been done elsewhere.'[146]

The reluctance of the Government to make haste with Town Planning legislation stemmed from several considerations. Firstly, the Government was already committed to a heavy legislative programme impinging upon planning issues; this included the Dublin Bill, the National Monuments Bill and a bill to protect wildlife.[147] Secondly, the introduction of the 1929 Bill had highlighted the lack of public interest in the whole question of town planning. Thirdly, the Government was particularly alarmed at the potential for compensatory claims which might arise under a planning act. This issue was spelled out clearly by the Minister, Mr Mulcahy, in an interview to the *Dublin Chronicle* in October, 1929:

> ... the conviction formed by me from the time I came to give consideration to this question, namely, that you can safely prepare your maps and your legislation for town plans only when you have settled your policy with regard to compensation. There has been a certain amount of impatience on the part of many persons, and of the Press, because of the delay in providing legislation. There has not, however, been any serious attempt in public discussion to face this question of compensation, without a solution of which, acceptable to public opinion, there can be no progress.[148]

Finally, there was the inescapable fact that little development was taking place due to the lack of financial resources. The conflicting demands for scarce funds were clearly highlighted by a note written by Mulcahy on 2 March 1929 setting out twelve alternatives and deserving uses which could be made of the £40,000 collected for a war memorial which had been proposed for Merrion Square.[149]

Not surprisingly, the new Town Planning Bill promised within six months from March 1930 had a much more lengthy gestation period, during which time planning remained focused upon local issues of immediate concern. One of these was the long standing and unresolved problem of slum areas. The other was a new and lengthy concern with the planning of the 'Blue Lagoon' near Sutton, Co. Dublin. Although almost 5000 dwellings had been erected in Dublin between 1923 and 1930, the Minister informed the Dáil that a further 18,000 new dwellings were required to deal with Dublin's housing problem.[150] There was particular concern that, despite the erection of new dwellings, there had been little reduction in the scale or extent of slum areas.[151] The Housing (Miscellaneous Provisions) Act, 1931, was introduced to simplify the procedures for the clearance of unhealthy areas and to extend the powers of local authorities to redevelop clearance areas. Using this legislation, local authorities, especially Dublin Corporation, launched a reinvigorated attack on the clearing of slum areas. Amongst the many areas designated for clearance, the most notable was a 40-acre site lying to the east of O'Connell Street (Fig. 1.7b).[152] The controversy surrounding any return to housing on central city sites was exacerbated by a parallel decision favouring the erection of blocks of flats, flying in the face of arguments that 'flat life is an unnatural thing,'[153] 'never ideal for children'[154] and disregarding the evidence of the City Architect that 'a central tenement flat costs £22 per room more than a suburban cottage'.[155] Against a backcloth of such controversy, it is hardly surprising that the energetic use of the clearance provisions of the 1931 Act resulted in an abundance of long lasting central area derelict sites, as the pendulum quickly swung back in favour of suburbanisation.

With the abandonment of the proposal for a Greater Dublin Council and with the exclusion of the North Coastal Area from urban jurisdiction, the 1930s witnessed the initiation of a twenty year controversy about the planning of the 'Blue Lagoon' and the use of the Bull Island (Fig. 1.7a). On 12 October 1929 the *Irish Builder* resurrected the 'proposal to construct the 1,000 acre marine lake (now popularly known as the 'Blue Lagoon') to cover the repellent swamp and slobland which now divides the Bull Island from the mainland,'[156] complete with drawings suggesting a Dublin version of Morecambe. Welcomed by P. J. Meighan, then Commissioner for Howth,[157] the proposals were attacked in the *Sunday Times* as nothing more than an attempt by developers to establish 'an Irish Coney Island'.[158] Proposals for the area were further elaborated in the *Irish Builder* in October 1930.[159] Following a costing of proposals made at a 'Marine Lake Conference',[160] the Borough Surveyor estimated development costs at £60,000 and in February 1931 the matter was referred to a committee of Dublin Corporation.[161] The debate on 'the Blue Lagoon' was kept alive largely by Ernest Aston and the issue was not finally laid to rest until 1949.[162]

While the debate was largely fruitless in relation to the development of the Bull Island and of little national significance, it served as a successful means of highlighting the importance of town planning and the need for a regional dimension to metropolitan planning.

The Town and Regional Planning Act, 1934

As if a reminder were needed, the enactment of the Northern Ireland 1931 Planning and Housing legislation served to emphasise the continued failure of the Irish Government to discharge its

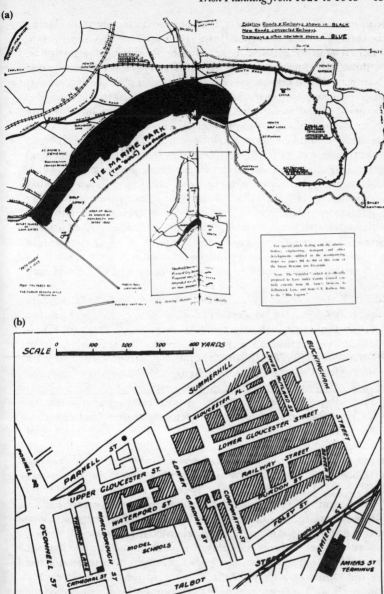

Fig. 1.7 (a) The Blue Lagoon Scheme; (b) Redevelopment Proposals for Gloucester Street Area. (Source: *Irish Builder and Engineer*).

commitment to bring forward planning legislation. Though repeatedly promised, the Bill did not finally emerge until August 1933. In both a comment on the absence of planning legislation and in the hope of an imaginative Act, Manning Robertson observed that 'we have no reason to suppose that Irish men are less proud of their country, less interested in its future, less observant of its beauty, than men of other nations, and we must hope that the stigma that we alone amongst civilised countries have taken no steps to organise by statute will be removed'.[163]

The principal cause of delay appears to have been the difficulty of framing what were deemed to be workable proposals on compensation and betterment. Among the many experts consulted was Raymond Unwin, who acted as advisor to both the Stormont and Dublin administrations.[164] The Town and Regional Planning Bill, although much more elaborate than the 1929 Bill, was also closely inspired by existing English legislation in spite of the repeated arguments as to the desirability of looking to other models of potentially greater relevance. The Bill consisted of eight parts as follows:

 I   Preliminary and General
 II   Planning Authorities and Areas
 III Preparation of Planning Schemes
 IV   Contents of Planning Schemes
 V   Execution of Planning Schemes
 VI   Construction of Planning Schemes
 VII Permission and Prohibition of Erection, etc., of Structures
 VIII Compensation and Payment for Betterment in Respect of Planning Schemes

Under the proposals in the Bill every county borough, borough, urban district and each county would become planning districts. Planning districts could come together to constitute planning regions and the Cork and Dublin planning regions were defined. Under Section 26 a planning authority could proceed to pass a resolution to prepare a planning scheme; such a resolution could not subsequently be revoked by the planning authority. Planning schemes prepared under the legislation would have to be approved by the Minister and laid before each House of the Oireachtas. Under the Bill persons initiating development would be required to seek and obtain planning permission for developments, once the Act was adopted. The Bill contained detailed provisions covering the payment of compensation as well as proposals for the payment of 'betterment' 'whenever the value of any property is increased by the coming into operation or enforcement of any provision contained in a planning scheme' etc. (Section 72).

The Bill was introduced on 9 August 1933 and received its second reading on 11 October 1933. It was clearly aimed at regulating development 'in the Cities of Dublin and Cork, which comprise more than half of the entire urban population.'[165] The Bill received a lukewarm reception in the Dáil with much of the discussion confined to specific issues or to the problems of local areas. Deputy James Dillon expressed the hope that the legislation would provide a rational framework for the proper planning of Dublin's housing emergency. While the response to the Bill in the Dáil had been muted, the Minister also revealed that no local authorities had taken up his invitation to comment or criticise the Bill.[166] In the Senate the Bill was welcomed by Senator Johnson, who had sponsored the earlier Bill, and who welcomed the powers bestowed upon local authorities under the new Bill.

Kevin Nowlan who examines the 1934 Act in detail in the following chapter suggests that the Act had considerable potential but that there was an absence of an adequate will to implement it. In particular he points to the very slow rate of adoption of the Act by local authorities, especially before 1939. The mixed public reaction given to the Bill in 1933 pinpointed many of the issues which were to militate against the effectiveness of the measure. Having outlined the contents of the Bill, 'Artifex' writing in the *Irish Builder*, failed to identify any major omissions. He went on: 'If exercised with imagination, courage, skill and sympathy the powers so to be invested would seem to be sufficiently comprehensive to secure 'orderly development'. But the 'if' is a very big 'if' indeed . . . . Efficient administration . . . is much more important than wise legislation.'[167] The same author also highlighted the likely consequence of failing to establish planning regions on a statutory basis: 'Having regard . . . to the known psychology and habits of local authorities, it may be assumed that few, if any 'regional' authorities will be created by the measure in its present form.'[168] The *Irish Builder* repeatedly returned to the possible problems likely to be created by the confusion of 'regions within a region'[169] and later called for the Minister 'to handpick a National Planning Council whose functions would be the co-ordination of all local planning operations and the determination of all issues which the Bill reserves to the Minister'.[170]

The *Irish Builder's* doubts about the practicability of the suggested Dublin region (Dublin County, Wicklow, Kildare and Meath) were shared by the Dublin City Manager, Mr Sherlock.[171] Sherlock saw such a region as too extensive and workable only if all authorities were prepared to operate in agreement. The Act did not formulate any operational procedure to overcome problems of disagreement between contiguous authorities. Ultimately, the fate of the Act was dependent upon public support and the Minister emphasised 'that progress could not be hoped for unless there was a demand for it in this direction, and a public opinion behind the demand.'[172]

To stimulate professional and public support, the professional institutes organised a large number of public meetings and lectures on planning issues. The case for regional planning councils had been argued in a lecture by the City Surveyor of Belfast, R. B. Donald.[173] In October 1933 Unwin delivered a lecture on 'Town and Country Planning Principles' to a distinguished audience in Mansion House[174] and on the 24 January 1934 Thomas Adams delivered an address in the RDS on 'Metropolitan Regions' with special reference to New York.[175] Alongside these international speakers, Manning Robertson was using every media outlet — radio talks, newspapers and lectures — to encourage a commitment to town planning. Amongst the lecture topics covered by Robertson at this time were 'Our Cities and Towns', 'Town Planning and Slums' and 'The Towns We Live In', while his *Cautionary Guide to Dublin*, prepared for the RIAI, illustrated the visual advantages of a degree of regulation to control indiscriminate advertising. In this, as in his other writings, Robertson demonstrated his profound conviction that effective action was utterly dependent upon public support:

> Without a sound public opinion our position will be without hope, since no legislation can instill a cultural attitude of mind, neither can we expect our Local Authorities to exert adequately any powers of control that may be conferred upon them if they know that the electorate is indifferent or hostile to any restraint exercised for the public good.[176]

Although subject to the philosophy of 'making haste slowly', the Act was in force and tentative steps were being taken to ensure its implementation. The 1934 Budget included a provision to supplement the Local Loans Fund by annual contributions from taxation so as to build up a reserve fund for planning purposes.[177] By 1937 the Department's 'Model Clauses for Use in preparation of Schemes' had been published.[178] A succession of advisory reports prepared by Manning Robertson and others also illustrated the potential social value of the Act. But more than any other single fact, Robertson's indomitable optimism and enthusiasm served as a catalyst for action. Referring to the new Act, he wrote:

Although late, in point of time, in comparison with other countries, it holds great possibilities since it coincides with a period which promises to be one of considerable development, and we in Ireland, having been spared the worst of the industrial phase, are not so badly hampered as are most countries by mistakes made through ill-considered development in the past.[179]

Advisory Reports Prepared under the 1934 Act

The credit for initiating modern town planning in the Greater Dublin area must go to Dun Laoghaire, whose manager P. J. Hernon secured a Council resolution on 14 March 1935 for the preparation of a planning scheme for the district. Manning Robertson was appointed Town Planning Adviser to the Borough Corporation and in 1935-6 undertook a detailed survey of the resources of the borough.[180] In this report Robertson presented a comprehensive inventory of the physical, scenic, industrial, institutional and demographic resources of the area. In the tradition of Civic Surveys, this was the first step in the preparation of a statutory town plan. For him a town plan should not be seen as a threat to private rights; rather its implementation was dependent upon individual initiative. Instead of being a restrictive straight jacket, 'the virtue of a town plan is that it can forestall mistakes which would make the execution of desirable schemes impossible'.[181] Welcoming 'this beautiful book', the Minister for Local Government and Public Health used the opportunity to stress the importance of implementing town plans:

> No Local Authority can afford to neglect to use the powers which a well-considered plan of development confers. In some plans the conditions of to-day may not disclose an immediate problem, but, as we know so well, conditions change very rapidly and unobtrusively, and it is only by intelligent planning for the future that proper development will succeed.[182]

No final plan was ever completed by the Dun Laoghaire Corporation at this time.

In 1935 Galway Borough enacted a resolution under the 1934 Act and D. O'Toole was engaged to prepare a 'Sketch Development Plan for Galway City'.[183] The Sketch Plan included the findings of a survey of geology, history, buildings of note, housing, open space and industry. The plan proposed that residential layouts should be in the form of neighbourhood units lying between radial routes.

These neighbourhood units would have 4000 to 6000 persons and would be further sub-divided into residential areas or social groups of 500 to 1500 persons. O'Toole calculated that the optimum size of a city was one of 80,000 population at 50 persons to the acre on 1600 acres. A green belt was proposed to limit Galway's growth and provide land for farming, recreation and landscaping. A somewhat similar set of proposals had been prepared for Limerick by 1937.[184]

Manning Robertson was commissioned to prepare a plan for Cork and its neighbourhood.[185] The proposals put forward by Robertson covered housing, health, recreation, zoning, reclamation, neighbourhood development, boundary extension and regional planning. He proposed the thinning out of the population of the centre city with a network of new roads to improve central area accessibility. The decentralised central city population would be rehoused in suburban developments. In relation to the long term development of Cork Robertson applied 'an accepted principle in planning the future of a city, that some definite limit must be set to its size';[186] accordingly Cork was planned to accommodate a maximum population of 254,000 persons on 11,000 acres and surrounded by an extensive green belt, with Blarney and Ballincollig as islands therein (Fig. 1.8). As in the other plans, many of the

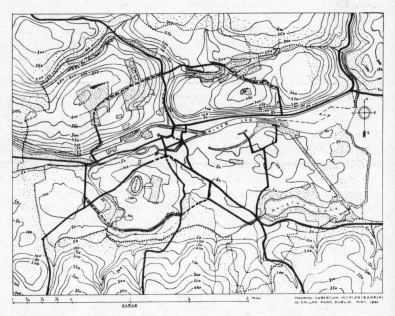

Fig. 1.8 Regional Scheme for Cork Area. (Source: *Manning Robertson, 1941*).

proposals related to territory outside the jurisdiction of Cork Corporation and in the absence of an agreement with the adjoining county were quite unrealistic. The application of green belts to cities of the size of Cork, Limerick or Galway was never adequately justified by the authors.

In a preliminary plan prepared for Waterford in 1943, Frank Gibney put forward a more balanced and less theoretically constrained set of proposals.[187] His proposals, set in a regional context, included an industrial estate to the north-east of Ferrybank, a new bridge, new docks and the erection of over 1000 dwellings to accommodate persons then living in the slums.

But, as in previous decades, it was Dublin which was to be the principal focus of planning action and to receive most attention.

TABLE 1.1

Principal characteristics of advisory reports prepared under the Town and Regional Planning Acts

Study Area	Date of Study	Adv. of Plan	Implementation*
Dun Laoghaire	1936	—	No
Galway City	1936	Yes	No
Limerick City	1937	Yes	No
Cork and Environs	1941	Yes	No
Waterford	1943	yes	No
Dublin	1939	Yes	No

*This does not deny that many of the proposals may have influenced decisions in an ad hoc manner.

Planning Proposals for Dublin

The late 1930s saw the initiation of three separate investigations into Dublin's planning, its administration and its housing policies. All three reports had implications for the organisation and planning of the city. Pursuant upon a resolution of 6 January 1936, Dublin Corporation appointed P. Abercrombie, S. Kelly and M. Robertson to prepare a Sketch Plan for the Dublin area. The consultants' report was submitted in 1939 and was published together with the Corporation's views in 1941.[188] The 1939 proposals for the city centre are in sharp contrast to Abercrombie's 1914 recommendations.[189] The desire for a Beaux Arts type re-development of the centre was greatly subdued although proposals for a new civic centre, a new cathedral and government offices were prominent. The report placed considerable attention on the residential function of the centre with particular emphasis upon adequate open space for the citizens of the central area. Within the centre city the consultants recommended policies to encourage the expansion of the middle class population, while much of the working class would be moved out to the new suburbs. In the commercial centre the consultants' policy was to encourage a 'gradual evolution towards a logical predominant use of different quarters'.[190]

The consultants' overall proposals for the Dublin area could have had profound implications for national and regional policy, if implemented. The consultants argued 'that no solution is, in our opinion, possible unless a further influx of families from the country is prevented'.[191] They therefore recommended that the growth of the built-up area should be limited by the establishment

TABLE 1.2
Land Areas and Populations for Dublin, 1939

(a)	Free Entry land between existing city boundary and deferred Development Land	13,500 acres
	Add reclamations	900 acres
		14,000
	Deduct:	
	Open spaces, Public 12½ per cent local)	15 per cent
	Open spaces, Public 2½ per cent city)	
	Private (including institutions)	15 per cent
	Balancing Land	20 per cent
	Non-residential	10 per cent
		60 per cent
	Leaving 5,760 acres	
	Population (including existing) at 30 per acre	172,800
(b)	Deferred Development Land	
	Area	5,200 acres
	Deduct 60 per cent. as above, Leaving	2,080 acres
	Population (including existing) at 30 per acre	62,400

Future population in area bounded by green belt when built up as contemplated above:

District	Acres	Population
Dublin within existing boundary	18,740	477,000
Dun Laoghaire	4,180	40,300
Howth	2,295	4,800
Free Entry Land, including reclamations	14,400	172,800
Increase in Dun Laoghaire and Howth	—	8,000
(a) Free Entry Land	40,245	702,900
(b) Deferred Development Land	5,200	62,400
Total, including Free Entry and Deferred Development	45,445	765,300

of a four-to-six mile wide green belt, thus only allowing the city to extend over an area of 45,455 acres and accommodating a maximum population of 765,300. The green belt could be used for agricultural, institutional or recreational purposes. The following quotation from the report pinpoints the consultants' general policy as to the size of the city:

> Table 1.2 indicates the population we envisage. We base it on the assumption that the population of 477,000 within the present boundary can remain fixed since the residential land, still unbuilt or within the present boundary, is capable of accommodating some 70,000 people which is a sufficient approximation to the number to be removed from central areas under the 'thinning out' programme.[192]

(see Figs. 1.9 and 2.2 for details)

Table 1.3 shows that within the green belt a number of centres would be allowed to expand and the whole proposal foreshadowed the 1944 Greater London Plan. Within residential areas the approach to development was similar to that in the Mark I British New Towns, although smaller in scale.

TABLE 1.3
Area and Population of Satellites within Green Belt

Name	Present Population	Free Entry	Holding at *20 to acre	Deferred Land	Holding at 20 to acre
		Acres	People	Acres	People
Malahide					
Portmarnock	2,000	600	12,000	400	8,000
Swords	1,000	300	6,000	220	4,400
Lucan	1,000	80	1,600	80	1,600
Blanchardstown					
Castleknock	1,000	200	4,000	150	3,000
Clondalkin	600	300	6,000	120	2,400
Tallaght	500	80	1,600	80	1,600
St Margaret's	—	80	1,600	80	1,600
	6,100		add 32,800 new 6,100 existing		add 22,600 new 38,900
			38,999	Final total including existing rural population	61,500

*To allow of open spaces etc.

To a large extent the consultants' general proposals had been put forward in 1936 in a memorandum by H. T. O'Rourke, the City Architect, to the Gavan Duffy Tribunal on Local Government. Arguing that the maximum size of town in modern times must allow for easy access to countryside, O'Rourke went on to say that in the case of Dublin 'the approximate ultimate radius from the centre, to provide quick and cheap transport, is suggested at five miles. Within this radius, with future controlled development, a maximum future population of 750,000 persons is suggested ...'[193] He proposed a descending scale of suburban densities as one moved towards the municipal boundary, beyond which 'an agricultural permanent belt of land should be reserved not less than 2 miles wide'.[194] He also proposed that no satellite town should be developed inside a radius of ten miles from the centre of the city and that such satellite towns should have populations of 50,000 to allow for self-containment. O'Rourke's proposals can thus be seen as an early precursor of the consultants' recommendations.

In addition, proposals by the planning consultants had to be examined in relation to recommendations from concurrent inquiries into both municipal boundary changes and working-class housing problems. Evidence before the Dublin Housing[195] Inquiry indicated a need for a sizeable increase in the number of new dwellings being erected annually, especially by the public authorities. Whereas the Dublin Corporation had erected 14,884 dwellings between 1887 and 1939, the inquiry concluded that at least 18,000 new dwellings were required to meet arrears and, to deal with the housing emergency, the Corporation's entire output would need to be increased from 1175 dwellings per annum to something over 3000. Such an increase in dwellings was likely to give rise to demands for more land and to cause further urban expansion.

The Local Government (Dublin) Tribunal had proposed a Dublin Metropolitan Corporation 'to administer a unified Dublin Metropolitan Borough, bounded by the present boundary of Dublin County and by the sea, thereby including the present Dublin County Borough, the Borough of Dun Laoghaire, the Urban District of Howth and the Dublin County Health District'.[196] In turn this new Metropolitan Borough would be divided into a 'rural portion' and an 'urban portion' with most services, including town planning, being provided on a unitary basis to the whole borough. Special services relating to provision of housing, water and scavenging would be provided in the 'urban portion' consisting of the old city area, Dun Laoghaire and a peripheral zone incorporating land out to Malahide, Swords, Finglas, Lucan, Tallaght,

Dundrum and Shankill.

Abercrombie, in an addendum to the Sketch Plan, equated the proposed green belt as corresponding to the rural portions of the proposed Metropolitan Borough and concluded that 'the findings of the Tribunal would thus apply as well to our proposals as to those put forward by the Tribunal'.[197]

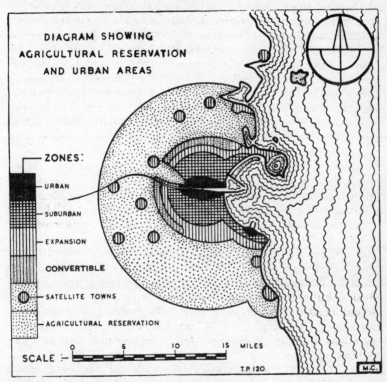

Fig. 1.9 Abercrombie's Sketch Proposals, 1941.

While the Dublin Corporation was prepared to initiate a planning scheme for the area under its own jurisdiction, many of the Consultants' proposals were not suitable for inclusion in a statutory scheme and were to 'be kept in reserve'.[198] By 1946 plans prepared by the City Engineer and the Town Planning Officer clearly favoured the development of contiguous suburban tracts within the city boundary (Fig. 1.10).[199] The Corporation abandoned the idea of satellite development because:

we plumped for fringe development as we feared to develop

by way of satellite towns we would be creating a transport problem, since without special powers to deal with the movement of industry and all it entails, the Corporation might find themselves with a number of dormitory satellites having people at considerable distances away from their work.[200]

It was also apparent that the proper planning balance between considerations of beauty, convenience and economy were being set aside and that infrastructural dictates were to shape the growth of the city "in order to get the most economic form of development for existing and future services, the green belt should . . . be related to drainage areas".[201] Progress towards the preparation of Dublin's Draft Planning Scheme was to prove painfully slow and, as Nowlan indicates below, the outcome faced the Department of Local Government with a very embarrassing problem.

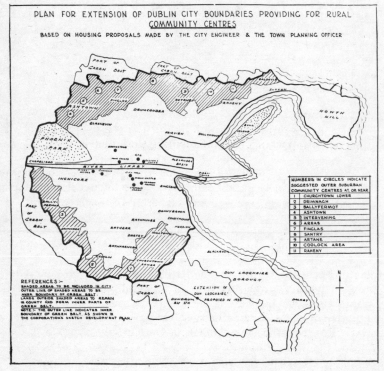

Fig. 1.10 Corporation Scheme of Peripheral Expansion. (Source: *Irish Builder & Engineer*).

Towards a National Planning Policy

Any acceptance of the restrictive policies implicit in the Dublin Sketch Plan would have implied a degree of central government control which the Government probably did not have and which it most certainly was not prepared to use. This was particularly true in respect of migration from rural areas to Dublin; but while it was the universal hope of social reformers 'to stem citywards drifts of population, and to induce immigrants to return to our depopulated countryside . . . the means to achieve such ends yet remain to be discovered'.[202] Replying to a paper by Abercrombie,[203] Justice Gavan Duffy pointed out that the prescribing of maximum city populations 'will call for legislation on this troublesome problem'.[204] Any such countering of traditional migration trends also presumed the existence of a scheme of national development.

The notion of a national planning framework had been raised by Ruthen in 1919 when he spoke of a national housing and planning scheme based upon 'the proper development of the national resources, agricultural and industrial, mineral and metaliferous'.[205] In the 1930s, as planning was seen to have a concern with the orderly development of all aspects of life — not just housing, there were to emerge repeated calls for a policy of national planning and development. A pamphlet on National Economic Recovery (1935) proposed a National Economic Development Commission to deal with the problem of unemployment.[206] Working to the Commission there would be a sub-Commission on 'Land Reclamation, Drainage and Forestry' and a second on 'Housing and Town and Country Planning'. The objects of the planning sub-Commission were:

1. To provide good and reasonably priced housing.
2. To compel local authorities to plan and implement schemes.
3. To fund the implementation of such schemes.
4. All schemes to 'conform to a general scheme of town and country planning to be approved by the Commission'.[207]

The report of the Commission of Inquiry into Banking, Currency and Credit echoed the need for a national development policy and one of the Minority reports explicitly called for the state to prepare 'a national plan of reconstruction and development capable of putting all our unemployed people to work'.[208] There was also a reappearance of the idea of an Economic Development Commission with a 'Commissioner' to be responsible for Housing and Town Planning. Under this proposal money would be advanced, interest free, to solve the housing crisis and good planning would ensure a more beautiful and fully occupied country:

> Town plans for the improvement and development of all Irish towns, and plans for the preservation of the beauty of the countryside should be drawn up. All grants of money should be made conditional on the works undertaken fitting in with approved plans, to prevent the country being disfigured as it is at present. Money should be advanced to local authorities for the improvement of towns and villages when local and suitable labour is in need of employment.[209]

While not incorporated in the majority report, these proposals do indicate the continued pressure for a national plan of development and reconstruction. The need for a national development policy stemmed from the chronic and related problems of rural decline, village decay,[210] rising unemployment and the imbalance arising from Dublin's 'more varied and vital part in national life'.[211]

The development of any national development policy was seen to entail a promotion of regional development and regional planning. The maximisation of regional resources within a national development policy was given a sense of urgency with the advent of World War II. The appointment of Sean Lemass as Minister for Supplies for the duration of 'the emergency' also offered a ray of hope and the *Irish Builder* stressed his 1941 speech in which he emphasised that the Government's objective 'in war or peace, however it might be expressed in terms of organisation or production, was the reduction of unemployment. If unemployment persisted, the economic system did not deserve to survive.'[212] In his capacity as Minister of Supplies, ably assisted by John Leydon, Secretary of the Department, Lemass assumed an increasingly important role in ensuring the country's wartime economic survival and in charting the course for post-war recovery.

One of Lemass's first actions was to establish an inter-departmental Committee to 'examine the problems which would arise in the event of isolation or invasion of this country'.[213] The inter-departmental Committee recommended on 5 July 1940 that 'Counties should be grouped so as to provide a district that will be reasonably compact and which can be covered without undue difficulty by the officer having charge of it'[214] — the 'Regional Commissioners.' There were to be eight emergency regions, almost identical with the existing army commands of that date,[215] with a regional commissioner named to assume full responsibility for each region in the event of invasion effective from 3 September 1940.[216] (See Fig. 1.6b). The designation of regional areas seemed to herald a new era of regional consciousness. Speaking on the Relief Works Bill in the Dáil in October 1940, the Minister for Local Government and Public Health, Mr Ruttledge, indicated ways in which his department proposed to apply the hitherto inoperative regional provisions of the 1934 Act, particularly in relation to Co. Dublin.[217] The Bill had proposed that public utility works should proceed regardless of local authority boundaries. The *Irish Builder and Engineer* saw in this a sign of a new beginning and an end of the situation where inter-municipal issues were 'treated as matters of inevitably acrimonious controversy between local and central authorities' — the first step towards 'a national planning authority'.[218]

The *Irish Builder and Engineer* expressed a strongly-held professional belief that 'the Regional Commissioners should be instructed to proceed with surveys of their respective areas'[219] and that the Commissioners be kept busy on useful work pending any unwanted invasion.[220] In this way the eight 'emergency regions' could help replace some of the multiplicity of small local authorities and 'should become permanent links between country and urban authorities and Government Departments'.[221] But regional planning could only succeed in the context of a national plan. Speaking to an inter-professional group in Dublin in Spring 1942, Manning Robertson had emphasised the importance of a national survey 'which would put us in the position of being able to organise the country to an immensely increased degree of efficiency'.[222] Robertson was calling for a National Plan and this implied some form of national planning organisation, an idea raised by Frank Gibney in 1940.[223]

From Robertson's suggestion sprang the idea promoted by the *Irish Builder and Engineer*, of a National Planning Exhibition — 'focus point and a sorting office for ideas of planned Reconstruction'[224] — whereby:

> accredited representatives of town planning interests, of rural organisation movements and of tourist agencies, could be induced to sit around a table, not to deplore the failure of the Government, or any other party, to appreciate their particular points of view, but to discover and propound some policy and practical programme of common interest.[225]

In this Aston was once again assisting the professional groups and championing the cause of a broadly based national planning policy, supported by Deputy Erskine Childers, who later became Parliamentary Secretary to the Department of Local Government. Childers had been deeply involved with the Civics Institute of

Ireland and in 1941 he responded to Michael Scott's proposal for 'the Village Planned' with a call for:

1. Compulsory town planning under a special Town Planning Commission having wide powers.
2. More education in town planning for civic authorities.
3. Architects to design all housing schemes.
4. A fine and inspired set of village models to be available to the Town Planning Commission.[226]

Childers wished to see Ireland first rate in everything, including planning, rather than slavishly copying second-rate English models. Responding to the challenge, some forty individuals met in Dublin in June 1942 to form the National Planning Conference — a loose federation of some twenty-five organisations and agencies committed to the future wellbeing of Ireland — including representatives of the Planning Institute, Muintir na Tíre, the County Councils, the Tourist Board, the Trades Union Congress, the Dublin Chamber of Commerce and the Civics Institute.[227] The Conference adopted the following memorandum:

> It is agreed: That plans should be prepared in advance for post-war developments in Éire.
> It is suggested:
>
> (1) That such plans should include the co-ordinated results of proposals to be prepared by
>
> (a) Local authorities under the provisions of the Town and Regional Planning Acts.
>
> (b) Regional planning authorities — to be responsible for the design of services which overlap local boundaries, and for the preparation of local plans in cases where county or urban councils may fail to apply for powers under the Town and Regional Planning Acts; and
>
> (c) A national planning authority in respect of such services as transport, and communications, harbour developments, electricity supplies, arterial drainage and the distribution of industries.
>
> (2) That the eight 'regions' portrayed on the accompanying sketch-map would be convenient geographical and economic units — to provide 'links' between local bodies and the national planning authority. (Fig. 1.6b).
>
> (3) Reasons and precedents for the selection of the regions delineated include the facts:

(a) That the proposed groupings of counties are those adopted by the Government as 'Emergency Regions'.

(b) That the counties of Dublin, Wicklow, Kildare and Meath have already been officially defined as a regional planning unit.

(c) That analogous groupings of counties have been adopted as planning regions by the Government of Northern Ireland; and

(d) That the groupings proposed for Éire are those of counties which possess many common interests and well-defined characteristics.[228]

The Conference received the warm approval of the Government 'in its efforts to direct the minds of citizens to certain aspects of post war reconstruction'.[229] Although De Valera feared that 'we are far too far from being out of the wood for post-war planning, yet, to be a very active preoccupation',[230] his department was concerned at the abysmal failure to implement the 1934 and 1939 Acts,[231] and the Conference received his encouragement.

The National Planning Conference set itself the task of bringing together a major exhibition of Ireland's human and natural resources using data in departmental reports, initiating surveys and an examination of detailed conditions in particular regions. The fifteen major topics to be researched were set out in Conference's Information Bulletin No. 1,[232] while a second bulletin was devoted to an analysis of population and migration trends.[233] Under the Chairmanship of Fr J. E. Canavan, much of the Conference's work was done by Manning Robertson.

The development of a national policy received a practical injection from two works by Frank Gibney in 1943. Developing his ideas of 1940, Gibney produced a 'Framework for An Irish National Plan', a Garden-City style, decentralised model of Ireland with a new capital city to the north of Athlone with full employment, good communications, adequate infrastructural services, proper education for all and a devolved system of participatory democracy.[234] The stylised nature of the illustrations in this proposal belie his more pragmatic hope that

> All our activities should be co-ordinated in a way to produce a coherent pattern and a single machine of national endeavour, wherein all parts work in unison without friction and waste and geared to the power of the State. The Plan visualises the State as a pyramid, the base being our Natural Resources, the body the Population, and the point, or summit of the design, the well-being of the Individual.[235]

Of potentially greater significance to national planning policy was Gibney's 'Suirbhéaracht Éireann' or proposals for an Irish National Survey and the draft for a National Atlas which would provide a basis for planning and reconstruction.[236] This volume contained a total of 338 maps dealing with the physical, human and economic interests on the island as a whole. Such a daunting task of national stocktaking was not to be repeated until the Royal Irish Academy, with the help of a vast team of researchers, compiled *The Atlas of Ireland* in 1979.

Meanwhile work was proceeding on the proposed planning exhibition under the auspices of the National Planning Conference, with Manning Robertson taking the opportunity to stress that 'Town Planning and Agriculture are as much interdependent, — different facets of the same problem — as chemistry and physics are partners in the body of Science'.[237] Planning was also the focus of considerable attention within the Commission on Vocational Organisation. The Commission's 1943 Report highlighted 'the sectional, local, piecemeal and balanced' attempts 'to plan, regulate and direct industrial life'.[238] Having examined the approaches to planned development in a number of European countries, the Commission proposed a National Vocational Assembly which amongst other things would prepare and implement plans of national development:

> The second main function of the Assembly, following necessarily from the first, should be to plan. A survey of social and economic conditions will reveal many defects that could be remedied, much new work that could be done and progress that could be achieved. The existence of unemployment and emigration is a constant reminder of defects that call for attention. It should be the duty of a National Vocational Assembly to consider such problems, to examine remedies, to calculate their cost and to propound for adoption the policy or procedure that is possible with given resources in a given time, as well as to indicate how this could be geared up to secure the maximum effort in case of emergency . . . .
>
> Towards that end political leaders and legislators should bend every effort; but they alone cannot achieve success. The whole organised economy of the country should devote itself to the task so as to secure that planning would not be external, imposed, unwisely contrived and regardless of cost, but would be the deliberate achievement of a free people. We do not see any way in which a democratic people can organise itself for planning the maximum development of its resources

in a wise and just scheme of national scope other than by means of a National Vocational Assembly such as we recommend, wherein shall be gathered the representatives of every sphere of its economic life.[239]

The Commission was deeply conscious of the distasteful connotation of the word 'planning' in some quarters, and they stressed the importance of co-operation in planning to ensure economic security and civic freedom.[240]

This report was seen to have made an important input to the International Labour Organisation's investigation of 'Collaboration between the Public Authorities, Workers' Organisations and Employers' Organisations' and a summary of the Report was prepared by the ILO.[241] However, the Irish response to the report was generally lukewarm and, most surprisingly, Lemass castigated the report for its inadequacies even though it dealt with a set of problems with which he appears to have been more deeply concerned than most of his Cabinet colleagues.[242]

The year 1944 was to be one of frenetic energy for planning, with several significant publications and the holding of the Conference's National Planning Exhibition. In *The Green Book,* the president of the Architectural Association defined the broad components of a national plan:

> It is, in a broad sense , the proper organisation of the country on economic, social, political, cultural and spiritual lines. In the physical sense, it has to do with the orderly development of the country's resources, convenience and suitability of transport, work, play and educational facilities, the production of food, clothing and shelter, health and general amenity.[245]

Associated with the exhibition, a number of pamphlets on planning or related to planning were issued. Under the general heading of 'Reconstruction Pamphlets' and with the motto, 'Ireland is ours for the making; let us make it', Robertson wrote a pamphlet on *Town Planning,*[244] with special reference to citizen participation, while Noel Moffett compiled one on *Leisure.*[245] In keeping with the all-Ireland spirit of the National Planning Conference, Manning Robertson and R. S. Wilshere joined forces to produce a small publication on *Town Planning in Ireland,* with sections on 'Éire' and 'Northern Ireland'.[246]

The National Planning Exhibition was held in the Mansion House from April 26 to May 5 1944.[249] The exhibition aimed to stimulate 'thought and energy in the minds of every well-wisher of Ireland';[248] it embraced all sections of Irish life — urban, rural, industrial, agricultural and professional, and its collection of exhibits filled the Round Room and adjoining rooms. While De Valera's opening speech reflected his jaundiced view of planning, the platform was representative of all sections of Irish society[249] — rather reminiscent of Geddes's Dublin Civic Exhibition of some thirty years before. The creators of the exhibition 'had succeeded in high degree in their aim of compressing into the Round Room, Ireland as she is, and Ireland as she might be, without concealing cloaks of party or vested interests'.[250]

In strongly Geddesian fashion, the centrepiece of the exhibition was a map on which the thousands of visitors saw depicted, with the aid of cameras, the whole interrelationship of Ireland's physical, economic and social resources.[251] A detailed account of the exhibition's contents appeared in the *Architects' Journal*.[252] The exhibition was complemented by a programme of lectures on topics such as 'Towns, Villages and Rural Life' by Rev. J. M. Hayes, 'Public Health' by J. M. Shanley, and a seminar on 'Finding the Money for Planning'.[253] As a permanent legacy of the exhibition there was the *Handbook* containing a series of papers on an equally diverse range of topics, including 'Planning in Northern Ireland' and 'The Parish as a Planning Unit'.[254]

With its wide base of support, the National Planning Conference demonstrated the innovative capacity of Ireland to produce a broadly based comprehensive planning movement of particular relevance to a relatively undeveloped, poor and predominantly rural economy. Indeed the unique involvement of Muintir na Tíre in the Conference was of special significance and later in 1944 the Chairman of that organisation made an impassioned plea for urban-rural co-operation and the preparation of 'Civic Weeks, Study Circles and above all, ensuring the spirit of harmony and co-operation among all citizens'.[255] The Conference demonstrated the type of development plan which was relevant to all of Ireland's needs. That the Conference did not have lasting success was due to many factors, including political and ministerial apathy and the inability of Government to come to terms with such a radical movement with inter-departmental implications. The inertia, the lack of staffing and the lack of finance to provide more staff are highlighted in the following extract from a memo of 21 April 1944 from The Department of Local Government:

> No change in planning law in this country is suggested at this stage but if progress is to be made under the existing law it is

very necessary that the Department of Local Government and Public Health should be put in a position to take more positive action in pressing forward the preparation of planning schemes by planning authorities. The lack of specialised staff in the Department of Local Government and Public Health who could devote themselves whole time to planning problems has been responsible for the very poor progress which has so far been made in this country and unless technical staff can be specially assigned within the Department for planning duties only, there is not much prospect of any better progress being achieved in the future.[256]

The Status and Professionalism of Planning
The development of an Irish planning movement reflected an alliance between the existing design professions and socially concerned and civic minded individuals and groups. Inevitably, planning was all too often viewed as nothing more than an extension of a particular profession. Thus, in an article on 'Building and Order', O'Gorman left his readers in little doubt that he viewed architects as the pre-eminent group in planning.[257] Somewhat similar distortions of planning as 'architecture writ large' were seen in a paper by Hill on 'Town Planning In Cork'[258] and in Michael Scott's proposal for the 'Village Planned'.[259] Likewise, the engineering professions saw planning as largely an engineering function[260] and, while there might be room for special survey staff or advisory town planning specialists, engineers would be responsible for implementing the 1934 Act.[261] This was certainly the case in Dublin where Michael O'Brien had been appointed Planning Officer but retained his partiality for engineers, as indicated by his 1943 comment that 'the Engineer is not as closely identified with town and county planning as some of us would wish to see'.[262]

Howevver, there had been moves to bring together, formally or informally, those professionals concerned with planning, and the professions of architecture and engineering both took early steps to obtain a measure of competence and proficiency in planning. Thus, by 1922 the Royal Institute of the Architects of Ireland had set up a 'consultative Town Planning Committee'[263] and in 1935 E. Murphy proposed a 'Planning Circle' within the Institute of Engineers to assist with matters of publicity and co-operation on town planning matters.[264] The Circle would act to safeguard engineers and architects in performing their duties under the Town and Regional Planning Act. In 1936 a Joint Committee of Architects, Surveyors and Engineers was set up to deal with town planning.[265] Lectures in town planning were offered to engineering students from 1946 onwards, while UCD architectural students also received some formal lectures in town planning. At a more general level the Civics Institute functioned throughout the 1920s and 1930s as a broadly based advocacy group seeking 'systematic co-operation in voluntary social work, by bringing into closer relationship Public Departments, Local Authorities, Official bodies and individuals engaged in works of Civic Development and Reform'.[266] The Institute functioned as a significant pressure group for town planning and housing reform[267]; it was an important centre of education in all aspects of civics and it played an important role in integrating approaches to the social and physical improvement of Dublin.[268]

Town planning was also deemed sufficiently important to have a place in the Diploma in Public Administration offered by Trinity College, in which the Civics Institute collaborated, and for which Manning Robertson wrote a general overview of 'Town and Regional Planning'.[269] But there was also a recognised need for some form of professional institute of planners if the Act was to be fully implemented. In 1936 Robertson identified Ireland's need for a planning course; he also recognised that 'we should have in mind the ultimate formation of a Town Planning Institute of Ireland'.[270] Such an institute should not be formed in haste since 'we must be sure that such a diploma (*sic*), if given, would not fall below the standard set by existing diplomas in architecture, engineering and surveying'.[271] Owing to lack of numbers, Robertson's aspiration for an Irish institute of planners was not realised for almost forty years; instead, the small band of existing Irish planners formed an Irish Branch of the Town Planning Institute in October 1941.[272] The founding members were Manning Robertson (Chairman), H. G. Simms (Vice-Chairman), M. O'Brien (Treasurer), R. Hogan (Secretary) and Desmond Fitzgerald. Over the succeeding years the Irish Branch was a consistent voice calling for advances in planning practice, improvements in planning education, and some of its members were to play a significant role in shaping and implementing the 1960s planning legislation.

However, while the 1930s and early 1940s saw cautious advances in planning within the professions, achievements at Government level were unspectacular. The report of the National Planning Conference recommendations favouring mandatory planning, greater integration of town and country, and the initiation of regional and national planning under the direction of a Ministry of Planning and Public Works came to nothing.[273], although such a Ministry had been proposed in the *Irish Times* in 1941[274] and the appointment of Erskine Childers as Parliamentary Secretary to the

Department of Local Government was seen as a ray of hope.[275] It was not until 1946 that a Planning Section was formed within the Department of Local Government [276], progress remained slow and the Department failed to exercise influence in Cabinet, at least on planning matters.

In so far as the torch of planning survived, it was a tribute to the tenacity of a small band of committed people including Ernest A. Aston, Manning D. Robertson and Frank Gibney.

The Pioneers of Irish Planning
Ernest A. Aston (1873-1949) was undoubtedly the greatest Irish name associated with the promotion of modern town planning prior to the 1960s. He must also rank as one of Ireland's most committed and public-spirited citizens. He was the Hon. Secretary and organiser of the Cork Exhibition 1907. He became closely associated with the work of Geddes and Lady Aberdeen in Dublin after 1911. In 1913 he presented a most imaginative set of proposals for Dublin's planned development in his evidence to the Departmental Housing Inquiry on behalf of the Dublin Citizen's Housing League. He was the founder and Hon. Secretary of the Irish Proportional Representation Society and in the 1920s he was the driving force behind the Greater Dublin Reconstruction Movement. He worked with Frank Mears and Lady Aberdeen to develop the Killester garden suburb for ex-servicemen. He was the initiator and persistent champion of the Blue Lagoon scheme. Under his own name and the pseudonyms 'Artifex' and 'Nomad' he contributed to virtually every issue of the *Irish Builder* for well over forty years. In this capacity and as sub-editor in the *Irish Times* he availed of his opportunity to advocate planning, to castigate mediocrity and procrastination and to pursue his policy to 'astonish Dublin', his beloved city, into positive action. He was a close acquaintance of many British and Irish politicians, a frequent critic of Ministers of Local Government, but a longtime admirer of the ability of Sean Lemass to get things done. An obituary by Smyllie, editor of the *Irish Times*, speaks for the man:

> To his dying hour he was a pioneer and a crusader. An unrepentant champion of lost causes, he was quixotic in his impulses, spending a great part of his waking hours in the unrewarded services of others. I never knew anybody who helped so many lame dogs over stiles. His charity was limitless. He would go to infinite pains to take even a complete stranger out of a difficulty, ignoring and even sacrificing, his own interests in the process. Needless to say, he was imposed

on constantly; but that never bothered Aston. He would sit up all night to do a good turn, and he always had a ready excuse for those who let him down.

He was an aggressive and violently persistent pioneer, who got things done by his sheer strength of character. One of his failings was that, once having seen a project well under way, he would leave it to somebody else to tie up the loose ends, and start off with equal enthusiasm on another trail.

Many of his daring dreams remain to be fulfilled.

Manning D. Robertson (1888-1945)[277] was an architect and town planner of international repute. A native of Co. Carlow, he was educated at Eton and Oxford where he studied architecture. His first two major publications were *Laymen and The New Architecture* (1925) and *Foundations of Architecture* (1929). Robertson settled in Ireland in the mid-1920s and quickly immersed himself in organising the Dublin Civic Weeks of 1927 and 1929. He remained deeply committed to the work of the Civics Institute. He was a prolific writer on all aspects of planning and contributed to international journals and to Irish publications; he was a successful user of newspapers and radio to promote an interest in all aspects of the environment. Robertson was largely responsible for the 'Cautionary Guide to Dublin' by the RIAI and he had a large influence on the shaping of the Town and Regional Planning Act, 1934. He used every avenue to promote the implementation of that Act and he himself acted as planning consultant to Limerick and Cork Corporations and to Dun laoghaire Borough Council. He was deeply involved with Patrick Abercrombie and Sydney Kelly in the preparation of *Dublin: A Sketch Plan*. He was the driving force behind the inter-professional Joint Committee, the founding of the Irish Branch of the TPI and the formation of the National Planning Conference of 1942-4. In addition he retained an interest in architecture, being a member of the advisory committee for the recording of Irish buildings; he also designed a number of housing schemes, including Temple Hill, Dun Laoghaire. His unexpected and untimely death in 1945 robbed Irish planning of its most prominent practitioner, although he had already left an important legacy to this country. Alone amongst Irish planners, he had recognised that Ireland's planning problems 'were as much sociological as physical'.

Frank Gibney (1905-1978), architect and town planner, served as planning consultant to Tralee Urban District Council, Drogheda, Meath and Navan. Reference has already been made to his realistic approach to the re-planning of Waterford where he was involved in a number of local schemes and projects.

The Beaux Arts nature of some of Gibney's sketches, for both Dublin and the country, conceal a philosophy of social concern. This concern manifested itself clearly in his submission to the inter-departmental Committee on Public Works in 1935.[278] The employment-generating schemes put forward by him included the building of a Dublin civil airport, cleaning the Liffey bed, riverside promenades, cleaning public buildings, refuse removal, road widening, tree planting, creation of flower gardens and construction of the Clontarf Marine boulevard. In an era when geographers had only a limited involvement in planning, Gibney's *Suibhéaracht Éireann* was an enormous and innovative undertaking with profound geographical and planning significance.

But it was Gibney's work for Bord na Mona which was to prove most evident in the Irish landscape. Complementary to its peat works, Bord na Mona erected in excess of 700 workers' houses at some nine locations, including Coill Dubh, Rochfortbridge, Kilcormack, Lanesboro and Cloontooskert in Roscommon.[279] These attractive schemes were designed by Gibney in a style and to a standard well above that normally provided in conventional local authority schemes. Gibney had many ideas which have a continuing relevance for Ireland including a clear and detailed understanding of the content of District Planning Schemes.[280]

Conclusion

The inter-war period provided a hostile and difficult environment for planning. The domestic problems of the new state, the country's isolation, its rural dominance and the slow pace of industrialisation all contributed to a lack of momentum in most areas of public policy, including planning. Where planning proposals were advanced, it is possible, with hindsight, to understand the futility of seeking to apply to Irish conditions schemes, policies and legislation which evolved in a different political and cultural milieus. As Manning Robertson advocated, we must adopt procedures 'of a kind to suit our particular needs'. But the unfortunate decision to do nothing in respect of many aspects of development inevitably cost the country dearly in terms of job creation, economic growth and national prosperity. Indeed this failure probably contributed to the country's unpreparedness to capitalise on post-war economic development and contributed to the perpetuation of bad housing and poor social conditions for many of its population. The new state, born of idealism, had lost its dynamism and had fallen victim to 'the inevitability of gradualness'.

The lack of attention given to planning casts a general reflection on the commitment of a succession of Ministers who held responsibility for the Department of Local Government. In addition, De Valera's caution 'to beware of the seductive occupation of planning' did little to foster enthusiasm.[281] Alone amongst all Irish Ministers, Sean Lemass exhibited both an interest in planning and evidence of understanding of the nature of planning suited to Ireland's needs, an activity confined 'to broad outlines of policy, leaving private enterprise to deal with matters of detail' with the planning authority 'answerable to the people and removable by them'.[282]

Under pressure from Lemass, De Valera had set up a Cabinet Committee on Economic Planning in 1942, inspired by an urgency regarding a possible return of 400,000 Irish from Britain. Though the Committee met almost sixty times, it lost its sense of urgency and had ceased by the end of the war.[283] Given his commitment to development and his success as wartime Minister of Supplies, it is not surprising that there were calls for a National Planning Authority and that 'Mr Lemass, in command of an expert staff, is the fit and proper person to undertake the work of reviewing and co-ordinating all plans for national reconstruction and development.'[284]

This was not to be, and planning settled down to a much less ambitious role of which Cronin was to say later:

> In some areas Local Government ignored the Acts altogether, in others it made permanent a temporary device provided for in the Acts: and control of development, a wholly negative frunction, masqueraded before the public as the totality of planning. Compensation provisions in the Act not only permitted but were found to accommodate this debasement of the legislation and the planning function.[284]

Irish Planning from 1921 to 1945 was sadly a story of "what might have been achieved."

CHAPTER TWO

THE EVOLUTION OF IRISH PLANNING 1934-1964

Kevin I. Nowlan

Any examination of planning legislation in the period after 1934 must have regard to the general climate of opinion in Ireland and the general context for planning as set out by Bannon in Chapter 1. In this chapter it is proposed to discuss, first of all, the 1934 and 1963 Planning Acts and then make some comment on their implementation and effects. But, the point will emerge more than once that the general public had little interest in planning and this lack of interest was and is evident among local and central government politicians. Now, they are deeply interested in their powers but not in the objective of proper planning and development. It is also well to remember that in 1934 relatively few people had even heard of the words 'town planning'.

The Town and Regional Planning Act, 1934
The preamble, or long title as it is now called, to the 1934 Act reads: 'An Act to make provisions for the orderly and progressive development of cities, towns and other areas whether urban or rural and to preserve and improve the amenities thereof and for other matters connected therewith.' It would have made a fully satisfactory preamble to the 1963 Act.[1]

The Act was of its time. It reflected the realities of development pressures, as they were seen. It did make a contribution to the orderly control of development and the protection of amenities. it did not include such words as ecology or environment. During a debate on the 1962 Bill[2] from which the 1963 Act evolved, the meaning of the word ecology was vainly sought in the Chamber of Dáil Éireann. In 1934 the county management system did not exist. Only three of the four county boroughs had been subjected to the management system.³ However, the basic difference in concept between the 1934 Act and the 1963 Act is very much less than is popularly imagined. Each required that a Planning Authority put some of its cards on the table, i.e. a local authority was empowered to make a plan and it was required to implement that plan.

An examination of what each Act would allow a Planning Authority to put into its plan leads to the conclusion that the more things change the more they remain the same. The second schedule to the 1934 Act lists the matters which might be included in a Planning Scheme. The third schedule to the 1963 Act includes four lists which display a very marked similarity to those of 1934. Section 40 of the earlier Act provides for use zoning in words that might, from some points of view, be more suitable than those used in Section 19 of the 1963 Act.

There are two important differences though they are peripheral or administrative rather than fundamental. Under the 1934 Act no town or county council was obliged to make a town plan. Though most urban authorities did, in fact, during the life of the Act, decide to make a plan, the choice was left to the council. The 1963 Act imposed a duty on every town and county council to make a plan and it also specified certain minimum provisions. The 1934 Act did not prescribe any minimum planning content for a planning scheme.

The second important difference is to be found in the nature of the plans when made. A plan when made and put into operation under the 1934 Act was intended to have the force of law. The system now called development control would not have remained. A duty was imposed on developers to comply with the plan.⁴

The local authority was given power to take legal and physical action to secure that development would not contravene that plan. The onus was cast on the land owner to ensure that his developments were in accord with the law. The arrangement proposed had advantages as well as disadvantages. The enormous bureaucracy of current planning administration would not be consuming such a volume of human and financial resources, and imposing such great costs on development through delay and consequent interest charges, if the 1934 procedure had been continued.

An argument against the making of plans, or planning schemes as they were called, was their cumbersome method of adoption and the rigidity of their nature. The validity of this argument now appears suspect, especially if regard is had to the delays encountered in making, reviewing or implementing a Development Plan under the 1963 Act. Thus, in the case of Dublin Corporation the first review of the Development was not completed until 1980, sixteen years after the commencement of the Act. Whereas the law requires that plans be reviewed every five years, it took four years from the time the Draft Review was displayed in 1976 until its adoption in 1980. In the case of Dublin Co. Council the delays are even lengthier. It has been suggested that a Planning Scheme under the 1934 Act could have been changed in nine months — about the length of time necessary to secure a decision from An Bord Pleanála[5]. Nothing of what is stated above should be interpreted as argument that the 1963 Act was unnecessary or inappropriate. The 1963 Act has been remarkably successful. Most of the criticism of it has been misguided and would be more properly directed at the administration than at the legislation, and it would probably be true to say that its success has been something of a surprise to those who were involved in its shaping. It is probably true also that the success story, if such words are appropriate, is a different story from that envisaged at the time of its enactment. One problem which was foreseen by a distinguished opposition member of Dáil Éireann during the debates is the vast bureaucracy that has come into existence in the wake of the legislation.[6] It is unlikely that those who framed the Act anticipated such an outcome.

It will again be necessary to refer later to similarities and differences between the two Acts. In doing this, the references will be primarily to the 1934 and 1963 Acts. In planning terms, the 1976 Act is of little real importance and its alterations in the law were far more important in administrative terms than in planning terms. This possibly reflects in some degree the weight of the bureaucracy on planning and development and the weakening of planning as a development tool. In contrast, the 1939 Act had much greater planning impact on the 1934 Act.[7] It would have been possible, with common sense and some skill, to have made useful Planning Schemes under these Acts. Though skill was in short supply during the 1940s and 1950s, common sense was only as scarce then as it appears to be now.

Planning schemes which included, or Development Plans which include, lists of objectives which are way beyond financial possibilities could not and cannot command respect from those who take the trouble to do simple arithmetic. They may and did make convenient topics for the superficial journalistic comment which the public at large appears to enjoy and pay for. The Town and Regional Planning Act, 1934, provided a framework within which each Town and County Council could, if it so decided, make a Planning Scheme for its area. The almost total town planning inertia of the Department of Local Government and Public Health at that time ensured that no pressure was applied to the Councils throughout the country to make themselves into planning authorities by passing the appropriate resolutions. The lack of ministerial interest in planning may be deduced from the fact that the first and only planning officer appointed in the Department took up his post after 1940 and a Planning Section was established as recently as 1946.[8] So far as it can be discovered, the aids to planning authorities issued by the Department consisted of a booklet of 'Model Clauses' and a circular about the location of petrol stations. During the two years 1945/47, the total number of appeals reached the dreadful number of 196 compared with 45 in the two years 1943/1945. The level of action or progress in local authorities at that time was not such as to disturb too greatly the corridors of power in the Custom House. The same Minister continued in office from 1932 to 1939 and another from 1941 to 1948, neither regarding planning as a top priority.

Procedures for Implementation

If a local authority decided to make use of the Act, it was required to publish notices in its area and by formal irrevocable resolution decide to make a Planning Scheme 'with all convenient speed'. It was necessary that a majority of the members of the authority vote for the resolution. It was not sufficient that a majority of those present should support the resolution. If the authority then performed the self-imposed duty of making a Planning Scheme, the Act required that it be submitted to the Minister who was given considerable power under the Act. He could have approved the Scheme or have requested its modification in such a manner as he thought fit; he could even require that a new Scheme be prepared and submitted to him. If the Minister made an order approving a Planning Scheme, he was required to lay the order before the Oireachtas. Either house was empowered to annul by resolution the order of the Minister granting approval to the Planning Scheme.

In comparison with the Development Plan of today, the formality of final adoption of a Planning Scheme was considerable, but it must be noted that the possible effects of a Planning Scheme could have been more fundamental than those which *necessarily* follow from the making of a Development Plan. As will be seen later, the putting into effect of a Planning Scheme could have created liabilities for land owners and the local authority, though it did not necessarily do so. Under a somewhat surprising power of Section 44 of the 1934 Act, regulations, bye-laws and Acts of Parliament, could have been suspended by provisions of the Planning Scheme. The procedure for compulsory acquisition of land in furtherance of the scheme was slightly simplified though not to the degree now available under the Housing Act procedure which is now used for most compulsory acquisition of land by local authorities.

A number of possibilities were created. A local authority could pass the necessary resolution to make a plan for part or all of its area. The total planning effort of Mayo County Council in thirty years appears to have been the passing of a resolution to make a plan for the Knock area; similarly, Longford County Council passed a resolution to make a plan for the environs of Longford town.

Regional Planning Schemes
Adjoining local authorities could decide by appropriate resolutions to create planning regions. The word region was not defined in the Act. Such a region could have been made up of the areas of adjoining authorities joined together for the purpose of making a regional plan in the normal meaning of the word or it could have been a 'joint planning area' for all the purposes of the making of a Planning Scheme. These powers are some of those which could, with advantage, have been incorporated in some form in the 1963 Act. The only and somewhat remotely similar provision is that in Section 42 by which Special Amenity Areas overlapping the boundaries of adjacent planning areas may be declared. So far as can be ascertained, no regional resolutions were passed by planning authorities. Such resolutions would have been subject to the approval of the Minister for Local Government and Public Health.

The advantage which could have been derived from the setting up of voluntary planning regions is considerable. The most obvious benefit would have been a continuity of policy across county or urban boundaries. These, fixed in most instances eighty years ago, do not relate in any way to the spheres of urban influence or to the activities of a population whose mobility has changed beyond the possible imaginations of those who fixed boundaries in 1901. An administrative and financial advantage could have been achieved by the joint employment of planners, whose cost could have been distributed. Some staff hierarchical problems evident today could have been avoided.

A further co-operative power provided by Section 21 of the 1934 Act enabled the council of an urban area to add to its planning district the contiguous parts of an adjoining County Council area for planning purposes. Thus, as early as 1940, Tralee Urban District Council availed of this Section to secure control of the adjoining County area. Several years later Dublin Corporation failed in an attempt to acquire planning powers or development control over a large part of County Dublin.

Though Dublin City attempted and failed to obtain control of the day-to-day planning in a large part of the county area, it could, under Section 20, have taken regional planning powers for the entire region consisting of the county of Dublin and its adjoining counties. A similar power was given to the city council of Cork in the 1934 Act. Neither Dublin nor Cork availed of the power offered to them by Section 20, probably because the Act required the regional authority in such case to confine the exercise of its powers to those matters which might affect the city. The county authorities were not to be interfered with in their normal planning or other operations. The extensive provisions for regional planning of the 1934 Act contrast markedly with the complete absence of the word 'regional' from the text of the 1963 Act.

The Question of Betterment

The absence of any reference to regional planning in the 1963 Act is matched by the absence of reference to betterment[9] and the omission to make any provision for its recovery by the State or by the Planning Authorities. The importance of recovering betterment to the minds of those who drafted the 1934 Act lay in the vague belief that somehow betterment recovered would balance any compensation payable after the coming into operation of a Planning Scheme. It is unlilkely that any real projections were made which would have justified such belief. Even with the sophisticated methods and techniques of today such projections would be uncertain.

Section 72 of the 1934 Act empowered planning local authorities to demand from property owners three-quarters of the increase in value brought about by provisions of the Planning Scheme or by the execution of work by the Authority in pursuance of a provision of the Scheme. Many years later, the Uthwatt Report in Britain proposed that three-quarters of increments in value of property be recoverable at five-year intervals.[10] It is probable that the Uthwatt proposals were unworkable and would have led to injustices and hardship. It is equally probable that some of the provisions of the 1934 Act were workable and that they included a sufficient safeguard to preclude injustice. This safeguard was provided by an option on the part of an owner of the property subject to a claim for betterment, to undertake not to change the use of the property involved. In such circumstances, the Authority was precluded from recovering betterment for fourteen years unless the property changed hands or was otherwise changed.

It is now over fifty years since the enactment of these betterment provisions. If they were re-enacted, numerous changes would be necessary to the details. It is, however, the belief of this writer that the legislation, as enacted in 1934, could have worked and could still work. Its failure followed from a number of situations which have, in the main, disappeared. The basic reason for failure of the 1934 betterment provisions is that no Planning Scheme was ever put into effect. Even the single Scheme (Dublin City) that was made ignored the betterment provisions of the law. Behind the failure lay the complete rejection by professional and business communities of the concept of payment for betterment and, only to a slightly less degree, a rejection of the concept by each landowner that he could not use his land exactly as he wished. The rejection was most complete among small property owners. The great estate proprietors had, in general, accepted the idea of control because they understood its value to their own estates. The rejection by small landowners of the concept of control, and the accord which this rejection still finds in the minds of local councillors, is evident today and can be seen in the unfortunate development of bungalows in the Dublin and Wicklow mountains, along the coasts of Galway and Cork and in the ribboning of many of the national routes. The availability of even the powers of Section 72 of the 1934 Act could have been a very useful and effective restraint and much of this unfortunate development would probably not have taken place if that power had been used.

The fate of the 1934 Act was in part determined by a continuing flow of information or mis-information from Britain where the equivalent Act of 1932 suffered from defects apparently not reproduced by our 1934 Act. The Irish Act also suffered from the same rejections by professional groups as in England. It suffered, as did the 1932 English Act, from ignorance amongst planners and the valuation professions. The valuation profession in Ireland, if at that time it was entitled to the name profession, had not advanced very far from the cattle market approach to valuation. The very sophisticated methods now practised were then unknown in Ireland.

On the other hand, planning authorities are now, in the 1980s, attempting unlawfully to collect betterment; they even use the name betterment. Section 26(2) of the 1963 Act does empower planning authorities to demand, as conditions attached to a Grant of Permission, contributions towards the cost of works which facilitate the development for which permission is being granted. A contribution towards the cost of doing particular works may, in truth, have little relation to betterment. Developers — not land owners — pay these demands in the knowledge that the eventual owners, whether ordinary householders, manufacturers or shop keepers will pay the contribution plus profit. In general, the real beneficiary in increased land price escapes though, like everybody else, he must pay his personal taxes including capital gains tax.

In much of the country, compensation and betterment had little relevance. It did not have any real impact on planning problems outside the large urban areas but the spectre of compensation provided a self-justification and excuse for administrative staff to do nothing and to advise councils to do nothing. The total inertia at Ministerial level provided a negative pressure throughout the country. In Britain, where planning has become part of life, there has been a continuing flow of advice in all forms from central to local government. The growth of planning in Britain was aided both by strong Ministerial commitment and by forceful Departmental staff.

Changes under the 1939 Act
When introducing the 1939 Act to Dáil Éireann, the Minister responsible said 'in the large majority of areas, very little attention has been given either to the provisions of the Act of 1934 or the model clauses prepared by the Department. The areas in which planning schemes are *under consideration* are the areas in which the largest development is taking place.'[11] That speech was made in October 1938 more than four and one half years after the main Act had come into operation. This second Act of 1939 appears to have been like many a flower born to bloom unseen — almost. It made no fundamental change in the basic law. It closed a number of gaps in procedure and made one important contribution towards reducing the rigidity of the planning scheme. It did this by providing that certain areas could be defined in the Planning Scheme as areas to which a 'restricted development provision' would apply. For such areas, a form of 'local plan' could be prepared and put into operation after the making of the Planning Scheme. This change foreshadowed in some form development control as we now know it. The smokescreen behind which the administrative machine of the Department of Local Government hid its lack of enthusiasm for planning was created by claims or allegations that large sums in compensation would be payable on the coming into operation of a Planning Scheme. The fact was that each Planning Authority was completely free to choose from the schedules to the Act the matter for inclusion in its Planning Scheme. There were no compulsory items, though the Minister did hold the power to insist that a Planning Scheme submitted to him be modified in such a way as he might direct. In ordinary circumstances, a local authority could

have adopted a Planning Scheme without costly proposals. It could have made a plan which contained nothing except zoning proposals which would not attract a penny in compensation. If it wished to recover betterment consequent on the execution of works by itself, those works would have, of necessity, been included in the Scheme proposals. For example, if an authority proposed to lay a sewer to drain certain lands, it could have included the sewer proposal in the Planning Scheme and recovered three-quarters of the increase in value of the lands drained by the sewer. It is not obvious why similar powers could not have been included in the 1963 Act. It must, however, be remembered that the astronomical increase in land values and prices which occurred since 1963 could not have been contemplated.

The Need for Strong Central Government Commitment

The 1934 and 1939 Acts did not produce the results expected of them or of which they were capable. They did have defects but in the context of their time, these defects were not fundamental. The fact that so little damage was done to the country and its amenities is testimony to the low level of development pressure. Population was falling and emigration was very high. Both industry and agriculture were suffering from the inward-looking and very nationalistic policies of government and from 1939 to 1946 the war concentrated the nation's activities on survival. It is probable that the propaganda which led to the making of the 1934 Act had little effect on those in a position to actually do something about making plans. There were few votes in town planning. For planning to be effective there must be real guidance and pressure if not control from the centre. The major reports of the 1930s and 1940s in Britain advised that a strong planning function should exist at central government.[12] In Britain, it was recognised that the importance of this function justified the appointment of a Minister for Town and Country Planning.[13] That office has disappeared but a strong central organisation was created with its research and advisory functions in addition to the appeal and general administrative responsibilities. It is possible that the inevitable hiving off of the appeal function in this country under the 1976 Act, away from the Minister to an independent Board, may have reduced the already inadequate service offered to local authorities in planning matters by the Minister for the Environment.

Implementation

It is not at all easy to assess what was achieved as a consequence of the 1934 and 1939 Acts. It is not unlikely that many public

80 Planning: The Irish Experience

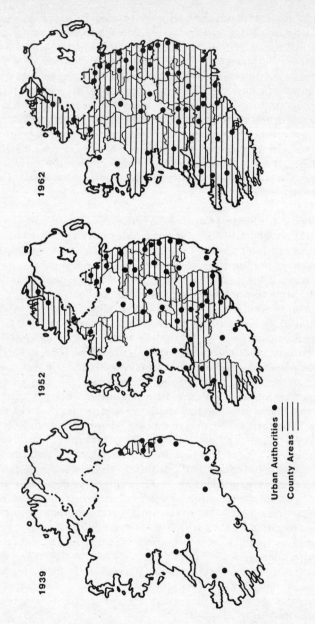

Fig. 2.1 Planning Authorities which passed Resolution to adopt the *Town and Regional Planning Act*, 1934. (Source: Reports of Departmental of Local Government.)

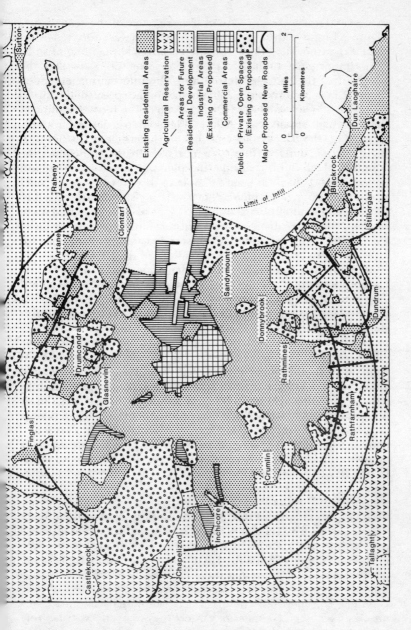

Fig. 2.2 Dublin Sketch Development Plan: Metropolitan Area.
(Source: Abercrombie et al. 1941.)

representatives were unaware of the existence of the second Act. Figure 2.1a shows the extent to which the Acts were adopted — i.e. the local authorities which considered physical planning of sufficient importance to justify the preparation of maps and the adoption of the required resolution. The information on which Figure 2.1a is based has been obtained from the speech of the Minister for Local Government in Dáil Éireann at the second reading of the Bill which became the 1939 Act. Figure 2.1b is derived from the reports of the Department of Local Government 1948/49/52. Figure 2.1c is derived from the reports of 1960/62 and shows the counties which did not decide that planning had a place in local government. It has not been possible to discover which of the 87 planning authorities which adopted the legislation attempted to prepare any kind of plan at all. Such plans as were prepared were, in the main, unrealistic, almost entirely unrelated to the likely availability of finance and they transcended administrative boundaries and even exceeded the legal realities of the 1934 Act.

Many of these defects became evident in a *Sketch Plan* for Dublin Corporation prepared by Abercrombie, Kelly and Robertson.[14] The general proposals are shown in Fig. 2.2 above. While it is sound planning practice to examine, study and take into account the facts and trends in adjoining areas, it would now be thought impolitic, unprofessional and impractical to prepare plans for the adjoining area. Planners in the Ireland of forty years ago suffered from no such inhibitions. Populations were allocated to towns and villages miles away from the area of the authority preparing to make a planning scheme.[15] It is not too unfair to say that almost nothing that this map predicted has come about. It is also probable that no human agency could have predicted the opulence and activities of today. The unreality of the 1941 plan (Figure 2.2) is in strange contrast to the extent to which the 1922 zoning proposals for the city have been realised.[16]

Planning of Dublin

Much of this chapter is related to the Dublin scene and there are many reasons why this must be so. It is thought, though facts are not easy to ascertain, that outside the Dublin area only three authorities employed qualified planners on their staffs as planners. At the time of the presentation of the Dublin *Sketch Plan* in 1939 there were very few professionally qualified planners in the country. A proportion were architects who practised as such but naturally accepted commissions where they were offered. Planning to them was a design-orientated operation. The concept of a planning processs responding to pressures and changes was contradictory to the design and master plan concept. The Planning Scheme of the Act helped to further this concept where, as was usual, consultants were employed who could not have continuing connection with the administration of the area planned and who were quite unfamiliar with the legal and political basis of local government.[17] The saving of planning and the protection of amenities lay largely in the extremely low level of development which took place. What was at the time called the 'economic war' led to the near destruction of agriculture and the self-isolating policies of industrialisation brought the economic activities of the country to a very low level by the 1950s. During the period 1951-1961 there was a net loss of people from the Dublin area of more than 70,000. At one period Dublin Corporation found that 1500-1600 of its houses per year were being abandoned by their tenants. The upswing of the 1960s led to the adoption of the 1963 Act (see Bannon, Ch. 5). Outside Dublin the pace of development was even slower and changes in the landscape were minimal. Even in Dublin City, the making of a Planning Scheme came about under quite extraordinary circumstances. It came about primarily because compensation for the provisions of the Planning Scheme, and to a lesser extent interim (development) control[18] decisions, was payable only when a Planning Scheme came into operation.

A building company was advised that certain decisions of Dublin Corporation created a right to compensation which would become real only when a scheme came into effect. Correspondence between the company and the Authority was terminated by a decision to continue 'interim control'. There was no indication that the making of a Planning Scheme with 'all convenient speed' as the Act required would proceed. Years of litigation followed and the proceedings occupied weeks in both the High and Supreme Courts. It is possible that personal antipathies rather than public interest inspired some of the action. Finally, the Corporation admitted defeat and under threat of the imprisonment of the Lord Mayor, Aldermen and Burgesses, a Planning Scheme was drafted in 1957[19] and submitted to the Minister. This author was deputy to the city Planning Officer at that time and inevitably had a major part in its preparation.

The plan, like much of its successors, attempted too much. It was initially intended to be based on a twenty-five-year projection, divided in five periods. At some stage, each five year period was extended to eight years and it became a forty-year plan by simple resolution. Nothing else changed. The excessive list of road proposals has been more than mirrored by the excessive list of road proposals in the 1980 Development Plan.

The Scheme was politically inept. In general, a plan implies constraints of one kind or another and most of these must be negative or objectionable from the point of view of some house or landowner. They give rise to objections which may be formal, made in accordance with some law, or they may be political by protest, lobbying or propaganda. A plan which claims to set out objectives covering a period of thirty to forty years after its proclamation must give rise to disquiet among those who are aware of the realities of government and among small property owners who fear that the indicated proposals may become realities and damage their interests. In the event, 3600 objections were lodged with the City Council. A very high percentage of these took the form of 'objections to proposal to take part of my property for road widening'. The next largest group consisted of objections to proposed taking of land for public housing sites. These latter had some relation to reality because the local authority had a history of activity in slum clearance and re-building. On the other hand, building is only now, in progress on many of the sites blighted by the 1957 Scheme. The objections to most of the road proposals could have been avoided because the Authority had no prospect of obtaining the money necessary for the road works proposed. In addition, many house owners were disturbed and the value of their property affected by long-term proposals — about which little has yet been done — and which took the form of incorporating front gardens of houses in widened roads. Such a reservation had no useful effect of any kind. Existing law prohibited building on the land reserved and if by any remote chance the road improvement were to be undertaken, the normal powers remained untouched by the Planning Scheme. Compensation would have to be paid for damage suffered by the house owners. Everybody, including the house owners, would have been better off by the omission of such proposals from the plan.

The Plan as made, in all probability, could have been adopted by the Authority if the 1963 Act had been in operation. It provided for the four essential elements of a Development Plan under the 1963 Act. The less controversial provisions of the Planning Scheme, that is, the zoning and amenity protection clauses, formed a useful basis for the control of development. Many of these passed in modified or updated forms into the Development Plan of 1971.

Quite independently of the planning law of the time, the City Council did attempt to acquire and redevelop the area now occupied by the recently constructed 'ILAC Centre'. It made an order to acquire the land compulsorily under its Housing Act powers but was constrained by a court order. During the Court proceedings, the judge expressed sympathy with the intention but condemned the means chosen. There were, in fact, no other powers available but if a Planning Scheme were in operation it could have provided the power required.

Conclusion
The fate of the Dublin Plan and the Town and Regional Planning Acts became inextricably linked. After adoption by the City Council, the Plan passed to a Government Department where its arrival could hardly have been less welcome. Whatever about some of its contents, it was competently put together. Many of its objectives were sensible. During its life, it did prove to be a useful statement of policies. To dispose of it in one way or another was essential. It was a hot potato in the hands of a Department ill-equipped to deal with it. The group of builders which had supported the litigation against Dublin Corporation remained unhappy. Parliamentary questions were asked and there were threats of further litigation. In justice to certain offices of the Department it must be said that efforts had from time to time been made to amend the 1934 and 1939 Acts. A committee of officials, together with some members of the Town Planning Institute, had met from time to time but the political will was not aroused until the necessity of doing something about the Dublin Plan brought compulsion. The Local Government (Planning and Development) Act, 1963, was the result. It repealed the Town and Regional Planning Acts of 1934 and 1939. The legal basis for the Dublin Plan was removed and never again would a Planning Scheme or Development Plan embarrass a Ministerial or Departmental desk with a demand for appraisal or approval.

CHAPTER THREE

ENVIRONMENTAL CONSERVATION CONCERN AND ACTION, 1920-1970

Ken Mawhinney

The other chapters in this volume are largely concerned with the history of creative or innovative aspects of planning, where planning is seen as one means of remedying problems of a social, economic, public health and general environmental nature by creating, or controlling the creation of, new environmental conditions. This chapter deals with another role of planning — conservation — which seeks to retain, safeguard and make good use of those elements in the environment which are given a special value by society. These elements include buildings of architectural and historical importance, archaeological monuments and sites, areas of botanical, zoological and geological importance, and landscapes of special scenic attractiveness. In recent years attention and concern have been broadened to include not only these special values, but the good qualities of the environment generally: wildlife, trees, woodlands, hedgerows, clean water, clean air, pleasant landscape and townscape.

This chapter examines, in an exploratory way, environmental conservation in the period 1920 to 1970 in terms of the growth in concern expressed by the public and the resulting action taken by Government and voluntary organisations. But first it is necessary to take a brief look at the period prior to 1920.

Before 1920
Prior to 1920 we find comparatively little concern for conservation — or its less dynamic sub-categories, protection and preservation — expressed in public debate, in the policies of various organisations, or in the legislation. The main exception to this generalisation was 'ancient monuments', structures and sites of the eras up to

and including the Middle Ages. Here, it is pleasant to record, Ireland had provided a lead, almost by chance, as a by-product of the Irish Church Act of 1869, which disestablished and partially disendowed the Church of Ireland.

Section 25 of this Act provided that:

> where any church or ecclesiastical building or structure appears to the (Church Temporalities) Commissioners to be ruinous or if a church to be wholly disused as a place of public worship, and not suitable for restoration as a place of public worship, and yet to be deserving of being maintained as a national monument by reason of its architectural character or antiquity, the Commissioners shall by order vest such church, building or structure in the Secretary of the Commissioners of Public Works in Ireland to be held by such secretary, his heirs and assigns, upon trust for the Commissioners of Public Works, to be preserved as a national monument.[1]

A sum of £50,000 was set aside for the maintenance of national monuments under the Irish Church Act (until 1882 there was no provision in Britain for the care of monuments by the state).

The concern of the Commissioners of Public Works with national monuments dates effectively from October 1874 when the structures on the Rock of Cashel were vested in them. Later that year 13 more monuments were vested. By 1880 the score was 137 monuments or groups of monuments. The first Inspector of National Monuments (or Superintendent as he was called), Mr Thomas Newenham Deane, was appointed in March 1875.

The next major development was the Ancient Monuments Protection Act, 1882, the only Act of Parliament dealing with monuments to apply to Britain and Ireland as a whole. This provided, initially, for the preservation of an additional 29 monuments or groups of monuments (listed in a Schedule) and it is intriguing to note that until the 1930 Act there were two categories — 'national' and 'ancient' monuments — each funded separately in relation to works required.

In 1892 the Ancient Monuments Protection (Ireland) Act extended the definition of ancient monuments to include any ancient or medieval structure, etc. which in the Commissioners' opinion was a matter of public interest by reason of its historic, traditional or artistic interest. This Act extended the Commissioners' powers to bring additional monuments into their care.[1]

Various bodies were concerned with the study of archaeology, the Royal Society of Antiquaries of Ireland and the Royal Irish

Academy in particular. The former had built up a collection of artefacts which was deposited in the newly established National Museum in the 1890s.[2] Nevertheless, there seems to have been little concern recorded by societies and individuals about the need for a fuller and more widespread policy of conservation of field monuments. Threats in the form of technological, economic and social changes did not exist in sufficient scale or strength to be apparent, perhaps; decay and other natural processes associated with the passage of time were seen as the dangers. However, the impetus towards the development of tourism in Ireland in the 1890s caused R.A.S. Macalister to express some concern in 1897:

> ... any large influx of trippers will menace the safety of these monuments, indeed in several cases the mischief is already done, notably New Grange, which is in a scandalous state on account of scribbled names mingling with its wonderful sculpting.[3]

Buildings erected in the seventeenth and later centuries were not regarded as 'ancient monuments' and concern for their well-being was limited. The Georgian Society was founded in Dublin in 1908 in order to produce records of eighteenth-century domestic architecture and decoration. Meant to remain in existence for five years to do this task, the Society was not dedicated to preservation although the readers of its *Records*, published in five volumes, were urged "to induce those who live in houses containing good and interesting work both to take care of it and to have sketches and photographs taken for the Society's collection".[4]

Despite this exhortation, a fatalistic acceptance of the effects of time seems to have pervaded the Society to judge by a statement in the Introduction to the first volume of the *Records*: 'But alas, most of these monuments of a brilliant society are doomed to decay and disappear: many have already vanished.'

In 1877 William Morris had founded the Society for the Protection of Ancient Buildings. Originally founded mainly to protect medieval buildings, the Society soon turned its attentions to those of later periods. Morris argued:

> It has been most truly said ... that these old buildings do not truly belong to us only, that they have belonged to our forefathers and they will belong to our descendants unless we play them false. They are not in any sense our property, to do as we like with. We are only trustees for those who come after us.[5]

Despite the fact that Thomas Davis had made a similar point in one of his essays thirty years earlier — 'he who tramples on the past does not create for the future'[6] — no evidence exists of any impact made by the Society for the Protection of Ancient Buildings in Ireland. In contrast, a ripple from another preservationist body founded at the end of the nineteenth century, the National Trust, did reach Ireland. Founded to acquire and preserve for the nation places of historic interest and natural beauty, the Trust acquired one such property in Ireland — Kanturk Castle, County Cork, now a national monument in state care.

In the nineteenth century there was a widespread development of interest in nature, reflected by the growth of natural history societies. The emphasis was on the academic study of flora and fauna, with a strong flavouring of the Victorian mania for collecting. Much of this activity, rather than contributing to conservation, ran counter to it as enthusiastic amateurs collected rare plant species. The Killarney fern was one casualty. Sir Robert Ball in his *Reminiscences* recalled how this plant leaped into fame:

> Everyone was searching for it. There were, however, many places in Ireland besides Killarney where it could be found .... I have looked for it in recent years — not later, indeed, than last year (1908) — in County Kerry, but it was not to be found. It was about 1830 or perhaps earlier that my father found it growing magnificently in an exquisite spot known as Glendyne, on the Blackwater near Youghal. I have often heard how he was seen running down the glen in the greatest excitement, bearing an enormous handful.[7]

His father was later Honorary Secretary to the Royal Zoological Society of Ireland.

Much serious academic work was done, of course, and floras were published for Ireland (*Cybele Hibernica*) in 1866, and for Dublin 1904, Donegal 1898, and Kerry 1916, as well as for many smaller areas. The journal, the *Irish Naturalist*, was launched in 1892. However, a perusal of the index of the first eighteen volumes reveals only one entry concerned with conservation. The subject was the protection of wild birds and reflects the fact that birds were the pioneering area of conservation concern in the United Kingdom of Britain and Ireland with the founding of the Society for the Protection of Birds in 1889, later the Royal Society for the Protection of Birds.

Around 1915, what could have been a major development in the history of conservation in Ireland was initiated by the Society for the Preservation of Nature Reserves, a body analogous in many ways to the Society for the Protection of Ancient Buildings. The Society prepared a *Schedule of Areas in Ireland Considered Worthy of Preservation* containing twenty areas of Primary Importance and two areas of Secondary Importance. In the first category were the Burren ('great botanical interest'), the Lakes of Killarney and surroundings ('very lovely scenery of botanical interest'), Nagraiguebeg Lough, Galway ('Lusitanian flora'), the North Bull, Dublin, the Raven, Wexford and Sand Dunes near Wicklow. Six bogs of 'general and botanical interest' were also included. World War I and the political changes in Ireland in the following years arrested this interesting line of development and left us with the intriguing speculation of a historical 'might have been'.

1920-1945

Some space has been devoted to describing the period prior to 1920 for the reason that, to a very large degree, the decades after were similar in character. In relation to what is now termed environmental conservation, it was for a long time a matter of 'no change'. In some ways this is not unexpected. There was no surge of economic development following political independence which might have produced threats to the environment and, in reaction to this, concern and action among the public. Four decades had to pass before this phenomenon took place in Ireland. In a state where the development of industry and agriculture was minimal, where there was a low rate of urbanisation and a decreasing national population, the major threats to environmental values were still seen, by the few who were concerned, to be those of temporal decay.

For successive governments the priorities lay elsewhere, in political and economic areas, although perhaps one might have expected more attention to be paid to the conservation and restoration of certain elements of the national heritage which were symbolic of Irish nationality. Political independence is like marriage, perhaps, in that realities often oust romance once the blessed state is reached.

Another consequence of political independence was that the ripples — ideas, movements and initiatives — which used to originate in the centre of the pool (London/Westminster) now no longer reached Ireland, or reached Ireland only after a considerable time-lag or in a subdued form. The instances of the Society for the Preservation of Nature Reserves and the National Trust which would have developed in Ireland in the 1920s and 1930s have been mentioned. Other movements in Britain concerned with national parks and the protection of buildings of architectural interest seem to have had no counterpart in Ireland between the wars. In time, of course, Ireland developed her own ripples, but for a long time there was little movement on the surface of the Irish conservation pond.

In relation to the natural environment, the case for nature reserves and the protection of rare species of flora and fauna does not seem to have been taken up and presented in any active or forceful way. For example, a look through the major writings of Robert Lloyd Praeger, the most eminent naturalist of the day in the 1920s and 1930s, yields no pleas or advocacy on behalf of conservation, protection, nature reserves, etc. (It should be added, however, that Praeger was active later in the formation of An Taisce in 1948.) A. W. Stelfox in 1928, in a book for use in schools, made a plea for conservation,[8] but otherwise it was the ornithologists who gave the lead in the natural history field, as they traditionally have done.

In 1930 the Wild Birds Protection Act was passed, following urging and pressure by ornithologists over a number of years. The Act gave protection to most wild birds, and also provided the legal basis for the establishment of bird sanctuaries. The latter provision was put in at the suggestion of Father P. G. Kennedy, who had a particular interest in the protection of the birds of the North Bull. To quote his own words, 'There was great jubilation among all naturalists' when in July 1931 the North Bull became the first bird sanctuary legally established in Ireland.[9] In 1930, too, all game birds and the hare were given the protection of close seasons under the Game Preservation Act.

The year 1930 also saw the passing of the National Monuments Act which replaced the Westminster Acts of 1882, 1892 and 1910. This Act has provided the basis for the protection of archaeological sites, monuments and artefacts for the past fifty years. It was very much archaeological in spirit, in the sense that its provisions suited the protection of structures and artefacts of the medieval and earlier ages. The record of items protected bears this out, although one or two adventurous sorties into the post-1600 period have been made. Nevertheless, despite its limitations, the Act has enabled the Commissioners of the Office of Public Works to take into state care by 1982 some 569 monuments, with Preservation Orders covering a further 405 monuments.

Buildings of more recent periods, the seventeenth century onwards, remained unprotected and their cause was not supported in any widespread or concerted way. Architects and planners, such as R. M. Butler and Manning Robertson lamented the decay of the Georgian houses of Dublin, but placed their hopes for the future well-being of the city in the town-planning schemes that would be made under the Town and Regional Planning Act, 1934.

This Act had its origins in a draft Town Planning Bill prepared and submitted to the Government in 1923 by the Royal Institute of the Architects of Ireland. It lay dormant for six years until 1929, when Senator Thomas Johnson asked the Civics Institute of Ireland to prepare a Bill which he would sponsor in the Senate. The Civics Institute had published its famous *Dublin Civic Survey* in 1925 and was the principal protagonist for planning in the country. The Civics Institute drew on the earlier Bill, with the approval of the architects, and the result was introduced into the Senate by Senator Johnson as the 'Town Planning and Rural Amenities Bill', 1929. It gained the support of all parties in the Senate, was passed and went on to the Dáil. The Government intimated that it would shortly introduce its own Bill and there was then a pause until the Town and Regional Planning Bill, 1933, was introduced. This became law the following year.

The subsequent history of this legislation is covered in another chapter. In relation to conservation, its significance lies in the fact that it put on the statute book provisions to protect certain environmental values. These are listed in Part III of the Second Schedule, 'Particular Matters for which Provision may be Made by Planning Schemes'. They include the preservation of views and prospects; the amenities of places and features of natural beauty or interest; structures and objects of artistic, architectural, archaeological or historical interest; forests, woods, trees, shrubs, plants and flowers.

Since only one planning scheme was completed, it cannot be said that this Act contributed much to environmental conservation in practical terms. However, it gave legal expression to certain values which society had in relation to the environment and it provided the basis for and much of the wording of the preservation provisions of Part IV of the Third Schedule of the Local Government (Planning and Development) Act, 1963. For example, that poetic phrase 'views and prospects' which has intrigued so many planners had its origins here in the 1934 Act.

The inclusion of views and prospects in the 1934 Act is indicative of a broadening of conservation concern away from specific archaeological, historical, architectural, geological and botanical values to include the more general and complex one of scenic landscape. It was recognised in Ireland that the country was not under the same threat as England, where 'scores of towns are extending every day, eating up the country between them like dry rot in long ribbons of shoddy buildings'.[10] Nevertheless, it was felt that a danger did exist, particularly with 'isolated atrocities and individual acts of vandalism', and that in areas of attractive landscape 'one badly designed or badly placed building may ruin a whole neighbourhood'.[11] It is of interest to note that the danger to the tourist industry of such development in Ireland was pointed out by *The Builder*, a British publication, which said that 'unless something is done, and done soon, Ireland will become an outer suburb of England, complete with bungalows, villas and ribbon development'.[12]

1945-1960

The protection of areas of scenic landscape was a theme that was taken up in 1945 after World War II. The country was on the move again and exciting things were happening in Britain in relation to the crusade for National Parks. The excitement spread to Ireland: Sir Shane Leslie wrote a paper 'National Parks for Éire'[13] in which he asked:

> What material and opportunity, what rural spaces and scenic possibilities lie before those who would like to set aside parts of Ireland to tell the native and tourist, during the next thousand years, how beautiful was the land of Éire before it was industrialised (say) in the year 2000 or overbuilt, overinhabited in the succeeding millenium?

He went on to suggest that 'he will be a brave man, who, without making the most careful inquiries and undertaking journeys himself, will dare to set out the most suitable spots for making Ireland's National Parks'. Courageously, he then produced his own 'rough suggestion':

1. Killarney District
2. North Donegal Highlands
3. The Curragh
4. Wicklow Mountains
5. Clare Coast
6. Achill Island
7. Galtees and Knockmealdown Mountains
8. Dingle Peninsula
9. Bog of Allen

Leslie saw a necessity for local public participation:

> I am certain that the local interest must be first raised and, when the principal inhabitants have collected their data and have confabulated with their local councils, then and not till then, should legislation be introduced making the Park a thing of joy and beauty forever.

More realistically, and prophetically, he said, 'we always believe that we have a longer lease of time on hand than other nations .... We shall probably not hurry over our National Parks'.

Something was achieved, however, in the next few years, with the formation of An Taisce, the National Trust for Ireland, in 1948. The origins of this organisation lay in a meeting of concerned citizens in October 1946 in the Royal Irish Academy. The group included Dr Felix Hackett, G. F. Mitchell, the Earl of Rosse, Sean MacBride, Dr R. F. Browne (Chairman, ESB), Robert Lloyd Praeger and Cearbhall O'Dalaigh. The name of the group, initially, was the Association for the Preservation of Places of Interest or Beauty in Ireland.[14]

Re-titled as An Taisce, the National Trust for Ireland, the organisation held its first meeting of Subscribers and Directors in July 1948, and the first General Meeting of the Trust took place in September 1948. The President was Robert Lloyd Praeger, who in the following month gave a broadcast talk on Radio Éireann on 'Our National Trust'. Among the principal objectives of the new body were:

> To promote the permanent preservation, for the benefit of the nation, of land and buildings of natural beauty or national historic or artistic beauty; and as regards land to preserve (as far as practicable) its natural aspect and features and animal and plant life.
>
> To devote any of the above for the purpose of science or for the preservation of natural features and animal and plant life.[15]

A membership of 250 was soon achieved and in its early years the Trust concerned itself with 'nature conservation and matters such as the flora in the Burren, Co. Clare, the state of the area surrounding Killarney, Kanturk Castle, in Co. Cork, the possibility of using Powerscourt House as a Georgian Museum, etc.'[16]

An important ingredient in the concern that led to the formation of An Taisce came from the Blue Lagoon controversy centred on the North Bull Island in Dublin Bay. As early as 1929 proposals had been put forward for the development and urbanisation of the island, one of which had included the provision of dams at both ends of the island to form a permanent lake. All remained dormant until 1944, when the golf clubs on the island were informed that the Irish Tourist Board was preparing plans for the development of the island as a tourist resort. Subsequent disclosures in 1945 showed the positions of a cinema, a dance hall, a bus road running down the island for half its length and, at the end of this road, a second dance hall in the sand dunes. In 1946 further proposals by Dublin Corporation showed an embankment and bridge linking the island with the mainland at the Dollymount end, and the provision of a restaurant, dance hall, open-air theatre, amusement park and various other amenities, and the construction of a road along the northern edge of the Bull Island.

All these proposals incurred the opposition of a wide variety of interests among the public, including the Irish Society for the Protection of Birds and the Dublin Naturalists Field Club who were particularly, but not exclusively, concerned with the effects the proposals could have on the bird sanctuary. This opposition, together with other factors, led to the withdrawal of the Irish Tourist Board from the proposed development in 1950, and the subsequent intimation by Dublin Corporation that it would not be in a position to carry out the project unless the Government provided assistance. As Father P. G. Kennedy concludes in his book, *An Irish Sanctuary* (1953), which gives an account of these events: 'Thus the immediate danger to the Sanctuary was averted, but the threat was not withdrawn and there is no feeling of security for the future.' He also made the suggestion that 'the Bull Island should be left untouched and be handed over to the National Trust for Ireland'.

The Bull Island controversy may be said to have had another important effect: by assisting the realisation in tourist development philosophy that the conservation of Ireland's cultural and natural heritage was of paramount importance to the successful growth of tourism. This tenet was expressed in the 'Synthesis of Reports on Tourism' (1950-51) by the Department of Industry and Commerce and, in legal form, in the Tourist Traffic Act, 1952. This Act established Bord Fáilte Éireann as the statutory tourist body in the Republic, and gave the Board power to

> 'Protect and maintain and to aid in the protection of historic buildings, sites and shrines and places of scenic, historic, scientific or other interest to the public, and to facilitate visitors thereto by the provision of notices and the provision and improvement of means of access'.

Another indication of changing times and perceptions is provided by J. P. Brunker in his *Flora of the County Wicklow* (1950), where he draws attention in the Introduction to the threats posed by the 'bungalow menace' and the 'tripper mentality' to scenery and flora. He pointed out that a piece of wild country can become a rural slum and rubbish-heap. This is the fate that has overtaken Brittas Bay — classic ground for the field botanist since the time of David Moore and A. G. More, and still quite unspoiled less than twenty-five years ago, but now covered with shoddy buildings and the debris of picnics. Apparently none of the good plants of this district have been entirely obliterated, but they are yearly becoming harder to find.

One other event in the 1950s is worthy of mention in a survey such as this. This is the excellent and remarkably comprehensive paper, 'The Position of Nature Protection in Ireland in 1956' by Michael O'Ruadhain, published in the *Irish Naturalists' Journal* in October 1956. It covers many facets of the subject not touched upon here and makes suggestions which, if acted upon, would have advanced Ireland's position in nature conservation by two decades — for example, in the establishment of nature reserves. Another example of the foresight contained in this paper is the warning that 'a new and menacing form of water pollution may arise from the disposal of atomic waste into the sea and other waters'.

1960-1970

The period 1960 to 1970 (or more accurately 1958 to 1970) stands in remarkable contrast to the preceding decades in the area of environmental conservation — and, indeed, in most other aspects of Irish life. As Brendan Clarke puts it in his paper 'The Environment 1945-1970':

> If we study the post-war years, it soon becomes clear that the protection of the physical environment as an important public issue did not begin to gather real momentum until the period covering the first two national economic plans between 1958 and 1969.[17]

This was the period of dramatic economic development. (Professor Lyons borrows W. W. Rostow's term 'take-off' to denote the period in his *Ireland Since the Famine*, but prudently adds a question-mark.) It was also a period of social change, and a social historian in writing about this period would regard the growth in public concern about environmental matters as an important feature of this change. He might well go on to account for this increased consciousness of environmental matters in terms of various factors which acted and reacted with one another during this period: industrial and commercial development, urban development and re-development, population increases, increased car ownership, pollution, legislation, an expanding middle-class, improved education, television, international ideas and influence.

An attempt will be made to chart the growth of public environmental concern in this period. Appropriately, 1958, the year of Dr Whitaker's *Economic Development* and the First Programme for Economic Expansion, saw the founding of the Irish Georgian Society, 'on 21 February 1958, fifty years to the day after the founding of the original Georgian Society . . . to work on the preservation of Georgian architecture in Ireland'.[18] Its purpose contrasts with that of the earlier society. By 1969 the Society had some 5000 members, though not all these lived in Ireland.

An Taisce went through revitalisation and expansion in the 1960s. In 1966 it had 450 members, less than twice its 1948 membership, but by 1969 the figure had grown to 2500. The Irish Wild Fowl Committee was founded in 1965 with three aims: research, conservation and education. Five years later the name was changed to the Irish Wildfowl Conservancy and the society had 800 members. By 1969 there was a merger with two other ornithological groups to form the Irish Wildbird Conservancy, with Major R. F. Ruttledge as the first President. Also formed in the late 1960s was the Dublin Civic Group.

These are indicators of the growth of public interest in, and concern about, environmental matters. There is obviously a close relationship between this growth and the environmental issues that arose during the decade as a result of the economic development of the country. Many of these issues arose in Dublin and some of the most notable concerned the burgeoning office development in the city, especially in the areas of Georgian houses. The earliest, and longest running, was the proposed ESB offices in Lower Fitzwilliam Street. The controversy began in 1961 and continued until the opening of the new building in November 1970, when *The Irish Times* began its editorial of 3 November with the words, 'This newspaper has consistently and unequivocally opposed the demolition of the houses in Lower Fitzwilliam Street by the ESB.'

The controversy was very heated and generated voluminous correspondence to the papers — in the first year 'over 100 letters, articles and comments', which the President of the Royal Institute of the Architects of Ireland. L. P. Cuffe, had read over prior to giving his inaugural address to the Institute.[19] It is of interest to note how he finished his address:

> The third point that arises from the strife is the awakening of public interest in the appearance of our city. I think this is the

most heartening element in a battle that no one can really win. This interest I believe is not confined to Dublin and the Dubliners but is awakening throughout all our country. Admittedly much of this interest is misguided and ill-informed. It is the Institute's role to inform and guide this interest.

Public interest was also awakened by other environmental issues in Dublin in the late 1960s and early 1970s, some similar to the Lower Fitzwilliam Street case, others not: Hume Street (the Green Property Co.), Pembroke Street (Bord na Móna), the Grand Canal (urban motorway), Sandymount Strand (reclamation and industrial development) and Wood Quay.

A most important contribution to the question of development and conservation in Dublin was made by An Taisce in 1966 when it prepared the *Study of Amenity Planning Issues in Dublin and Dun Laoghaire*. This report was an attempt to view the amenities of the city in a comprehensive manner, and to put forward in a positive and constructive way proposals as to how they could be conserved and enhanced within the process of city development. Many of its proposals were incorporated in the first Development Plan prepared for the city.

In relation to the natural environment, An Taisce had prepared for the country in 1963 a preliminary list of species and sites which required protection, the list being subdivided into (1) botanical, (2) ecological, (3) geological and (4) zoological categories.[20] This list was the forerunner of the lists that were compiled by An Foras Forbartha from 1966 onwards and developed in the 1970s on a county basis.

Interest in the natural environment was not confined to the protection of sites of special value. The more extensive effects of industrialisation and other development on the environment were beginning to be recognised, and there was a widening of the concern which developed further in the more environmentally conscious 1970s. The Irish Wildbird Conservancy in its *Newsletter* for April 1969, for example, listed some of the problems: uncontrolled drainage of wetlands, pollution of rivers, bogs and estuaries by effluents, and the use of harmful pesticides. It is an interesting indication of the development of environmental awareness that although the Arterial Drainage Act had been passed in 1940 and the Turf Development Act in 1946, there was no widespread concern about their ecological consequences until the 1960s.

If one moves from the 'concern' side of this account of conservation to the 'action' side, then one readily recognises that the major achievement was the Local Government (Planning and Development) Act, 1963. This Act, which forms the legal basis of the Irish environmental planning systsem, is described and discussed elsewhere in this book; as with the 1934 Act, discussion here is confined to its conservation provisions.

The importance of the Planning Act in this regard is twofold. First, the Act gave a strong emphasis to conservation by extending the range of preservation or protection objectives which could be written into the Development Plan: thirteen categories in the Amenities part of the Schedule compared with seven in the 1934 Act. In addition, the Act provided the planning authorities with a battery of special conservation powers: Conservation Orders, Special Amenity Area Orders, and Tree Preservation Orders. Other general powers under the Act permitted a planning authority to develop or secure the development of land for any of its development plan objectives, including conservation; or to enter into agreement with landowners for this purpose.

For conservation, the second important contribution of the Act lay in the provisions it made to facilitate involvement by the public in the planning of their environment. This involvement had three forms: in the right of a person to object to an application for planning permission and to appeal against a decision of the planning authority; in the public display of draft development plans and the right of a person to make representations; and in the designation of Prescribed Bodies in the Act. The latter, who included An Taisce, were given a function to comment on planning applications which affected areas of special amenity, sites and buildings of scientific, architectural, etc. interest; and had to be sent copies of the written statement of proposed development plans.

Probably these public participation provisions of the Act had a greater effect on the conservative side of planning, as opposed to the developmental side — not unexpected, as people are more likely to object to proposals which would change their surroundings than to put up alternative suggestions as to how a locality, town or county should develop. The designation of An Taisce as a Prescribed Body gave status to this body and acknowledged the importance of voluntary organisations in environmental conservation. A similar designation for Bord Fáilte recognised the close connections between the quality of the environment and the tourist industry.

During the remainder of the 1960s Planning Authorities were learning to cope with the new process of development-plan making. The first generation of plans, appearing towards the end of the decade, aimed as best they could to formulate objectives for conservation, but they were made within the constraints of the limited time, manpower, data and professional expertise available. Despite their inadequacies, these plans were important in that they effectively began the process of environmental conservation through planning. This is a process which continued to improve in the following decade as experience, fuller staffing and improved data led to better development plans and development control. In contrast, the special conservation powers, with the exception of Tree Preservation Orders, have been virtually unused; one Conservation Order has been made and no Special Amenity Area Orders have been confirmed by the Minister.

The major institutional venture in relation to environmental conservation during the 1960s was the establishment of An Foras Forbartha, the National Institute for Physical Planning and Construction Research, in 1964. It was established by the Government, and operated in partnership with the United Nations Special Fund for the first five years, to undertake research and to provide training in, and advance knowledge of, the physical planning and development of cities, towns and rural areas. Within the Planning Division of the Institute work was done in the area of conservation and amenity planning in which the two principal publications were *Planning for Amenity and Tourism* (1966) and *The Protection of the National Heritage* (1969).

Planning for Amenity and Tourism sought to demonstrate how a county planning authority, through the planning process, could develop amenity resources for tourism and recreation, and at the same time ensure their conservation. An elaborate and logical procedure was presented, and although in practice it proved too complex and demanding of resources for the local authorities to use, its philosophy of balancing development and conservation has strongly influenced the character of Irish planning.

The Protection of the National Heritage was prepared by an advisory committee to the Planning Division of An Foras Forbartha — the Nature and Amenity Conservation and Development Committee. This committee of thirty-eight members representing a wide range of voluntary organisations, Government departments and state bodies, reviewed the extent and variety of the national heritage (Fig. 3.1) and the financial, legal and administrative measures which existed for its protection. It made recommendations as to what was required if the national heritage were to receive the protection it warranted. Some of these, such as the national heritage inventories initiated and carried out by An Foras Forbartha in the 1970s, have been implemented; others, such as financial assis-

Environmental Conservation, 1920-1970   101

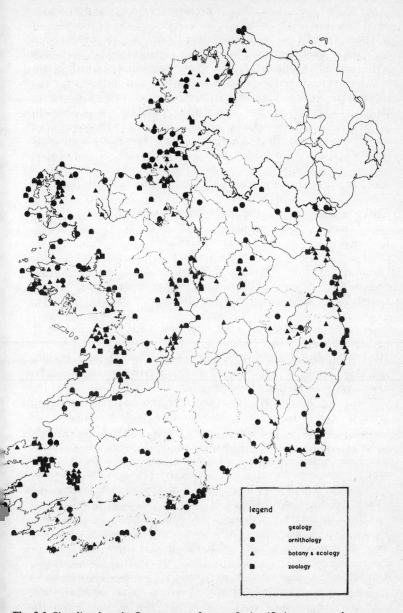

Fig. 3.1 Sites listed on the first surveys of areas of scientific interest are shown on this map, published in *The Protection of the National Heritage*. (Source: An Foras Forbartha, 1969.)

tance to owners of buildings of architectural importance, and the establishment of a Heritage Council, have yet to be realised.

The year 1970 has been taken as the terminal date for this review for a number of reasons. This year was designated by the Council of Europe as European Conservation Year and it marked the start of a decade when public concern about the environment developed in an unprecedented fashion. This concern no longer concentrated largely on special environmental values but embraced the whole environment and viewed it as the habitat of man, where destruction and damage could affect safety, health and the quality of life. Pollution of water and air, and the wastage and irrational use of scarce and non-renewable resources, became areas of concern. A list of some of the controversies of the 1970s in Ireland illustrates this:

Cork Harbour	proposed lead-zinc smelter
Bantry Bay	proposed oil refinery
Dublin Bay	proposed oil refinery
Ovens	asbestos products factory
Clonmel	proposed pharmaceuticals factory
Shannon	proposed pharmaceuticals factory
Lough Sheelin	agricultural pollution

This concern is also reflected in some of the legislation in this period including the Wildlife Act, 1976, the Local Government (Water Pollution) Act, 1977, and the Local Government (Planning and Development) Act, 1976, which made provision for the making of environmental impact statements.

The years since 1970 have seen Ireland become increasingly open to, and influenced by, ideas from outside the country. The realisation that we are all part of 'Spaceship Earth' has grown, a process assisted in 1973-74 by the so-called 'energy crisis'. Various European campaigns have affected public awareness of environmental matters: European Conservation Year 1970, European Architectural Heritage Year 1975 and Urban Renaissance Year 1981. This internationalisation process has been intensified by Ireland's membership of the European Community, particularly through the Community's directives on environmental controls and standards, beginning with the first Environmental Action Programme of the Community, 1973. By 1980 some fifteen EEC Directives relating to water, waste and air had been issued, as well as Regulations dealing with waste and air. Once more Ireland is aprt of a larger pond, this time affected by decisions and initiatives emanating from Brussels.

PIONEERS OF IRISH PLANNING IN THE INTER-WAR ERA

Patrick Abercrombie

Manning Robertson

Frank Gibney

Ernest. A. Aston

NATIONAL PLANNING CONFERENCE 1944

Among members of the conference, during which the photograph was taken, were the Rev. J. C. Canavan, S.J. (president, Civics Institute) in the chair; Messrs. Barry Walsh (Muintir na Tire), T. Condon (Co. Councils Genl. Cncl.), Manning Robertson (T.P. Inst.), S. Fitzgibbon (Dublin Cptn. Planning Dept.), L. F. Giron (R.I.A.I.), J. P. O'Brien (I.T.A.), M. Costello and N. Moffett (National Research Group), C. O'Shannon (Trade Union Congress), J. H. Webb (Rotary Club), K. Nowlan (Dublin Co. Commissioner's Office), Senator Brennan and J. V. Downes (Maritime Inst.), Dr. T. O'Higgins, T.D. and Dr. J. P. Shanley (Irish Medical Union), Senator Rowlette, M.D., and Dr. C. J. Murphy (Royal College of Physicians), H. S. Robson (A.A. of I.), R. Hogan (T.P. Inst.), E. D. Buckley (Safety First Assocn.), F. Ryan (Inst. C.E.), T. B. Byrne (Inst. County Eng.), C. J. Callaghan (Dun Laoghaire Borough), R. Henderson (Nat. Health Insce. Socty.), P. O'Caoimh (N.A.I.D.A.), C. J. Buckley and J. O'Dea (Engineers Assocn.), N. O'Dwyer (Joint Town Planning Board), D. Coyle (Dublin Chamber of Commerce), P. P. Russell (Dublin B. of H.), Senator Healy and S. McCaul (Municipal Authorities Assocn.), M. P. Linehan (I.N.T.O.), Misses M. Keane (Civics Inst.), M. Gahan and M. McDonald (Countrywomens' Assocn.). To right of chairman—Mr. Keogh Nolan, joint hon. treasurer, and Mr. F. J. Ryan, hon. secretary, of provisional committee who issued invitations to conference.

CHAPTER FOUR

THE CONTROL OF DEVELOPMENT AND THE ORIGINS OF PLANNING IN NORTHERN IRELAND

John Hendry

The original aim of this chapter was to look at the development of planning for housing, industry and amenity in Northern Ireland in the post-war period, examining the factors which led up to the adoption of the Matthew Report, and to conclude with a summary of its proposals. However, this happens to be the exact theme of a well-researched and quite perceptive article by Alan Murie which appeared in *Town Planning Review* in October 1973,[1] and it would appear of little value to cover the same ground again. The very fact that one might consider that the history of physical planning up to 1970 could already have been adequately summarised in a single article perhaps underlines the rudimentary nature of planning up to that time. It certainly reflects the absence of any notable contribution to the general theory of planning, as the system which evolved relied entirely upon successive adaptations of the British model. Therefore, rather than investigate in further detail the content of either the plans produced or the enabling legislation, it would seem more profitable from the outset to accept this dependence on British experience and to examine the context in which the system evolved, concentrating upon those local factors which have proved particularly relevant to the outcome.

There was, for example, one particular feature which immediately placed planners in Northern Ireland in a unique and in some ways unenviable position. It is a small region of 5240 square miles and a population of roughly 1.5 million, which for over fifty years enjoyed a large measure of autonomy, electing twelve representatives to the United Kingdom Parliament whilst maintaining its own House of Commons and Upper House from 1921 to 1972. Most government functions were devolved to this local Parliament which was free, within the bounds of overall Exchequer control, to pass its own laws, allocate grants for various services and generally run its own affairs. Jean Forbes has clearly expressed the problems of planners working within this framework:

> This telescoping of national and regional roles leaves Northern Ireland planners in an unusually isolated position. On the one hand, their territory is rarely included in a British level national overview of spatial planning policy ... the Irish Sea renders redundant any need to co-ordinate the regional strategies of neighbouring regions across the sea. On the other hand, Northern Ireland cannot be included in an all-Ireland 'national' overview of planning strategy.[2]

Thus, planning in Northern Ireland has had to be undertaken largely without the guidance of a wider national policy framework, and the solutions to existing problems have almost invariably had to be sought within boundaries which were created in a manner which ignored the area's natural sub-regions as might be defined according to the existeing settlement pattern or other geographic features. To complete the planners' isolation, planning in Northern Ireland evolved against a background which did not reflect the same concern with social issues shown by either of the major British parties, whether currently in government or not. In fact, for the most part, planners in Northern Ireland worked in a hostile atmosphere because of local resistance to change which planning per se was seen to represent. They could not therefore count upon the same degree of government support enjoyed by their British counterparts. It is with the effects of the political response to planning issues during the life of the Stormont Government that this chapter will mainly be concerned.

Early Background
Planning in Ulster is by no means a phenomenon confined to recent times, for the seventeenth century settlement of Ulster by the British Crown was preceded by a regional plan produced in 1609. In *The Town in Ulster* Camblin remarks that 'the methods used were very much the same that would be adopted in similar circumstances today'.[3] By this he apparently means that they appointed a committee and commissioned a survey and report. He continues:

The planners took the view that the lands in Ulster, although containing large areas of forest and bog, were capable of supporting a greatly increased population if the resources of the Province were properly exploited, and if the population became settled in towns and villages.[4]

Whilst one may admire this early regional plan for the way in which it shaped the future settlement pattern, it also provides a telling background against which reactions to later planning endeavours may be viewed. It was imposed by the British Government and set out to 'exploit' the resources of Ulster, presumably for the benefit of British commercial and political interests, and it is in this same light that planning has since been regarded by many sections of the local population.

At a somewhat later date, Belfast itself experienced two phases of planned development. From the original axis of the city along Castle Street the present line of Donegal Place was laid out in 1784. 'The plan was deposited at the estate office and interested persons were invited to inspect it and to make proposals for building in the new streets.'[5] Had he been writing some years later, Camblin might have cited this as an early exercise in public participation. Thereafter, a plan dated 1823 shows further planned developments laid out by a surveyor named Hill:

> To the north ... was laid out in a regular gridiron of streets. York Street, the central artery, had a width which challenged that of the avenues of European renaissance cities. South of the town a second sector of rectangular blocks was planned. This was centred on the White Linen Hall, which broke the monotony of the grid ... the subsequent development of the two planned sectors was very different.[6]

As R. S. Wilshere concludes in a paper to the Irish Association in 1944:

> Unfortunately the industrial pioneers of the nineteenth century, faced with a hard economic struggle, took the short-sighted view that any expenditure on amenities was an unnecessary luxury, and that open space unoccupied by buildings represented a possible loss of profit.[7]

Upon another amenity project for a city almost devoid of green space he further commented: 'The formation of the Boulevards to the River Lagan in 1924 might have been Belfast's most interesting and impressive Town Planning improvement . . . it must be admitted that the scheme as carried out, is aesthetically really little better than a flooded railway cutting.'[8] Thus the unwillingness to spend money or provide space from which profit could not be made has been a recurring factor in the implementation of planning proposals in Northern Ireland.

From the 1830s onwards 'Belfast entered its period of maximum growth and thereafter little effort was made to control the sprawl of new buildings as the city outgrew the planned extensions of the Georgian town . . . within the nineteenth century a small town of about 20,000 people had become a city of 350,000.'[9]

To complete the picture we might look at the reaction of one of the first generation of professional planners, Sir Patrick Abercrombie:

> Belfast suggests a town begun in a leisurely manner, with a designed centre, not indeed very remarkable, but having the dignity of a large central square where stands the city hall, a regular, artificial, and urban arrangement. But it has been suddenly overwhelmed by a rush of prosperity; the lava streams of irrupting urbanism seem to flow blindly in natural devastating confusion.[10]

Preservation and Amenity
The roots of modern planning in Northern Ireland — the statutory regulation of development — evolved throughout the latter half of the 19th century and, as in the remainder of the United Kingdom, are principally concerned with the preservation of historic monuments and with the demolition of unfit housing. Since 1869 ecclesiastical buildings throughout Ireland which had fallen into disuse were placed in the care of the Commissioner of Public Works. By the end of the last century some 180 monuments were preserved in this way with £1000 spent annually upon their upkeep. At the time of Partition this sum was divided between North and South and the Northern Ireland Government found itself awarded £117 annually to cover the cost of maintaining the seventeen monuments which were in the six northern counties. Thereafter the British Ancient Monuments Act of 1913 coloured the approach to architectural conservation for the next sixty years. The Ancient Monuments Act (NI) 1926, required the Ministry of Finance to produce a schedule of monuments — a duty which it duly carried out, listing some 200 monuments in all, of which one half were in public ownership. An Act of the same name in 1937 then permitted financial aid to owners of scheduled monuments, although in

practice funds were limited to a few hundred pounds a year. The attitudes noted by Wilshere towards investments which did not show a chance of profit certainly applied in the case of the conservation of the national heritage.

In 1953 a committee set up under the Chairmanship of Sir Roland Nugent recommended the listing of buildings in Northern Ireland in accordance with the British Town and Country Planning Act, but no action was taken to preserve the built environment for almost two decades. The passing of the Amenity Lands Act (NI) in 1965 actually permitted a degree of protection to be afforded to the countryside which was not available for buildings. It was in the late 1960s that the Ulster Architectural Heritage Society became active as a broadly based pressure group, claiming with some justice that Northern Ireland was fifty years behind the times in its attitude to its heritage.[11] Following a campaign of intensive publicity and lobbying, provisions were finally included in the Planning Order (NI), 1972, which brought Northern Ireland generally in line with British practice regarding the listing of buildings and declaration of Conservation Areas.[12] This illustrates a pattern which we will see repeated time and again, where there have been unjustified delays in taking legislative action to implement the recommendations of advisory committees. Changes in legislation are consequently less frequent than elsewhere in the United Kingdom and more marked in their effects as the legislators eventually attempt to catch up on the changes which have meanwhile taken place in British practice. This obviously is neither likely to tailor the resulting legislation to local needs, nor to foster the political and public support which is normally required to fund the implementation of such major changes in direction.

Housing and Redevelopment

Housing legislation in Northern Ireland has also shown a remarkable resistance to change. For instance, until 1956 the Housing of the Working Classes Act, 1890, remained the principal enabling legislation under which slum clearance might have occurred. The British Housing Acts of the 1930s which provided for increased local authority involvement in housing were not enacted locally, and the Planning and Housing Act (NI), 1931, continued to place redevelopment at the discretion of individual local authorities and consequently was not acted upon. In its report on housing in 1944 the Planning Advisory Board commented:

> We believe it is true to say that these powers have not been used to any appreciable extent by any local authority in

Northern Ireland. The reason for this was that the Acts made no provision for financial assistance by the Central Government. In Great Britain, however, after a period of house building to meet general needs, special grants were given from 1933 onwards for the provision of new houses for slum dwellers. No such grants were made available to local authorities for this purpose by the Northern Ireland Government.[13]

Housing conditions in Belfast were probably no worse at the turn of the century than those in comparable industrial cities throughout Britain. However, only 13 per cent of the housing stock in Northern Ireland was built between the wars compared to 27 per cent in Britain, and of this local total, 82 per cent was constructed by private developers. In Belfast itself 29,000 houses were built in this period, but only 2562 (8 per cent) were provided by the local authority. Wilshere refers obliquely to the 'so-called Housing Scandal' in Belfast after which the Corporation withdrew entirely from the housing field.[14] The lack of profit to be made from housing development can only partly explain this lack of activity. It is certainly true that the city benefited more from commercial development and wished to see housing confined to the suburbs so that it might retain desirable central sites for highly rated development, but this was equally true of cities elsewhere in the United Kingdom. The essential difference would seem to be that housing did not become a major issue between political parties as it did in Britain. When a dominant party can be assured of its return to power by a traditional voting pattern, there is little need to entertain reforms in housing legislation which will prove difficult and costly to implement.

In Northern Ireland during World War II 3200 houses were destroyed and a further 50,000 badly damaged. Increasingly, voices were raised against low standards of housing, especially as a result of the figures revealed by the Planning Advisory Board:

> We have now for the first time a comprehensive picture of housing conditions in the Province. The survey shows that to provide decent housing conditions approximately 100,000 houses will be required. This is a tremendous task. About 50,000 houses of all types were built in the twenty years from 1919 to 1939, and it will be appreciated that the most energetic steps will have to be taken if the task is to be completed within a reasonable period of years after the end of the war.[15]

The Report concluded: 'After full consideration of the alternative proposals ... it has been decided to recommend the setting up of a Housing Department in the Ministry of Health and Local Government.'[16] However, local authorities were loath to relinquish their housing powers and argued that these could not be divorced from other services such as the provision of water and sewerage facilities. In fact, it was twenty-seven years later in 1971 that the alleged misuse of these powers finally gave rise to the creation of a central housing authority — the Northern Ireland Housing Executive.

The Board's comments on the need to initiate an organised slum clearance programme also had to wait twelve years before they achieved official Government support. It was the ponderously titled Housing (Miscellaneous Provisions) and Rent Restriction (Amendment) Act (NI), 1956, which finally required each local authority to estimate the number of unfit dwellings in its area and to submit proposals for dealing with them. The results, published in 1959,[17] showed that out of 376,324 dwellings in Northern Ireland 95,364 were unfit — one quarter of the entire housing stock. In Belfast 18,440 houses out of 114,995 were found to be unfit. In 1960 proposals were finally put forward for the establishment of thirty redevelopment areas and in 1964 a further twenty areas were added, but it was not until 1966 — twenty-two years after the Planning Advisory Board's initial report — that the first programme involving 28,000 houses was actually approved.

Despite the neglect of redevelopment, the immediate post-war years marked the introduction of a series of important Housing Acts, providing subsidies for local authorities and private builders alike,[18] and setting up the Northern Ireland Housing Trust to supplement the efforts of local authorities.[19] Under these provisions the rate of house building grew from 2500 dwellings per year between the wars to 7500 per year between 1946 and 1971. Of the 191,960 dwellings built in this latter period 37 per cent were provided by local authorities, 36 per cent by private enterprise and 24 per cent by the Northern Ireland Housing Trust.[20] The target of 10,000 houses a year by 1970 was virtually achieved by 1968 and reflects the emergence of a new faction within the Government at that time which recognised that good housing was required as part of the basic infrastructure necessary to attract investment into Northern Ireland.

Planning in the 1940s and 1950s
Turning from housing to the development of actual planning legislation, the Northern Ireland government was equally slow to provide the legislative and administrative structures required for

either the control or promotion of development. In fact, the Planning and Housing Act (NI), 1931, remained the basic planning measure until as recently as 1972. This was similar to the 1932 Act in Britain and, being permissive in the use of its powers as already noted, it proved equally ineffective in the planning as in the housing sphere up to the time of World War II. It was adopted in only Belfast and Londonderry, caused no development plans to be produced, and allowed planning to become more or less an appendage to bye-law control.[21] Attempts to attract new industry were separately introduced under the 1932 and 1937 New Industries Development Acts, as for the first time Government intervention was admitted to be necessary to promote development, but planning at a local level was solidly resisted. The tradition existed that anyone wishing to carry out development first enlisted the services of his elected representative on the local council. Thus suggestions for the approval of formal development plans were seen by councillors to undermine their function and the means by which they built up their support in the community.

Truly constructive thought on planning matters dates from 1942 when the Government, advised by W. R. Davidge — past-president of the Town Planning Institute — set up a Planning Commission and Planning Advisory Board. The Commission was comprised of the senior professional officers of the County Councils, County Boroughs and various government and semi-state bodies; the Board consisted of elected representatives of local authorities, learned institutions and various commercial and social bodies. The Government commanded and published nine reports by the Board between 1943 and 1951 and, although it did not endorse the reports, the act of setting up these bodies in itself marked the realisation that radical changes were necessary if the economy was to survive through the attraction of external investment. The reports of the Board are remarkable both for the range of their coverage and in that their recommendations form a pattern-book for the plans of the 1960s and 1970s.[22]

What then were the main recommendations which were made? The first was the need for the centralisation of authority. In the *Preliminary Report on Reconstruction and Planning*, published in 1944, the Board stressed the need for a comprehensive plan to be prepared by a central planning authority — a recommendation which was not put into effect until a five-year development programme was produced by the Government in 1970.[23] Similar recommendations were made for the provision of public services. In its report on *Problems of Water and Sewerage*, published in 1943, the Board recommended that the eighty existing authorities should be reduced to four, but that again had to await the reorganisation of local government in the early 1970s. In *Road Communications in Northern Ireland*, published in 1946, the need for a reduction in the number of road authorities was recorded, and similar comments regarding housing authorities have already been noted earlier. In all of these fields, opposition was met at a local level, and this opposition was strong enough to prevent Government action. Murie comments:

> Planning legislation has been slow to emerge and has operated within a political and administrative climate which has a direct and significant influence . . . . Where political survival requires the maintenance of a coalition of interests there will be great reluctance to threaten the most jealously guarded powers and claims of these groups.[24]

Apart from the need for administrative reform, the Board investigated the physical changes required for the prosperity of Northern Ireland. Basically it highlighted the imbalance of industry and population, with two-fifths of the population and three-fifths of manufacturing jobs concentrated in the Belfast area.[25] It drew attention to the need to attract industry to smaller settlements, but recognised the difficulty of supplying amenities to towns of under 15,000 population. In order to attract external investment, the Board underlined the need for improved transport facilities with a network of trunk roads and motorways, especially related to the flow of traffic to and from Belfast.[26]

Finally, two reports were prepared on Belfast itself in 1945 and 1952.[27] These both expressed the degree of concern which was already being shown about the imbalance between development taking place in the Belfast area compared to that elsewhere throughout Northern Ireland. The reports recommended the control of suburban growth, the co-ordination of all forms of transport allied to the construction of a new major road system, the diversion of new industry away from the city, the redevelopment of unfit housing, the protection of open space and the creation of a green belt around the city — in fact, all of the recommendations to be found in the Belfast Regional Plan prepared by Sir Robert Matthew two decades later. The later review of progress in the 1952 report showed that, whilst the proposals of the 1945 report had been approved by the Belfast Corporation, 'the lack of machinery to co-ordinate effort forced local authorities to confine themselves to immediate problems facing their own areas'.[28] In short, the scale of necessary physical change was such that it could not be carried out without the centralisation of control. After 1951 still no action was taken and the Commission and Board ceased to function.

Towards the end of World War II it was recognised that some form of control would be needed to regulate the wave of development activity which peacetime would bring. The Interim Development Act (NI), 1944, based on the similarly-named British Act of 1943, therefore deemed all land to be subject to planning schemes and laid down a timetable for their preparation. Without the necessary staff or organisation available, this proved to be an impossible task, and so Outline Advisory Plans were substituted. These were 'in most cases a general extension of existing land use zoning together with road improvement proposals. They were not related to any specific programmes of development nor in many cases to any specific population figure'.[29] They were not statutory plans, nor were they based on any overall policy for the development of Northern Ireland.

So there came into being thirty-eight authorities of varying size and resources throughout Northern Ireland — consisting of the counties, county and municipal boroughs and urban districts — responsible for the administration of planning proposals set out for the first time in the form of advisory development plans. The largest was Belfast County Borough with a population of 416,000 and a penny rate producing £23,000, and the smallest was Dromore with a population of 2115 and a penny rate product of £60.[30] Planning in Rural Districts was carried out by the County Councils. Some of the smaller Urban Districts also surrendered their powers to the Counties, whilst others employed consultants as part-time planning officers. Architects in private practice appointed in this way prepared the Outline Plans, carried out the housing work of the authorities and reviewed each others submissions for priavate building development. They were furthermore appointed as necessary to act as Appeal Commissioners in cases of dispute. Even in 1965 the membership of the Royal Town Planning Institute in Northern Ireland stood at only forty-six practitioners, with one-half employed full-time by local and central government and the remainder generally employed in architecture with part-time involvement in planning as consultants to local authorities or as auxiliary inspectors appointed by the Government. Planning powers at this time were not uniformly administered, being applied most strongly in the urban areas and generally applied 'rather more strongly in the East than in the West'.[31]

One particular barrier to the enforcement of planning control under the 1944 Act was the ambiguity regarding the right to compensation for refusals or conditional permissions to develop.

This arose through the interpretation of the Government of Ireland Act, 1920, which provided safeguards to individuals against the taking of their interests in land. In England any possible ambiguity regarding compensation was removed by the Town and Country Planning Act, 1947, which nationalised development values, but in Northern Ireland the planning authorities operated in fear of claims which would become a charge against the local rates. This situation continued until the limitations on compensation had been clarified by legislation in Westminster and was only fully resolved by the Land Development Values (Compensation) Act (NI), 1965, which made the newly formed Ministry of Development responsible for all claims arising from planning decisions.

Planning in the 1960s

If the 1940s and 1950s were the decades of resistance to change, then the 1960s should be labelled the decade of the ambitious plans. This seeming reversal Wiener attributes to the emergence of a new faction within the Unionist Party, headed by O'Neill, Faulkner and Bradford, promoting for the first time with real conviction the interests of new overseas investors as opposed to those of traditional locally-based comercial interests.[32] The unplanned growth of the Belfast urban area in stark contrast to the stagnation of development elsewhere eventually produced sufficient pressures for the Government to appoint Sir Robert Matthew in 1960 to prepare a plan for the Belfast region. This was in fact the first Regional Plan in Ireland. Jean Forbes comments:

> The Matthew plan must be judged in the context of its time. Its greater contribution may be seen, in future, to have been its ground-breaking function rather than its planning proposals as such. It was produced in an atmosphere which was decidedly anti-planning, and in a community intensely suspicious of change. The Matthew plan provoked a rigorous public debate which still continues, and this has served to bring planners to public notice in Northern Ireland.[33]

The Report, published in 1964[34], was concerned principally with physical development, an economic plan being prepared in parallel by Professor Tom Wilson and published in 1965.[35] Sir Robert Matthew proposed to control the further development of Belfast by the application of a 'stopline', by initiating a system of radial motorways and by promoting eight growth centres outside the city (Fig. 4.1a). One of these was to be developed as a 'new city' of 100,000 population as a countermagnet to Belfast, and this

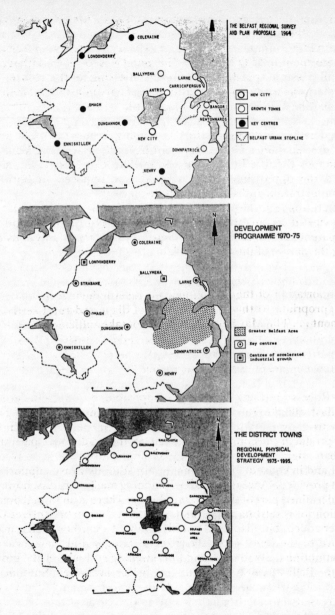

Fig. 4.1 Northern Ireland Development Proposals. (a) The Belfast Regional Survey, 1964; (b) Development Programme 1970-75; (c) The District Towns: Development Stratgey, 1975-95.

proposal was accorded the highest priority by the Government:

> An important and encouraging two-day debate took place at Stormont in May 1963 .... The mood was to get on with it at all possible speed. Acting on this 'blessing' of the House, a start was made on the recruitment of a team for the new city and the drafting of a New Towns Bill.[36]

Unionist support was solidified by naming the new town Craigavon — after Sir James Craig, Northern Ireland's first Prime Minister, who took the title Lord Craigavon in 1927. Conversely, this alienated the opposition whose support was required in both the administration and settlement of the new city.

In retrospect, the proposal for the development of a new city can be viewed as an attempt to emulate in Northern Ireland the apparent success of the British New Towns, without duly considering the nature of the local problem:

> Fundamentally there was little attempt to assess whether the importation of the British new town settlement system was appropriate to the Irish tradition of dispersed rural settlement ... The Matthew Report did not take sufficient consideration of trends in residential and industrial location patterns which cast doubts on the relevance of the British new town model of twenty years earlier.[37]

Sir Robert Matthew saw that the imposition of a stop-line around Belfast, allied to the full-scale renewal of its inner areas, would give rise to an overspill in the order of some 36,000 people. This he saw as producing a counter-movement to the traditional pattern of urban migration. However, the full implications were not worked out and in consequence the necessary administrative support was not provided. 'A weakness of the planning machinery has, however, undermined part of the Matthew design. There is no formal organisation for resettling overspill population.'[38] Some incentives were later added, but displaced families showed a marked preference to move to the inner growth centres of Bangor and Newtownards, commuting daily to work and thus swelling still further the growth of the Belfast region. The radiating motorway system, intended to lure industry westward beyond the Belfast region, has in fact increased accessibility to the centre and extended the commuting range of workers. The outer ring of growth centres have not been notably successful in attracting outside investment but, by offering conditions which compare favourably with those of the surround-

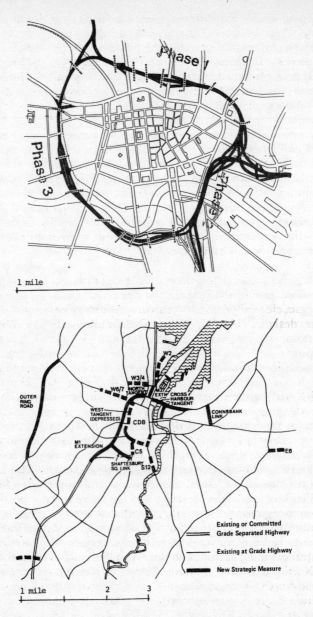

Fig. 4.2 Road Proposals for Central Belfast. (a) Belfast Urban Motorway Proposals (after B.D.P. 1969); (b) Belfast Road Proposals (Review of Transportation Strategy 1977).

ing countryside, have tended to draw population from the very areas where development was seen to be most needed.

Thus, the more recent history of planning in Northern Ireland 'is marked by the adoption of prestigious plans or projects which change their character and impact by a process of erosion through failure to implement the whole or by changes in parts without altering or reconsidering related parts'.[39] Those who commissioned the plans had been bound to act upon the main proposals — if only to justify their choice of consultants and the cost of the reports. Being then able to lay claim to have initiated a new city or a motorway system, there was subsequently a lesser inclination to proceed with the further implementation of the plans — especially where this might invoke political debate in sensitive subject areas. As Murie points out, 'Area Plans for the growth centres... departed from the Matthew recommendations... without any public discussion of the effects on other parts of the plan'.[40] (Fig. 4.1 a to c). Another over-ambitious plan which was never implemented was that for the Belfast Urban Motorway (Fig. 4.2). This was originally chosen by the Belfast Corporation as the prestige solution to the city's transportation problem.'The brief for the traffic consultants, Travers Morgan, clearly specified that an urban motorway should be part of their design.'[41] Although the abandonment of the motorway proposal was claimed to stem from citizen protest after the public enquiry in 1972,[42] even this may be seen as a face-saving excuse for relinquishing a solution which in practice constituted an impossible economic burden in a deteriorating economic climate and which had by then been shown to have disastrous consequences elsewhere.

Apart from its physical proposals, the Matthew plan called for the formation of a centralised planning administration to replace the thirty-four local authorities in the Belfast region (of which nineteen were planning authorities, thirty responsible for housing and twenty-two for roads), within the overall control of a Ministry of Planning and Development — thus effectively repeating the recommendations of the Planning Board in the 1940s. In 1964 a White Paper was produced on the *Administration of Town and Country Planning in Northern Ireland* with the main proposal of setting up a central planning authority to prepare a Regional Plan for the whole of Northern Ireland and Area Plans to outline development in broad-brush terms. Local authority participation was to be by 'Action Plans' but it was proposed that development control would become a function of central government:

Public reaction was disappointingly thin, although generally

> favourable.... The reactions of local authorities, on the other hand, were quite strong and, in the main, unfavourable.... Where the strongest opposition came was in the matter of development control by the central authority. It was apparent this was the strongest focus of local interest for councils and councillors.[43]

The proposal was fiercely debated within the Cabinet, with O'Neill's more radical supporters facing strong resistance from the more reactionary members who saw the centralisation of power undermining their own local support. Allen in fact alludes that 'only by a coup, whilst other ministers were on vacation, did he (O'Neill) establish such a ministry'.[44] So a Ministry of Development came into being with overall responsibility for planning, housing, roads, transport, water, sewerage and local government, although local authorities were permitted to retain many of their powers — in the case of planning including development control. O'Neill immediately appointed his Chief Whip, William Craig, as Minister and, with Brian Faulkner as Minister of Commerce, the new Unionist group appeared set to bring about at least a modest economic revival in Northern Ireland. However, the O'Neill Government was soon to fall and other members of his Cabinet subsequently since passed out of the mainstream of politics, even though the centralised structure they established was able to survive.

Postscript
In 1970 the McCrory Commission recommended that Government services should be placed entirely under the direct control of the Ministries concerned.[45] This was largely influenced by the 'troubles' which flared up in 1968, and the allegations of the misuse of local powers, especially in the fields of housing and planning. This reorganisation took place on 1 October 1973 when the Ministry of Development, subsequently restyled the Department of the Environment, became the sole planning authority for Northern Ireland. Similar steps were taken to centralise road services, water and sewerage disposal, so that at last the recommendation of the Planning Board of the 1940s was implemented in full. Local authorities were reorganised under twenty-six district councils which were left with responsibilities only for environmental health and the provision of community facilities. This arrangement assumed that a devolved government would be maintained at Stormont, but with the collapse of the power-sharing Assembly in June 1974 the Government of Northern Ireland passed under the

'direct-rule' of Westminster. Planning under this system is carried out under the Planning (NI) Order, 1972, which provides a synopsis of the legislation currently operative throughout Great Britain, but is stifled in two directions. From above it has frequently been repressed by a conservative administration which has shown a tendency to adopt only the safe alternative – and usually it is safer not to invoke changes, especially in the face of possible political opposition. From below, planning is open to attack by members of local councils who are now able to represent themselves as the champions of the local electorate against the imposed rule of central government. Perhaps the major impediment to planning in Northern Ireland is the continued failure to realise that British planning practice can only operate in the context of the British political system. By concentrating upon planning as a technical activity, successive administrations have refused to recognise that planning is essentially a part of the political process itself.

CHAPTER FIVE

DEVELOPMENT PLANNING AND THE NEGLECT OF THE CRITICAL REGIONAL DIMENSION

Michael J. Bannon

The renaissance of physical planning in Ireland after 1959 must be seen as part of the wider range of policy innovations with which a dynamic government was prepared to experiment in an attempt to meet its twin objectives of ending involuntary emigration and creating full employment at home. Following the deaths of Manning Robertson and E. A. Aston shortly after the National Planning Exhibition of 1944, the commitment to planned development waned. In the fifteen years up to 1959 there was little reference to the subject, publications on planning were few and far between[1] and progress within either the local authorities or within the Department of Local Government proved exceedingly slow.

The resurgence of interest in all forms of planning is closely associated with the rise to power of Sean Lemass, who became Taoiseach in 1959 and who had demonstrated a consistent commitment to planning over the previous thirty years.[2] Under his leadership, and with the support of a committed Minister for Local Government, there emerged a broadly based confidence in the role of development planning at local, regional and national levels. Indeed, Ireland's achievements in the field of planning in the early 1960s were to serve as a model to inspire action in other relatively underdeveloped societies and emerging nations.

This chapter provides an understanding of the background and ethos of Irish planning in those dynamic years. It looks at the concept of 'development planning' and outlines the reasons why the political objectives behind the 1963 Act remain unrealised to date. The chapter is subdivided into six sections dealing with the changing social and economic context, the inspiration behind the

1963 Act and its initial implementation; the chapter also examines the impediments which hindered the realisation of the positive objectives of the Act. Finally, the chapter outlines the achievements of planning to date and the role planning could play in helping to realise the socio-economic objectives of the country.

The Changing Socio-Economic Context of Planning

Any understanding of the reasons behind the introduction of the *Local Government (Planning and Development) Act, 1963*, must relate to the social and economic problems of the 1950s and early 1960s. In addition, any changes in the national perspective on planning must also be set in the wider context of socio-economic trends in general. In the course of the past twenty-five years Ireland has undergone a radical social and economic transformation. The persistently high levels of emigration which characterised the 1950s and earlier decades yielded to net population increase during the 1960s and to a sizeable inflow of population into the country during the 1970s (Table 5.1). Between 1961 and 1981 the national population increased by 19 per cent or 549,876 persons. From its position, with one of Europe's oldest populations in the 1950s, Ireland, by 1981 had the youngest and fastest-growing population in Western

Table 5.1
Changes, Natural Increase and Estimated net Migration in the Intercensal Period 1971-81 for each Planning Region and Dublin Sub-Region

Planning Region	Population 1971	Population 1981	Increase in Population	Natural Increase	Estimated Net Migration
East (of which	1,062,067	1,288,973	226,906	168,931	57,975
Dublin sub-region)	852,219	1,001,985	149,766	129,036	20,730
South-west	465,655	525,022	59,367	47,453	11,914
South-east	328,604	374,484	45,880	38,500	7,380
North-east	173,964	193,296	19,332	18,814	518
Mid-west	269,804	308,040	38,236	31,985	6,251
Donegal	108,344	124,783	16,439	9,373	7,066
Midlands	232,427	256,413	23,986	20,868	3,118
West	258,748	286,384	27,636	21,845	5,791
North-west	78,635	83,032	4,397	3,034	1,363
TOTAL	2,978,248	3,440,427	462,179	360,803	101,376

Source: Census of Population 1981, Vol. 1.

Europe, with over half the population aged 25 years or less. During this same period Ireland had been transformed from a rural and agriculturally dependent country to a rapidly urbanising industrial and service economy (Table 5.2). Ireland has moved swiftly from the agricultural to the information age.[3] The conservative social order of the emigration-dominated 1950s yielded to a more mobile, socially open, better-educated and more demanding and participatory society in the 1980s.

The geographic pattern of population has also changed. The widespread population loss of the 1950s, except around Dublin, gave way to more dispersed urban growth in the 1960s. But during the 1970s population growth was widespread in both urban and rural areas.[4] Seen in terms of the physical landscape, the derelict and abandoned houses resulting from decades of emigration have now disappeared; on the other hand, many rural areas are being swamped by an invasion of urban-generated houses, often of questionable aesthetic quality. In the present era, with public concern to provide adequate schools, housing, employment, amenities and services to accommodate an expanding population and labour force, it is easy to forget that a mere twenty-five years ago planning was viewed as an essential solution to problems of economic and social decline. The shift from a rural to an urban way of life, which had been evident even in the 1950s (Table 5.3), accelerated rapidly in the 1960s. Between 1961 and 1981 the percentage of the population residing in towns of over 200 increased from 53.4 per cent to 63.4 per cent. During the 1970s the growth of urbanisation accelerated in consequence of the high rate of natural increase, particularly in the East Region (Table 5.4), and as a result of continued migration from rural to urban areas as well as through in-migration from abroad. In spite of frequent calls to regulate the growth of Dublin,[5] 49 per cent of the total increase since 1961 has taken place in the Dublin area. Such a context of rapid population growth and urbanisation was a far cry from the 1950s when the economy was stagnating and emigration was widespread. The major cause of the continued economic decline of Ireland lay in the contraction of agriculture throughout the 1950s, coupled with the stagnation of the industrial sector. The proportion of gross domestic capital formation increased by a mere 50 per cent between 1938 and 1955;[6] by 1958 the real wages of the average worker barely equalled those of 1939 and unemployment, in the absence of adequate welfare supports, reached a peak of 78,000 by 1957.[7] Emigration – that 'centrifugal force pulling more and more of her children from their homeland' – was a national humiliation and a visible symbol of failure. So persistent was the emigration trend that some observers began to seriously question the survival of the Irish population, at least in Ireland.[8] Not surprisingly, the country suffered a national psychological crisis by 1956[9] in which the adequacy of institutions and the efficacy of most approaches to economic management were seriously questioned. This crisis of the 1950s highlighted the necessity of adopting a free-trade approach in place of protectionism and the need to follow a planned programme of productive investment.

It was the lack of capital investment which caused the national crisis of confidence in 1956 and, in turn, generated a need for investment programming which led logically to the inception of national economic planning in 1958. In this context it was quickly

Table 5.2
Employment Change by Broad Sectoral Classification, 1961-81

	1961	1971	1981	Changes Number	1961-81 %	% Share 1961	% Share 1981
Agriculture	379,491	273,079	189,500	−189,991	−50.1	36.1	16.5
Industry	257,178	322,749	360,800	+103,622	+40.3	24.4	31.4
Services	415,870	459,011	600,500	+184,630	+44.4	39.5	52.1
TOTAL	1,052,539	1,054,839	1,150,800	+ 98,261	+ 9.3	100.00	100.00

Source: Census of Population 1961 and 1971; data for 1981 from 5 per cent sample returns of 1981 Census of Population.
Industry includes mining, manufacturing, electricity, gas, water and construction.

Table 5.3
Change in Aggregate Rural and Urban Population 1926-61

	Aggregate Rural Population			Aggregate Urban Population		
	1926	1961	Percentage Change	1926	1961	Percentage Change
Leinster	554	457	−17.5	595	876	+47.2
Munster	682	516	−24.3	288	333	+15.6
Connacht	499	347	−30.5	54	72	+33.3
Ulster (Part)	278	191	−31.3	22	26	+18.2
TOTAL	2,013	1,511	−24.9	959	1,307	+36.3

Source: Census of Population 1961, Vol. 1.

accepted that physical planning played a major part in social and economic development and that there existed 'an intimate interrelationship between economic, social and physical planning'.[10]

Changes in Public Policy

From the early 1940s there emerged a growing recognition that protectionist policies on their own would not solve Ireland's unemployment problems,[11] and over the next thirty years protectionist regulations were dismantled in favour of attracting foreign investment, free trade and a policy of export-led growth. In the post-war era *Ireland's Long Term Recovery Programme, 1949-53*, the statement of claim for Marshall aid, reflected the increased attention to industrial development and the outlining of Ireland's advantages for foreign investment.[12] To help attract overseas firms foreign trade departments were set up in Irish embassies abroad from 1948 onwards[13], the Industrial Development Authority was established in 1950,[14] and the *Undeveloped Areas Act, 1952*, defined Designated Areas within which An Foras Tionscail could provide capital grants and other assistance to new manufacturing concerns. The scale of the grants and the extent of areas eligible for assistance were expanded greatly by the Industrial Grants Act of 1956 and over the next years the level of government assistance to manufacturing industry was to increase dramatically. The movement towards free trade received a major advance with the signing of the

Table 5.4
Average Annual Rates per 1000 of Average Population
1971-81

Planning Region	Births	Deaths	Natural Increase	Net Migration
East	22.8	8.4	14.3	5.1
South-west	21.0	11.4	9.6	2.4
South-east	21.9	11.0	11.0	2.1
North-east	21.7	11.3	10.4	0.3
Mid-west	22.2	11.2	11.0	2.3
Donegal	20.2	12.2	8.1	6.3
Midlands	20.2	11.7	8.6	1.4
West	19.8	11.7	8.1	2.1
North-west	18.1	14.2	3.9	1.6
TOTAL	21.6	10.4	11.3	3.2

Source: Census of Polulation 1981, Vol. 1, Table 9B.

Anglo-Irish Free Trade Agreement of 1965 and Ireland's accession to full membership of the EC in 1973.

Particular note has to be taken of developments taking place at Shannon Airport. As well as running an international airport, the Shannon Free Airport Development Company pioneered a number of initiatives aimed at promoting free trade, notably the creation of a Custom Free Zone and the payment of generous incentives to attract foreign investors.[15] Alongside these, Shannon also initiated a number of successful experiments in physical planning including the laying out of an industrial estate and the preparation of plans for a new town of 25,000 persons.[15] Thus Shannon served as a successful laboratory where new policies were tested before receiving nationwide application. In addition, the integrated model of economic policies and physical developments unfolding at Shannon was to bring home to Irish administrators the close and successful association between economic and physical planning.

The Advent of Economic Programming

The increased emphasis on free-trade policies, together with the attraction of foreign investment, went hand in hand with a new approach to capital investment. The proportion of national product devoted to capital investment in the early 1950s remained abysmally low[17] even though Capital Budgeting has been in use from 1950. Following the financial crisis of 1956, a Capital Advisory Committee was established, under the chairmanship of John Leydon, to determine priorities for capital investment.[18] Working along similar lines, Whitaker prepared for the Government a detailed programme of sectoral investment for the five years 1958-1963; Whitaker's study was subsequently published as *Economic Development*[19] and it also formed the basis of Ireland's *First Programme for Economic Expansion*,[20] a flexible programme for productive investment over the 1958-1963 quinquennium and following the French economic planning model as enunciated by Jean Monnet.[21]

Partly as a result of an upturn in world trade, and partly in response to new political leadership and dynamic economic policies at home, the years covered by the 'First Programme' were years of unprecedented growth. The modest target of 1 per cent growth rate per annum was trebled and the long history of decline was interrupted if not reversed. By 1963 the government could claim that 'the long-established excess of emigration over the rate of population growth was reversed'[22] and economic growth seemed assured. Subsequent exercises in planned management of the economy over the years 1963 to 1972 were less successful and politically unsatisfactory, since they over-estimated the likely rate of growth.²³

However, the advent of economic planning in 1958 did coincide with the initiation of a long period of successful economic development. From its initial success economic planning, and planning in general, was popularly associated with growth and expansion. One of the hallmarks of the Irish approach to economic programming was an abhorrence of 'planning in any rigid sense';²⁴ rather, 'flexibility is rightly recognised as being the essence of planning' as Whitaker later described it.²⁵ Another feature of the government's approach at this time was a willingness to innovate and to seek practical solutions by new means. As Lemass put it, 'the most efficacious administrative arrangements to give effect to a dynamic policy of economic progress is one on which some fresh thinking, and informative discussions, could help clear our minds'²⁶ In a lecture to the Irish Branch of the Town Planning Institute, Lynch stressed the necessity of having 'an energetic imaginative administration'.²⁷ The government was committed to expanding the creative role of the public sector in development through the modification of existing institutions and the introduction of such new institutions, procedures and legislation as was deemed appropriate. One such innovation was the implementation of a pragmatic, flexible system of development planning aimed at accelerating the pace of growth in an orderly fashion.

The Planning Act:
Enactment and Initial Implementation

The Abrams Report

By 1960 it was clear that the Town and Regional Planning Acts were unworkable and that they could inhibit development, especially of the derelict cores of larger urban centres. Accordingly, the government sought the advice of the United Nations on

> the feasibility of redeveloping cleared central areas with a view to making the process more economic and to reduce the burden on public funds such as by a mixed development of residential, commercial and industrial enterprises. This would involve examination of the possibilities of attracting such enterprises to these areas and of so designing redevelopment projects as to bring about an economic and balanced use of the available land.²⁸

The government also wanted guidance in particular on the following aspects of urban renewal:

(a) Land uses, based on the economic development programme for the city, indicating locations for different enterprises such as public and private housing, shops, office buildings, hotels and light industries;

(b) the kinds of investments that should be made to attract businesses and industry, including any facilities that should be provided;

(c) a financial plan necessary for the proposed redevelopment;

(d) the procedures to be adopted to ensure co-ordination of public and private interests and uses.[29]

Charles Abrams was nominated as consultant to the Irish Government by the UN and promptly adopted a more comprehensive remit, including a review of the planning and development legislation. Abrams advocated an unashamedly expansionist role for planning in accommodating the needs of both industry and business, especially in the case of Dublin which was 'both of national and municipal concern'. In his report Abrams dealt with the necessity for regional planning and he outlined the elements of the city planning process.[30] With reference to decaying areas and derelict sites, it was his view that 'a plan is needed, the will to push it ahead, a law to authorise it and the administrative apparatus to implement it'.[31] Arising out of his report, Abrams made a total of twenty-four recommendations to the Minister for Local Government, embracing the whole field of development regulation and planning and including proposals for a new Dublin plan and a new planning act. Since the Abrams report reflected the government's pragmatic approach, it is not surprising that most of the recommendations were substantially implemented.

The Local Government (Planning and Development) Bill, 1962
Accordingly, the *Local Government (Planning and Development) Bill* was introduced in the Dáil on 12 July 1962 by the Minister for Local Government, Neil T. Blaney.[32] The 'Second Stage' commenced on 12 November; the bill cleared both houses of the Oireachtas on 31 July 1963 and in general the Act was to have effect from 1 October 1964.[33]

In introducing the Second Stage the Minister spelled out the objectives of Irish planning:

> The object of planning is to make our towns, villages and countryside better places in which to live and work, by improving their appearance, their public services and facilities and other opportunities for employment and recreation.[34]

Planning was clearly viewed as a dynamic process which would 'pay dividends in economic and social well-being in the years to come'.[35] The Minister stressed the importance of planning in the case of a poor country like Ireland for 'the poorer the resources of a country, the greater is the need for careful planning'.[36] While the preservation of the heritage and the elimination of 'visual disfigurement' were part of the purpose of this Bill, particular stress was placed on the avoidance of economic waste through good planning. The new Bill was clearly and emphatically seen as assisting in the national development effort:

> Planning has a considerable significance in helping to foster economic development, especially in locations which offer prospects of becoming centers of commercial or industrial growth . . . planning for a better physical environment is of national economic importance . . . A good environment and prosperity are closely associated.[37]

There was clearly a close and complementary relationship between economic and physical planning in the mind of the government at this stage. The development emphasis in the Minister's speech reflected the tone of Abrams's approach, as well as the Minister's own experience of planning in North America.[38] No doubt the Minister was also conscious of the harmonisation of economic policies and physical planning then taking place in Shannon. The Minister made repeated references to the importance of this legislation in facilitating 'urban renewal and redevelopment particularly in the case of our bigger centres of population, such as Dublin City'.[39] In as much as there was a value system behind the Planning Act, that set of values was strongly motivated in favour of orderly development through growth and expansion.

In contrast to the situation in 1933, when the planning Bill was greeted with apathy both by local authorities and most members of the Dáil, the 1963 Bill was the subject of numerous discussions with local authorities and a series of conferences and seminars and even film shows were arranged to promote an understanding of planning.

The Bill was welcomed by all parties in Dáil Éireann, although there were serious misgivings expressed about certain of its powers. Many Deputies were concerned at the loss of control by the Oireachtas and the extent of the powers conferred on the Minister, especially in respect of appeals.[40] It was suggested that many of the powers proposed in the Bill were too sweeping to invest in authorities which had failed to operate the previous legislation, and the view was put forward repeatedly that the Bill might with advantage be confined to Dublin and the larger towns in its application:[41]

> The Minister would have produced a more acceptable and better type of Bill had he proceeded in the first instance by dealing with the larger sections of population, where there is a case for more elaborate town planning than in the smaller towns and villages. Not alone would it be the more prudent approach, but in that way, the Minister and his officials would get experience step by step.[42]

In general, however, the Bill was received positively and constructively in both Houses with Deputy Dillon paying a warm tribute to the Minister's handling of the debate in the Dáil.[43]

Principal Provisions of the 1963 Act

The Local Government (Planning and Development) Act, which was signed into law on 7 August, 1963, followed closely the Town and County Planning Act 1962, of England and Wales. The Irish Act was mandatory and its principal provision was the establishment of 87 planning authorities which were each required to prepare Development Plans for their areas.

The Development Plans, consisting of written statements and supplemented by maps, were required to deal with land-use zoning, traffic and circulation, the renewal of obsolete areas and the preservation and improvement of existing amenities. In non-urban areas the plan should also have regard to provision of services. Development Plans were to be reviewed quinquennially. Allowance was made for the making of 'variations' and minimum requirements on public participation in the plan-making process were stipulated. Section 22 enabled the Minister to co-ordinate the Development Plans of two or more Planning Authorities and to vary any given Development Plan.

The Act imposed an obligation upon everyone wishing to undertake 'development' to obtain planning permission from their local Planning Authority in advance and an appeal to the Minister either by the applicant or by a third party was allowed. Other sections of the Act dealt with Amenities, Compensation and powers of Land

Acquisition. Central to the objective of the Act was Section 77(1)(e), which enabled a Planning Authority to undertake the development or renewal of obsolete areas.[44]

During and immediately following the Dáil Debates on the Bill, a major programme of public information was launched through the publication of explanatory memoranda, the preparation of Planning and Development Circulars and the publication of 'Your Development Plan' – a layman's guide to the Irish Planning System. Under the aegis of the Department, and with the support of the professional institutions, a series of public lectures and technical seminars sought to inform all shades of public opinion on planning.[45]

The cause of planning was championed through the holding in Dublin by the Town Planning Institute of its 1967 Annual Conference and the associated publication of *Planning in Ireland*.[46] The Dublin meeting of The International Federation of Housing and Planning in 1969 provided another important forum for the promotion of planning. Considerable effort was made to generate a broad basis of support for planning. Reflecting on the operation of the Act during its first year, Delany pointed out that while 'nothing spectacular or unforeseeable has occurred, there has at least been a great deal of consolidation all along the front'.[47] As the *Architects Journal* saw it, Ireland had made a late start in planning but this could prove to be 'a great advantage to a country; it is the pioneers who make the worst mistakes, and latecomers learn from them'.[48]

Implementation in the 1960s
The main provisions of the Act came into operation on 1 October 1964, and all 87 planning authorities were required to prepare and adopt Development Plans for their areas on or before October 1967. For a country with a lack of a planning tradition or adequate technical staff,[49] this was a daunting task. Many Planning Authorities had to establish and staff planning departments *de nova*, while even Dublin, with its longer planning tradition, had to gear itself to meet the requirements of the new legislation.[50] Even the Minister for Local Government had to quadruple the technical staff of his department to deal with the expected increase in planning appeals.[51]

In May 1964 An Foras Forbartha, The National Institute for Physical Planning and Construction Research, was established as a state agency with United Nations assistance to 'undertake research into and provide training in and advance knowledge of the physical planning and development of cities, towns and rural areas'.[52] By 1966 this interdisciplinary environmental research institution had twelve Irish specialists and six UN staff giving 'a good and practical return for the funds invested'.[53] This early work included the preparation of planning manuals, specimen development plans, urban renewal studies and amenity and regional planning exercises.[54]

Preliminary to the preparation of the first Development Plans, the Minister directed Planning Authorities to prepare Provisional Plans. These were to be 'preliminary studies, routine in all planning activity, but with this difference: they were to be separated, given a status of their own and published'.[55] By way of example, inspectors of the Department of Local Government prepared an outline of a typical provisional plan and demonstrated its application to County Meath. A series of seminars was held around the country to demonstrate this approach. At one of these seminars, held in Galway, the Minister urged local authorities 'to press forward with the preparation of their provisional plans basing them on the model which they have seen demonstrated at this seminar'.[56] An Foras Forbartha participated in the preparation of a provisional plan for Galway City.[57] and the continuing relevance of provisional plans as a model for the making of Development Plans was demonstrated by Kreditor at a seminar in Dublin in 1966.[58] The local authorities were repeatedly urged to prepare 'realistic and flexible' plans[59] and, reflecting on these first planning attempts, Stringer concluded that they 'were very succesful and achieved their purpose,' acting as a dress rehearsal for the development plan and providing a fine opportunity to consider the issues in a comprehensive manner.[60]

The subsequent Mark I Development Plans, covering the years 1967-72, were also envisaged as rather limited in scope. 'The aim must be to draw up simple realistic plans which will serve while staff, skill, experience and data are accumulated.'[61] In general the plans adhered rigidly to the guidelines and recommended procedures as set out in the first two Departmental Planning and Development circulars. But the Minister retained a wider perspective and looked forward to 'plans which will be much more than a statement of development control policy and a programme of public works. We want plans which will reflect and further the new role of local authorities as development forces in their areas.'[62]

While it is dangerous to generalise about the plans prepared by 87 different planning authorities, with varying problems and expertise, many of the Development Plans fell far short of the Minister's expectations. Stringer has provided an overview of the limited quality of many of these early plans:

Most of the first development plans were based on a quick survey yielding minimal information, often using second-hand data which was well on the way to being obsolete. The analysis of the information gathered rarely deserved so fine a name. As a result, the fact-to-policy link often seemed very tenuous indeed . . . This weak fact-to-policy link is best seen in the first or policy sections of the development plans, which were often vague, imprecise and sometimes amounted to little more than pious sentiment. On the social and economic side the link was particularly weak . . . . The tactical components of the development plans were usually better than their policy statements. Yet the programme of intensive objectives was rarely more than the set of projects already in the local authority's files, with some amenity items added. There was inadequate allowance for change, for it was not sufficiently realised that we were trying to foresee or to forestall change. Much of the work was subjective and too many topics were left to that great loophole – further study.[63]

Whatever the limitations of these first Development Plans, a start had been made and for the first time much of the territory of the state was covered by planning policies.

Ironically, the major exception to this general coverage was in the Dublin area, where the intensity of problems had generated the need for the 1963 Act in the first instance. The preparation of the draft plan for Dublin City involved discussions with consultants undertaking a study of the Dublin Region[64] and, while the draft was published in 1967, it generated some 7000 objections and was not approved until 1971. The plan for Dublin County, which was prepared with the help of planners from the Department of Local Government and broadly followed the lines of the Myles Wright report,[65] took effect in 1972. Under the guidance of a single manager and with a joint planning officer, a coherent policy for Metropolitan Dublin was given effect.[66]

While Dublin was to adopt plans very belatedly, the plan preparation stage had started quickly; the Dublin Corporation had quickly availed of the new powers granted by the 1963 Act and invited Nathaniel Lichfield to advise on the redevelopment of the North Central Area of the city.[67] Such action had been very much within the spirit of the legislation, stimulated as it was by the desire to promote centre city redevelopment and to facilitate economic growth.

Whatever the limitations of the Development Plans, the government remained firmly committed to the principle of planning as a develoment catalyst at every level. For the government the 'local plans are the means by which expression and effect will be given to the role of local planning authorities as "development corporations"'.[68] This positive view of planning was reinforced by the Minister when he stated that:

> The wide scope of development plans and the range of positive powers made available to planning authorities show clearly that the intention of the Act is not to control or restrict development on the basis of vague aesthetic principles, but to enable each planning authority to draw up and give effect to a programme which is directly related to community development.[69]

Even as recently as 1969, An Taoiseach, Mr Lynch, stated that 'the emphasis in our interest in physical planning is on the positive contribution it can make in the process of national development'.[70] But by then the vision of a hierarchy of interacting plans had been largely abandoned and throughout the 1970s the emphasis slipped inexorably from 'development planning' to 'development control'.

By the late 1960s there was evidence of a growing conflict between the positive perception of planning as enunciated by the politicians and the more negative and regulatory concept of planning being implemented by the planning and legal professions. To a large extent this dichotomy derived from the legislators' own failure to reform institutions and to bring forward complementary legislation in relation to development and planning. The next section of this chapter examines a number of areas where a failure to reform and modernise was to undermine the ambitious concept of development planning.

Development Planning: The Reasons for Underachievement

The concept of 'Development Planning' as promoted by the government in the 1960s caught the imagination of the population who believed that planning had a positive and creative role in the orderly development of the country and in the attainment of national goals aimed at ending involuntary emigration and creating full employment. In practice, however, the link between physical planning and such national objectives was to prove increasingly tenuous and planning was to become obsessively concerned with details of control and regulation. In such circumstances the 'Forbairt' of the 1960s had given way to the 'Pleanáil' of the 1980s.[71]

This section examines why planning failed to live up to the original expectations and concludes that in at least four broad areas of public policy the government did not proceed with the necessary structural reforms to support the concept of development planning. In addition, many of the actions of government have served to undermine the status of local authorities and hence of planning, which had been seen 'as the mechanism by which they give effect' to their role as development corporations.[72] The following pages examine the suitability of the basic legislation, the relevance of central and local government institutions, and the conspicuous neglect of a regional planning dimension.

The Local Government (Planning and Development) Act in Context

As indicated above, much of the motive force behind the basic Irish Act had drawn heavily upon the aggressive, growth-oriented approach to planning as operated in North America. In contrast, the actual Bill introduced into Dáil Éireann in July 1962 was substantially modelled on the Town and Country Planning Acts of England and Wales. Such a model placed a high priority on planning as a regulatory tool, with limited concern for the linkage between local planning activity and the goals of national socio-economic development. It was singularly unfortunate that the adoption of the Irish Act just preceded a re-evaluation of the whole concept of Development Plans in Britain. In the United States, Land Use and Transportation Studies had demonstrated the inadequacy of the Master Plan approach and gave rise to a search for a new philosophy of planning.[73] In a paper to a Planning History Group meeting, Rosser spoke of the irrelevance of the Development Plan concept to rapidly changing cities in India and the Far East;[74] the search for a 'strategic' solution in such cities in turn influenced the *Planning Advisory Group* which had been reassessing the British system for some six months prior to the operation of the Irish legislation.[75] A recent examination of Dublin's planning problems confirms the original P.A.G. conclusion that the Development Plan System is, on the one hand, too divorced from resource allocation and strategic considerations while, on the other hand, the system is too far removed from the concerns of local areas generally.[76] Thus while England and Wales adopted the concept of 'strategic plans' with continuous monitoring from 1968 onwards, Ireland continues to labour under a network of five-year Development Plans whose antecedents lie in pre-war British planning philosophy. Some aspects of the basic legislation have proved unworkable to date, e.g. the implementation of Special Area

Amenity Orders, while many other sections have received little support in practice. The absence of any 'Betterment' provisions in the Act was to deprive the Planning Authorities of a meaningful contingency fund with which to acquire land, pay compensation or initiate development.[77]

Since the Development Plan was not given the force of law, a high incidence of planning appeals was likely; such a process was indeed facilitated by the procedure under the Act whereby both developers and third-party groups could appeal the decisions of the Planning Authority to the Minister for Local Government.[78] While political abuse of the appeals system may have been overcome by the establishment of An Bord Pleanála,[79] the volume of appeals remains high. The high level of appeals inevitably serves to undermine the role of Planning Authorities; more seriously, the Appeal process, while creating work for planning consultants and legal expertise, has tended to emphasize the judicial side of planning and to correspondingly downgrade the social and economic objectives of the process.

Ireland is unique in relation to other West European countries both in regard to the importance of its agricultural sector[80] and the involvement of the state agencies in industrial and commercial development. And yet both these groups were to receive special treatment under the 1963 Act. Most agricultural developments were defined as 'exempted development' and it was only with the enactment of the 1976 Act that an attempt was made to ensure that state agencies were required to follow the normal planning procedures before commencing development works. With the benefit of hindsight, it is evident that the Act failed in not specifying a much larger range of research, co-ordination and promotional functions to be undertaken by the Department of Local Government. In addition, some of the Act's statutory provisions, such as minimum arrangements for public participation, have proved hopelessly inadequate to meet the realities of a highly educated society, insistent upon a participatory role in the planning process.

At the local level, the lack of procedures for preparation of Local or Action Area Plans have proved to be a serious omission. But it was probably Section 77, enabling a Planning Authority to develop land, which has been the greatest source of false expectations. In practice this section facilitated development, but without a radical reorganisation of local government there was little likelihood of much development by the Planning Authorities. In many respects this section was central to the passage of the Bill through the Dáil and generated the belief that local authorities would become dynamic development corporations. Yet it was not until 1982 with proposals to establish 'Urban Development Commissions', that the Dáil considered giving any real development role to local agencies;[81] it is not without significance that the 1982 Bill also proposed that such commissions would have power to by-pass much of the negative bureaucracy that has attached to planning over the past twenty years.

It is clear that the Local Government (Planning and Development) Act, 1963 was an unsatisfactory instrument with which to achieve the objectives of planning as it was promoted in 1962. While there has been a critical review of some aspects of the operation of the Act,[82] there is reluctance to contemplate an overhaul of the existing legislative base of planning, with reliance being placed instead on a flexible interpretation of the Act coupled with modifications in the law relating to its administration. While it is true that the 1963 Act was ill-suited to the development objectives as advanced by the politicians, the major reasons for the lack of progress in development planning rest in the failure to undertake the necessary administrative reforms and restructuring of the public sector.

The Decline of Local Government

As outlined above, the Planning and Development Act had been envisaged as the mechanism which would enable local authorities to function as development corporations. In reality, this positive role for local authorities implied that they possessed the necessary powers and finances to act as development agencies, that their geographic extent related to existing urban and socio-economic realities and that they were allowed to exercise the type of 'energetic and imaginative administration' which had been anticipated from 1960 onwards.[83] Unfortunately the outcome has been a dismal failure to make progress in any area of local government with numerous examples, especially since the 1970s, of the continued erosion of the powers of local government.

To have extended full planning powers to eighty-seven planning authorities (Fig. 2.1), with a population range from approximately 500,000 down to 1500, and without regard to urban or economic realities, was probably a serious error, even if a reorganisation of local government was to follow. Most of these authorities could not support a planning team and for them planning could be little more than development control.

The necessary review of local government had been widely discussed during the 1960s. Barrington had consistently argued the need for local government to 'concern itself with new things as well as old'.[84] A presumption that the revenue basis of Local

Government would be strengthened had underlain the writings of T. K. Whitaker[85] and, accordingly, an inter-departmental committee was established to examine this subject. Various reports from this committee supported the concept of strong local government. The third report of the committee foresaw continued pressure for the improvement and expansion of local government services and the Committee proposed long-term financial arrangements 'to complement the long-term plans drawn up by them in other spheres, and especially in physical planning and housing'.[86]

The government also tackled the whole issue of reforming the functions of local government and reorganising its territorial extent. Thus, the 1971 White Paper on *Local Government Reorganisation*[87] proposed a strengthening of the system based upon the county unit, with a reduction of the role of Urban Districts and Town Commissions. A related report on *Strengthening the Local Government Service* re-enforced the recommendations of the White Paper.[88] In particular this report supported the idea of the county as the basic unit since 'from the standpoint of management effectiveness, urbans below about 12,000 population (including suburbs) do not and cannot have either the staff structure or the financial strength to be viable as independent units'.[89] In addition the report proposed that twelve adjacent small counties be administered in pairs.

The notion of a critical minimum population in a local authority area had direct implications for the delivery of planning services. Of even greater importance to planners was the proposal that each authority should have a Planning and Development Officer as head of a planning and development team with responsibility for land-use planning, development activities, long-range planning and who would report directly to the Manager.[90] Thus, for the first time, most authorities would be in a position to assemble a planning team or offer an attractive career structure to planners.

In a detailed analysis of the possibilities for reform in local government the Institute of Public Administration outlined a functional role for a hierarchy of sub-national tiers of government from which policy-makers could make a selection.[91] In relation to the developmental role of local authorities the IPA report stressed that a 'comprehensive approach to development becomes almost impossible if responsibilities are fragmented to the degree that exists in the Irish system of public administration'.[92] While there was widespread cross-party political agreement on the need for reform, there was disunity with respect to the form that reorganisation should take. In the event, after much discussion, a new government's 'selective and measured response' was to yield to pressure from the small urban authorities and no reforms were implemented.[93]

Instead, the 1970s witnessed the erosion of the financial autonomy of all local authorities, unifunctional state agencies adopted an ever more autonomous role in relation to their remit[94] and central government became increasingly powerful. In such circumstances, neither the view of local authorities as development corporations nor the allied concept of development planning had a real chance of success. Instead Ireland stumbled into the 1980s relying largely on 'the management methods of the small farm and the village shop'.[95] The failure to reform local government has generated increasing frustration as people came to realise that 'ultimately the surprise is not that it has not done better, but indeed that it has survived at all'.[96] Nowhere is this paralysis in reform more evident than in respect of a policy to enable local authorities to regulate the supply and price of development land. Despite a large measure of agreement on the desirability of such a policy, more than a decade has elapsed with no tangible result, other than the imposition of taxes on profits from the sale of development land.[97]

On the social dimension, the lack of reform has largely inhibited any serious response to the growing significance of community groups in society, thereby largely undermining the Ministerial hope that 'local development associations and other similar bodies can also play an essential part . . . in the task of improving the quality of environment in our towns and countryside'.[98]

Development planning by local authorities was thus deprived of the necessary financial and corporate structural supports while, at the same time, unable effectively to harness the energies and goodwill of voluntary associations and local groups.

The Absence of a Regional Planning Dimension

While Ireland has had a long and continuing concern for regional planning[99] and while Charles Abrams has emphasised the importance of 'a plan for regional development and for the resolution of jurisdictional conflicts',[100] the 1963 Planning Act makes no reference to regions and regionalism hardly featured during the Dáil[101] and Senate[102] debates on the Bill. Delany has suggested that reference to regions was omitted 'so as not to delay the passing of the Act whilst this highly delicate and controversial subject was being debated'.[103]

Whatever the reasons for such an omission, the absence of a statutory role for regional planning was to leave Ireland almost alone in Europe in not having legal provision for regional planning.

Such an omission was particularly serious since only through a strong tier of regional plans could the government achieve its objective of linking local planning to national, social and economic policies. The absence of any reference to regionalism in the Act was in complete contrast with the government's steadfast commitment to ensuring 'that economic and physical planning are properly co-ordinated at both regional and national level and that all major developments will be executed within the framework of a comprehensive physical planning system'.[104] The Minister for Local Government even went so far as to state that he was 'personally convinced that one of the most important tasks I have as Minister for Local Government is to establish a regional physical planning framework for our social and economic development programmes'.[105]

The practical importance given to regional planning by government was evident in the decision to establish nine regions for planning purposes.[106] Using his powers of co-ordination under Section 22 of the Act, the Minister appointed consultants to undertake studies of the long-term development of the Dublin and Limerick regions. Myles Wright was appointed to undertake the study of the Dublin region, while, in commissioning Nathaniel Lichfield to undertake the study of the Limerick region, the Minister stressed that the study should 'provide the framework needed to guide the planning authorities in the region in deciding upon the contents of their development plans and the general policy towards development in their areas for about 20 years'.[107] The subsequent regional plan was based upon a clear urban hierarchy (Fig. 5.1). The importance of regional planning was emphasised by the holding of a national conference on regional planning in Dublin in 1965 at which papers were delivered by a number of Irish and international experts on regional planning.[108] Lichfield saw the regional plan breaking down the national plan in an attempt to formulate the scale of development within a given region.[109] Curtin, on the other hand, relying on his Irish experience, stressed the positive role of regional planning, since 'it aims at achieving an increase in the contribution which each region can make to the solution of national economic and social problems'.[110] Thus, regional planning was the essential link between national economic planning and local physical planning[111] – a link lacking in statutory support in the Irish case.

The central importance of a regional planning dimension in the achievement of a balanced promotion of economic objectives was repeatedly recognised.[112] The interaction between the different levels of planning was elaborated by Turpin in 1967:

It is recognised that if planning authorities are to operate effectively in the promotion of economic and social development in their areas, there must be a means of communication and interaction between the local statutory plans and national economic planning.

The local plans must be consistent, in the aggregate, with the employment and population objectives in the national programme, and with the projections of capital availability. It is the task of regional planning to provide a means by which local plans may be geared to national and regional objectives. This is not simply a matter of achieving a regional breakdown of the national programme, though it is desirable that there should be a regional orientation in future national economic planning.[113]

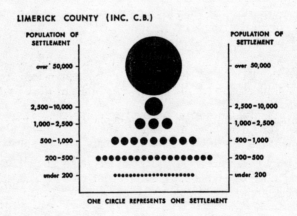

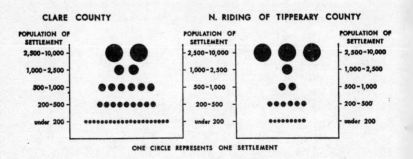

Fig. 5.1 Settlement Hierarchy for Limerick Region (after Lichfield, 1967).

Irish writings on regional planning clearly recognised the interactive relationship between planning at different scales and the necessity of having a hierarchy of plans in which the regional dimension was to be central to resource allocation and development. Thus, as C. H. Murray of the Department of Finance outlined the sequence, it was:

> only when all regional plans become available that the total demands on national resources can be seen, the necessary reconciliation with the supply of natural resources be effected, and final regional plans be published.[114]

All of the advisory regional reports envisaged some form of regional agency having responsibility for implementation of their proposals. Such a body was set up in Limerick, with representation drawn from all local authorities; in 1969 the government extended that concept to the whole country, establishing nine Regional Development Organisations charged 'to co-ordinate the programmes for development in each region'.[115] The White Paper on *Local Government Reorganisation* indicated a preparedness to give statutory powers to the RDOs 'as required'[116] but no extension of their powers took place despite the importance of a statutory basis for their work.[117]

The important national role of regional planning was stressed by Vincent Cullinane:

> the regional component in National Economic and Social Plans is to be fully recognised and the expected contribution that the regions have to make to national development is to be spelled out in future rolling plans then an objective should be to seek to achieve integrated comprehensive strategic planning at both national and regional level.[118]

In 1982 Sean Murphy of Limerick County Council spoke of the 'urgent need to strengthen the Regional Organisations' and to allocate 'power and resources to agencies other than Government Departments'.[119] However, any move towards the devolution of powers to a broadly based regional tier is likely to face continuing strong resistance from central government which successfully sought to curtail the powers of a proposed Western Development Board in 1977 and which kept secret the deliberations of a 1970s Committee on the role of sub-national units of administration.

The dilemma over regional planning highlights clearly the conflict between the politicians and their professional staff over the role, function and form of planning. The lack of a strong regional planning tier largely divorced local planning actions from the realities of public policy at national level. But in addition to confusion on the regional level, the government's desire for a national development strategy was to raise serious questions about the disposition of power within different government departments and the role of physical planning in resource allocation. It also was to highlight the inevitable conflict between long-term development time spans and short-term political necessities.

A National Strategy: The Role of Central Government

In an effort to solve a long-running dispute over the size, number and location of 'development centres'[120] and in order to provide a framework for regional and local plan-making, the government, with the support of the United Nations, commissioned Colin Buchanan and Partners in association with Economic Consultants Ltd and An Foras Forbartha to carry out regional studies of the remaining seven regions of the country. The brief stipulated that:

> The Consultant shall indicate economic growth potential, identify possible development centres, establish the level of change needed in infrastructure to facilitate growth and make proposals for policy decisions to be taken by the government, including measures to implement such proposals.[121]

Table 5.5
Estimated 1986 Population Under Hypothetical Alternative Strategies

REGION	1966 Actual	1986 Out-turn	Concentration in Dublin	Cork/limerick	Regional Alternative	County Dispersal
East	1,058	1,335	1,765	1,460	1,465	1,335
South-east	319	385	330	335	375	345
South-west(a)	718	852	705	1,010	805	765
Mid-west(b)	409	409	345	345	400	380
North-west(c)	436	556	350	350	380	415
TOTAL: State(d)	2,884	3,537	3,500	3,500	3,430	3,234

(a) includes all of the current South-west and Mid-west regions
(b) comprising Galway, Roscommon, Offaly, Westmeath and Laois counties
(c) All other designated area counties
(d) Figures rounded to nearest 5,000

Working within the policy context as laid down by the *Second Programme* and the Reports of the National Industrial Economic Council, the consultants examined the country's problems and resource possibilities and prepared a range of population projections which could result from the pursuance of a range of physical strategies. Table 5.5 indicates the differential scale of growth under each strategy, together with the regional distribution in 1986. The consultants concluded that the greater the degree of concentration, the larger would be the likely scale of employment growth and population containment within Ireland. But the greater the concentration, the more widespread the pattern of loss elsewhere in the country. In an attempt to balance the economic and social considerations, the report recommended a regional strategy based on an urban hierarchy, as set out in Fig. 5.2a. Central to the strategy was the idea that Dublin should continue to grow, but only at the natural increase rate.

Belatedly published in May 1969, the report was welcomed by the National Industrial Economic Council which argued that the likely diffusion effects of growth in these centres upon the rest of the country would be considerable.[122] For its part the government deferred judgment upon the recommendations pending further examination 'in the context of proposals for regional development generally'.[123]

Simultaneously, the government requested the newly established advisory Regional Development Organisations to undertake studies in each of the nine regions. Although these studies generally favoured a much wider intra-regional pattern of growth than Buchanan had proposed, the government in 1972 accepted the Buchanan target figures for the nine centres (Table 5.6) as 'planning-base' figures for the period up to 1991.[124] But these planning base figures were not supported by any evident policy instruments and to a great extent the location strategy pursued by the IDA from 1972 onwards[125] was not compatible with the government's targets as set out in Table 5.6. The failure to implement a national physical strategy left regional and local planning seriously jeopardised. The exercise also raised serious questions about the divisions of power within Cabinet with respect to forward planning and resource allocation. The national strategy proposed by Buchanan and later by the 1972 Government Statement was in effect a framework within which all public-sector investments would be made. The effective implementation of such a programme would have required an inter-departmental approach to planning, with ultimate policy vested in a Cabinet subcommittee. It was unrealistic to believe that the Department of Local Government

146   *Planning: The Irish Experience*

Fig. 5.2 National Development Strategy:

a) Buchanan's Proposed Growth Centres, (1969).

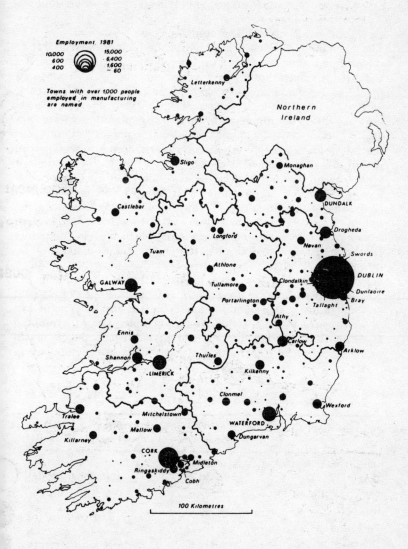

b) **Employment in Manufacturing Industry by Town** (after Gillmor, D.A., *Economic Activities in the Republic of Ireland: A Geographical Perspective*, Gill and Macmillan, Dublin, 1985.

(subsequently, the Department of the Environment) or indeed the proposed super-ministry of Regional Development (Fig. 5.3) would ever have received the freedom to implement such a programme.[126]

Development Planning: Concluding Note

The concept of 'development planning' had not borne fruit due to the interplay of many factors: the unsuitability of the basic legislation, the weakness of local government, the lack of regional planning and the failure to grasp the political nettle of planning at national level. After a glorious start in the 1960s, the 1970s saw a growing disenchantment with all types of planning in Ireland. There was an abandonment of national economic planning as recessions made prediction a hazardous art. Interest in regionalism within the county waned as the government sought to ensure that all of Ireland remained classified as a European underdeveloped region. Given the circumstances in Ireland with its 'post-colonial traditions of individualism',[127] the planners may have been too optimistic in attempting to redirect migration flows. In the event Myles Wright's warning that it 'is impossible for the government in Dublin to enforce a desired pattern of population distribution development'[128] has proved correct. It may even be, as Aalen suggested, that 'an expanding metropolis is a pre-requisite for growth in peripheral regions'.[129] In any event, hopes of a grand strategy of integrated planning had collapsed and local plans had to be prepared in the absence of a national plan and with minimal co-ordination at either national or regional levels. This is not to underestimate the contribution of local plans to development in

Table 5.6
Proposed Expansion of the Main Growth Centres 1966-86

Centres	1966 Population	1986 Population	1966-86% Increase
Dublin (sub-region)	795,047	1,125,000	+ 42%
Cork	122,146	250,000	+105%
Limerick-Shannon	57,570	175,000	+204%
Waterford	29,842	55,000	+ 84%
Galway	26,295	47,000	+ 79%
Dundalk	21,678	44,000	+103%
Drogheda	17,908	35,000	+ 95%
Sligo	13,424	25-30,000	+105%
Athlone	10,987	18,000	+ 64%

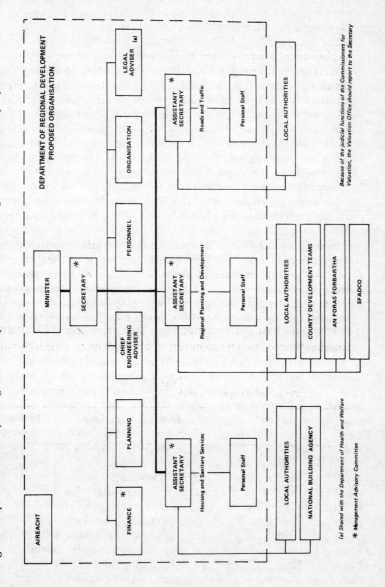

Fig. 5.3 Proposals for Ministry of Regional Development (after *Public Service Organisation Review Group Report*, 1969.

the 1970s or to assume that planning will not have an enlarged role in the 1980s. But the 1970s saw a shift in physical planning away from fundamental issues of national development towards an overriding concern with environmental management and control.

The Decline of Regionalism 1975-1987

While no statutory basis had been provided for regional planning, the regional dimension did flower during the years of the Lemass administration and, indeed, advisory regional planning studies were to provide the basis for the long term development of the Dublin region where the Myles Wright report on the *Dublin Region*,[127] together with the recommendations of the report on *Transportation in Dublin*[128] have provided the basis for the long term development of the capital city region (Fig. 5.4). Likewise, the advisory report by Nathaniel Lichfield in 1967 provided the basis for the strategic planning of the Mid West Region and it also provided a model for the establishment of the Regional Development Organisations.[129]

But from the late 1960s Government faltered in its support of the concept of regionalism and failed to promote an effective system of regional planning. By the mid-1970s there was also a weakening of commitment to the notion of regional development policies for areas within Ireland. There were two reasons for this change of emphasis. Firstly, the mid 1970s recession had adversely affected the older and hitherto successful manufacturing cities and towns of the east and south, while the traditional problem and 'designated' areas had improved due to a mixture of successful policies and the continued reduction of the intensity of congestion through emigration. The Government increasingly wished to have development incentives extended to the whole country and they were arguing that 'the approach to regional policy is now nationwide rather than confined to specific areas'.[130]

The other reason favouring an emphasis upon national rather than inter regional approaches arose from Ireland's accession to the European Community in 1973. Whereas the protocol governing the enlargement of the Community had repeatedly emphasised the intention of 'evening out regional differences in levels of development' and thus could have been expected to lead to a reinvigoration of domestic regional policy, the outcome was rather different. In having Ireland declared as a single region for the purposes of European Regional Development funding, the emphasis was to shift from internal regional disparities to a priority on bringing Ireland as a whole into line with the rest of Europe. As Lee has

Development Planning 151

Fig. 5.4 Development Strategy for the Dublin Area:

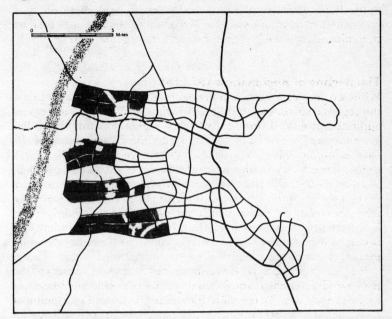

a) Myles Wright 1967.

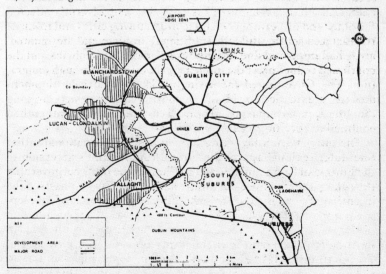

b) Dublin County Council Development Plan Strategy.

pointed out the designation of Ireland as a single region 'managed to abort a potentially dangerous discussion concerning regional policy'[131] and it also enabled the Department of Finance to dismiss Ireland's internal disparities as being 'insignificant compared with the disparity between Ireland and the rest of the EEC'.[132] Thus, while promoting strong arguments for a regional approach at the European level, Ireland adopted an increasingly centralised approach to development policy within the country. Particularly during the period of rapid growth in the 1970s, this centralised approach, in the absence of regional policy, resulted in the continued growth of Dublin and the spread of metropolitan influence throughout the East region.[133] The 1985 *Eastern Region Settlement Strategy 2011* provides a quantification of the extent to which the East region had come to dominate the remainder of the country in terms of employment and capital investment;[134] that report also points to the future consequences for all of Ireland of a laissez-faire approach to spatial planning policy.

One of the ironies of development policy has been the necessity, against a backcloth of increasing centralisation, to undertake a series of regional reports for Irish regions[135] and border areas[136] in order to assist in the co-ordination of local planning and as a basis for programmed investment under the European Regional Development Programmes. Many of these regional reports prepared between 1979 and 1987 were in fact largely funded by the European Community.

For the most part, these regional planning reports paid particular attention to the urban development strategies for the regions' settlement systems and the development of the necessary inter urban support infrastructures. See Fig. 5.5. The rural component of these studies remained particularly weak and confined largely to negative control proposals and to prohibiting the development of 'urban generated housing'. The lack of attention to rural issues, apart from tourism, reflects both the fact that most agricultural activity was deemed to be 'exempted' under the 1963 legislation and also the hard fact that to date Ireland has not developed a planning philosophy relevant to the country's rural traditions and culture.

An overview of the various 1980s regional reports and plans has concluded as follows:

> Although successful in highlighting regional problems and opportunities, the second round of regional plans clearly reflects the problems of operating without national planning guidelines. The lack of willingness at state level to designate

Fig.5.5 Regional Strategies: Urban Structure:

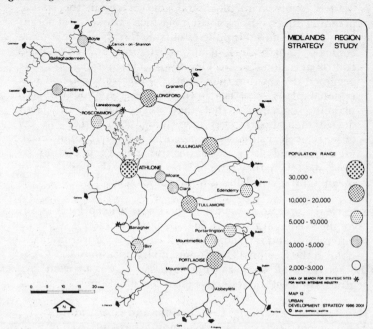

a) Development Strategy for the Midlands Region, 1981.

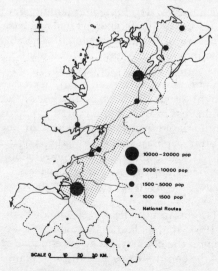

b) Donegal – Leitrim – Sligo Regional Strategy, 1987.

different parts of the country for different purposes; the limited involvement of central government in the spatial planning dimension (as a result of which state sectoral bodies have carried out their policies outside the physical planning context); and the lack of any substantial form of political control at regional or local level (which might otherwise have occupied the vacuum thus created) – all this has meant that regional plans have not been the clear, confident spatial planning documents that they might have been. Their developmental strategies have often been forced, in the absence of clear direction from national level, to follow existing trends and also to avoid positive spatial articulation. By the same token, they have also been denied the possibility of meaningful upward and downward linkages.[137]

The clear implication was that there was a need for a statutory planning system at national, regional and local levels which could be interactive and interdependent. Instead, the government chose to abolish the Regional Development Organisations and to curtail the activities of An Foras Forbartha in favour of even greater centralisation without effective local coordination.

Development Planning: Conclusions and Implications

The concept of development planning has not lived up to the expectations which were aroused by the notion in the early 1960s. The relative failure of development planning has been due to many factors including the inadequacy of its legal base, the unreformed and weak nature of Local Government, the absence of regional-national planning and the nature of the political and administrative systems throughout the country. In the absence of structural reforms in public administration, it was inevitable that the achievements brought about by the introduction of the Planning Act of 1963 would be less dramatic and more incremental in nature than had been anticipated. Any evaluation is made particularly difficult since planning operates through the political process and, consequently, clear and identifiable monuments to its success are difficult to identify. In addition, real success may lie in curbing excesses and in ensuring the more judicious use of scarce resources.

For all its limitations, the Development Plan process initiated under the 1963 Act has had many important implications for the development of the country. As a consequence of the Act all of the land area of the country has been subject to planning proposals and controls as operated by the 87 planning authorities. The process of plan making forced these planning authorities to make more explicit their proposals for long term developments; they were required to think in terms of at least a five year time horizon. Through the planning process, local authorities have been able to give effect to longer term schemes and proposals.

The Development Plans have also provided 'an indication for developers, land purchasers and prospective home owners of the types of development which would be acceptable in the area'.[138] The social importance of Ireland's planning process must also be emphasised: planning came on stream at a time when the Irish economy was experiencing unprecedented industrial and commercial expansion. Planning represented an important if sometimes inadequate modifier of market excesses during this period. It also offered a very great strengthening of the existing mechanisms for the protection of both the natural and the man-made environment.[139] Under the legislation and the Development Plans society has been able to establish reasonable development standards with respect to housing, open space and other uses.[140] While plan making has been hampered by the failure to develop a theory of planning relevant to Irish needs, much has been achieved especially where the development plan derived its rationale from wider and long term advisory reports which laid down the context for development by a number of local authorities in conjunction with other State agencies. This has been especially true in regard to the long term development of the Dublin and Cork areas as well as in the formulation of joint policies by a number of rural planning authorities.

However, much more might have been achieved had successive governments persisted with the positive and progressive concept of Development Planning and if steps had been taken to implement the reforms necessary for the modernisation and rationalisation of local administration and development policy. More than anything else, the neglect of the national-regional planning dimension necessitated that local planning operate almost in a vacuum; it also tended to divorce the operation of planning from the activity of development which was often undertaken by different agencies operating at a different scale. While there have been some reforms of the planning code, there has been no attempt made to reform the planning structure as laid down in 1963.

There is also a need for a reassessment of aspects of Ireland's spatial policy at different scales. To quote a recent evaluation of planning:

156 *Planning: The Irish Experience*

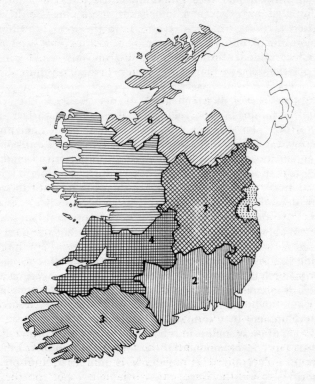

Fig. 5.6 Regions for Programmes for E.C. Funding. (Source: Dept. of Finance).

Re-assessment of spatial planning policy must take into account how it should relate to economic and social planning as well as how it can be most meaningful at different planning levels. In this context, the first premise must be that, while spatial planning at national level is bound to be of a different nature from that at local (development plan) level, it is none the less meaningful for that. In fact, if local development plans were stronger and more effective, some framework of national or regional planning would soon prove necessary to co-ordinate different plans and safeguard issues of national interest.

Perhaps the answer lies in a continuum where at national level economic planning forms the central objective leading to spatial planning policy, while at local level the spatial policy is central. The principle is that of a planning hierarchy to execute planning functions at all levels and facilitate upward and downward linkages. Primary responsibility to identify the social and economic problems (the 'why' and 'how' of development) would lie at the national level. Once these are identified, planners will be in a much stronger position to say what kind of regional policy is required.[141]

Despite the continued neglect of the regional issue in Irish administration, there is evidence of a growing body of opinion favouring devolution, regional development and regional planning. The current case for regionalism is founded upon a range of considerations including the failure of the centralised approach in terms of investment, production or job creation. Throughout Europe there is a growing emphasis upon economic development linked to regional cultures and it is argued that Ireland needs to develop 'a creative synthesis between state and community.'[142] There is a confusion of regional areas within Ireland with the Mid West alone having a regional development authority. The regional subdivision of the country for E.C. funding purposes compounds the problem by separating Dublin from its functional region (Fig. 5.6). Almost alone amongst the countries of Europe, Ireland has failed to develop its regional tier of administration and the country's arguments in Brussels are often seen as being at odds with practice at home in regard to spatial development policy. Much more serious has been the recent opinion of O.E.C.D. that Ireland's centralised bureaucracy is inhibiting innovation and growth[143] while the European Parliament report on the *Regional Problems of Ireland*[144] emphasises the need for devolution of power and the establishment of statutory regional development authorities to undertake integrated development programmes[145] and to take full advantage of funding from the European Community. However, Ireland's response, as announced in August, 1988, appears to favour a perpetuation of the centralised approach to local and regional development[146].

The issue of regionalism and of regional planning[147] is now a live issue at the European level. As Ireland seeks to play a full and vital part in the Single European Market, it must first ensure that its planning structures are reformed and modernised. The case for the integration and linking of development and planning within a comprehensive framework of statutory regional plans remains compelling. Such an integrated structure would facilitate good planning which, in turn, would enhance Ireland's social and economic development.

CHAPTER SIX
(Epilogue)

ENVIRONMENTAL AND PLANNING POLICIES IN THE 1980s

Michael J. Bannon

Introduction
The previous chapter has examined the reasons for the failure of the concept of a vertically integrated system of local to regional to national planning. Likewise, the notion of a national urban system with a rationally planned role for each level in the hierarchy was to prove illusory. Even the more modest goal of restraining the flow of migration from the rest of Ireland into Dublin was found to be outside the scope of planning and to involve a degree of political discrimination which was considered unacceptable.

In the absence of either a national-regional planning system or a grand strategy for urbanisation, planning in the 1980s has become much more incremental and much more local, with an increasing emphasis upon community problems and community based approaches to solutions. In the process, the focus of planning has shifted away from development and in favour of environmental concerns. The somewhat naïve belief that well planned land management could of itself alleviate all the major ills of society has been superseded by an increasingly specialised approach to environmental issues, leading to a priority for urban conservation, rehabilitation and renewal. The more modest expectations in respect of planning also reflect the currently held view that the state should play a diminished role in the management of economic and social affairs. Local issues rather than national strategies have become of central concern.

Environmental Awareness
Looked at in the wider context of the European Community,

surveys have revealed that Ireland has had a relatively low level of environmental concern and, traditionally, environmental problems have not been treated with the same degree of urgency as in many other European countries.[1] As President Hillery expressed it, Ireland has been travelling down 'a road of destruction' for too long in terms of its environment but at last 'forces of enlightenment' are awakening to the need to protect, manage and utilise the resources of both the scientific and the built environments.[2] In fact, there has been an upsurge of interest in all aspects of environmental issues in recent years. This growth in environmental concern arises in no small part from the rights and opportunities afforded to individuals and groups under the planning code to express their concerns and to seek a role in protecting and managing important elements of their national heritage.

One of the major contributory causes to the increased environmental awareness has been the growth in attention to environmental research and education. Throughout the 1980s and up to late 1987 An Foras Forbartha was engaged in an expanding programme of environmental research and in operating a conservation advice service for local authorities. One of the many fruits of this work was the compilation of a major report, *The State of the Environment*, which provided an overview of the nation's resources and problems in terms of both the rural and urban environments and containing specialist chapters on water, air, noise and waste.[3] Indeed, whatever else may be said about the decision to abolish An Foras Forbartha — the National Planning Institute — and to transform parts of it into an Environmental Research Unit of the Department of the Environment, it pointedly signifies a shift of emphasis from land use and planning towards environmental issues.

Over the past decade there has been a steady growth in the number and range of environmental science and environmental studies courses and research organisations. Chief amongst these has been the Resource and Environmental Policy Centre in University College, Dublin, endowed by The Heritage Trust to provide 'a focal point for the mobilisation of the university's intellectual resources in the cause of harmonising economic development and environmental quality.' Since its establishment the Centre has acted as catalyst for interdisciplinary research and the exploration of environmental issues. The major publications of the Centre include a comprehensive review of Irish environmental policies under the title *Promise and Performance*[4] and *Managing Dublin Bay*,[5] an interdisciplinary inventory of the problems and the resources of the bay and its environment. Among its other activities, the Centre promoted an *Options* exhibition aimed at having the public, particularly young people, better informed about their own environment and more involved in the making of choices and understanding the consequences of such choices.

Another important development was the establishment of The Environmental Awareness Bureau with the objective 'of fostering, at all levels in our society, a greater appreciation of environmental values and a more caring attitude to the environment'. The E.A.B. was responsible for organising Ireland's involvement in the European Year of the Environment, during which in excess of one hundred local environmental projects received support. From July 1988 the functions of the Environment Awareness Bureau have been incorporated with the new Environmental Research Unit of D.O.E.

Indeed, environmental awareness and protection is increasingly an area of European Community involvement. The Environment Directorate (D.G.XI) together with The European Environmental Bureau is open to advise on environmental concerns and also to hear and to examine complaints from individuals and organisations throughout the Community.[6] An increasing range of environmental legislation has had a mandatory effect in such areas as water quality, air pollution, chemicals management, waste disposal and noise control. Of particular importance is the Directive on *Assessment of the Effects of Certain Public and Private Projects on the Environment*, requiring that all projects likely to have a significant environmental effect be subjected to a detailed environmental impact statement with effect from mid-1988. Likewise Council Regulation 1094/88 – 'the Set Aside Directive' – seeks to withdraw land from arable and other intensive agricultural production, thereby making more of Europe's land available for amenity, leisure and recreational use.

Planning for Environmental Improvement
The increased investment in environmental education and research has resulted in both a heightened awareness of environmental issues and in the need to plan for environmental areas by all levels of government. Thus, new National Parks opened by the Office of Public Works include Letterfrack in Connemara, Glenbeigh in Donegal and the Burren in Co. Clare. There is an expanding network of Forest Parks including Ards in Donegal, Doneraile in Cork, Killykeen in Cavan, Rossmore in Monaghan and Donadea in Kildare. A large number of nature reserves and local heritage parks have been established and the Slieve Bloom mountains have been designated as an Environment Park under the control and management of the local authorities. The opening

up of the Wicklow Way provides a 132 km walkway through some of Ireland's most scenic countryside. The Office of Public Works has completed an examination of the Royal and Grand Canals and the Barrow Navigation as linear amenities linking Dublin and the countryside,[7] while the Wicklow Mountain Environmental Group have developed proposals to designate much of the Wicklow mountains as a National Park (Fig. 6.1).[8] In this, as in many other

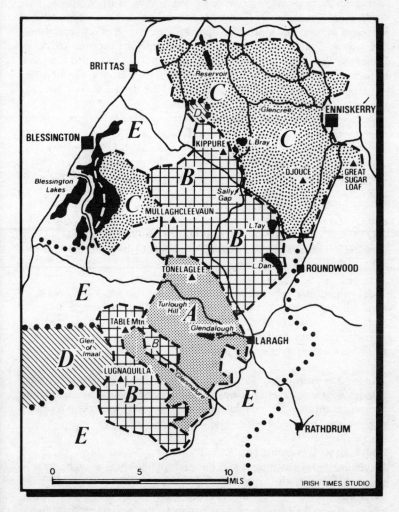

Fig. 6.1 The Proposed Wicklow Mountains National Park. (Illustration supplied by *Irish Times Studio*).

amenity projects, the problems of land acquisition and the costs of compensation can either delay a project or render it prohibitively expensive. Land acquisition and pricing remains a problem.

Many of these new parks and amenities link the urban and rural areas through the provision of scenic rural environments for urban recreation. In order to meet the increasing needs of an expanding urban population for recreation and amenity lands and facilities, urban authorities have provided a hierarchy of open spaces and parklands. Thus Dublin County Council has a total of almost 3,000 hectares of land designated as open spaces, much of it in the splendid regional parks at Malahide, Newbridge Demesne and Ardgillan House to the north of the city and at Marlay, Tymon and Corkagh demesne to the south west. Likewise, Cork County Council has developed the Ballincollig regional park while the Cork Corporation is assembling the Glen River park.

A growing urban population with increased leisure time requires a network of parks and recreational facilities. As that population becomes more highly educated more mobile and environmentally sensitive, the demands for high quality landscapes and amenities for an increasingly diverse range of activities will continue to expand.

However, the importance of the environment cannot be judged simply in terms of amenities or meeting recreational demands. The quality of the urban and rural environment is central to the economic success of the country. The point has been made forcefully by Philip Mullaly that:

> If we produce a better environment, we can get a pay-off in the form of tourist revenue and in the form of leisure activity for our own people. A living environment is an essential national asset, and this asset should be wealth producing, and should have job creating potential.[9]

As tourism promotion becomes central to the Government's recovery programme, the enhancement of both the rural and urban environment is of crucial importance in the reinvigorated programme of Bord Fáilte – the Tourist Board.

The Urban Environment
Environmental awareness and concern probably is at its highest in respect of both the quality of the urban environment and the constant threat to the heritage of buildings and streets, most especially in Dublin. In many respects the urban environments resulting from Ireland's brief period of economic expansion in the

1960s and 1970s left much to be desired. There was considerable evidence of water pollution; there were also problems of air pollution with too little regard for the problems of noise or traffic congestion. Some, if not all of these have been ameliorated through a mixture of domestic legislation, compliance with E.C. standards and, not least, in consequence of the closure of many older industries.

But it is perhaps the approach to the built environment which has left the greatest legacy of problems. In general, the ethos of the society turned its back on the old and on the heritage. Generous grants and loans were available for new developments with little or no subvention for conservation, rehabilitation or renewal of the old. Indeed, free market forces favoured redevelopment and resulted in the demolition of many historic buildings and the violation of the integrity of historic streets and cultural areas. This emphasis upon new buildings and redevelopment went hand in hand with a philosophy which presumed that the decentralisation of people and industry was ideal. Suburbanisation became the norm and the inner areas of Ireland's cities and even of the smaller towns[10] suffered both a decline in their residential population as well as a serious contraction of the social spectrum of their residential populations. Both the physical and the social fabric of the urban areas came under imminent and widespread threat.

Urban Rehabilitation

The environmental awakening of the 1980s gives grounds for optimism that Ireland will adopt a more sensitive approach to its cultural heritage of buildings in the decades ahead. Papers in a recent book on building conservation show that: 'How we manage our buildings depends upon a host of factors which can be grouped into four interdependent categories: economic and financial, cultural, institutional and technical.'[11]

Until recently, most of these factors did not as a rule favour the older building stock or its protection. However, there are increasing signs of hope. Many public agencies, institutions and major companies have undertaken the cleaning and restoration of some of Ireland's notable buildings in recent years. These include the Royal Hospital, Dublin Castle, the Custom House, the Bank of Ireland and the Casino in Dublin. While the An Taisce *Urbana – Study of Dublin*[12] highlighted the endangered nature of the 694 listed houses which it examined, there is currently reinvestment and rehabilitation work under way on some of the key buildings in this collection. Perhaps it is symptomatic that the Electricity Supply Board has painstakingly restored two houses on Merrion Square when, twenty years ago, it forced through the demolition of most of one side of Fitzwilliam Street for its modern offices. While it has to be accepted that there are major difficulties facing privately funded rehabilitation for residential purposes,[13] the endeavours of the North Great George's Street residents demonstrates what can be done. While the Dublin local authorities have undertaken little or no rehabilitation of residential properties in recent years, the restoration of parts of the Shandon area and Douglas Street in Cork by Cork Corporation has proved successful. In the case of Waterford city urban renewal has embraced detailed excavations and conservation while housing rehabilitation and modern infill together have led to a revitalisation of the city's core. In Galway, a unique heritage of stone warehouse buildings serves as the centrepiece of the city's rehabilitation successes. The rejuvenation of the urban centres of many of the larger urban places has been accelerated in response to the incentives made available under the Urban Renewal Act of 1986.

One of the few examples of Irish legislation favouring the existing building stock was the rehabilitation grants scheme in respect of pre-1940 buildings which operated from 1985 to 1987. Under this scheme grants of up to £8,000 could be secured towards cost of rehabilitating and upgrading older properties. This scheme was availed of by many individuals and smaller landlords. It encouraged a move back from the outer suburbs and it enabled many buildings in the inner suburbs to be reconverted back to single family occupancy. Finally, the scheme was also available to larger landlords to help initiate the rehabilitation of some of the major working class schemes – e.g. the Iveagh Trust and the schemes erected under the Artisans housing legislation.[14]

Another contributor to the rehabilitation of historic buildings in both urban and rural areas has been the use of a variety of social employment schemes to simultaneously provide trainees with construction skills while also securing the restoration of buildings, including old mills, schools and churches for use for community or business activities. The various AnCO schemes also contributed to major restoration projects as in the case of the Tailor's Guild Hall in Dublin or the Roscrea Heritage Centre and Damer House in Roscrea.

There is a belated but strengthening recognition that 'our built environment is a physical tapestry which is taken up and worked upon by each succeeding generation' but with each recognising that 'the pride of a nation is best marked by what it conserves and cherishes as it adapts to development and to changing needs'.[15] But building conservation and rehabilitation must be seen as part of a wider concern with urban renewal and regeneration – a process of reversing the trends evidenced in Irish urban areas since the mid 1920s – and of restoring the social and environmental quality of cities.

Urban Renewal and Envioronmental Improvement
Having examined the long-term consequences of the centrifugal forces leading to inner area decline in cities and towns, the National Economic and Social Council in its report on *Urbanisation: Problems of Growth and Decay in Dublin* set out an agenda for urban renewal which, though developed for Dublin, was relevant for all the cities and major towns.[16] That inner area agenda consisted of some fourteen issues as follows:

1. Planning to achieve a more compact centre.
2. Strict land zoning to prevent commercial expansion into residential areas.
3. Public acquisition of lands around the business area.
4. A shift of emphasis in favour of public transportation in the inner city.
5. The stimulation of high quality architecture and design.
6. Environmental improvement of the centre.
7. Increasing both the population size and the range of social groups living in inner areas.
8. Ensuring a wider mix of inner city housing.
9. Progressive renewal using environmental areas and local community areas.
10. Rehabilitation of inner city flats.
11. Expansion of local job opportunities for inner city residents.
12. Priority educational programmes for disadvantaged groups.
13. Return to community based systems of welfare and area management.
14. The establishment of an inner city fund drawing in part of EC aid.

In the interim since these proposals were enunciated a considerable degree of progress has been achieved, at least in some of Ireland's cities and towns. Thus it is now recognised that central business areas will not expand indefinitely and that, in many instances, the most appropriate use for redundant factories and commercial sites is residential. In pursuit of this, many urban authorities have acquired such properties as part of their renewal programme. In the decade from 1978 to 1988 Dublin Corporation erected in excess of 1,500 new inner city dwellings on thirty-eight sites around the business district. Cork Corporation has developed a number of inner city infill schemes, including a joint venture with a voluntary group at the Marsh, while Waterford has renewed much of its derelict inner core with tastefully designed inner housing schemes. On the debit side, few of the developments have involved private investment nor have they yet succeeded in encouraging the middle classes to return to the inner city.

Many of these housing schemes have involved high standards of housing design while pedestrianisation schemes and environmental improvements have made the urban cores safer and more attractive. The proposals emanating from the short-lived *Dublin Metropolitan Streets Commission* caught the public imagination[17] and many of the proposals have been taken up by Dublin Corporation. The rehabilitation of older local authority flats is now beginning and is coming onto the political agenda.

In the case of urban transportation policy, it is possible to draw a stark contrast between the approaches and the achievements in Cork and Dublin. In the former case, Cork has put in place a programme of road improvements, parking controls and traffic management procedures acceptable to the public at large and which have avoided major negative impacts on the urban environment.[18] In contrast, the situation in Dublin is one of considerable conflict between road proposals and the urban environment on the one hand[19] and between roads engineers and community groups on the other.[20] In such circumstances the decision in 1987 to abolish the Dublin Transportation Authority remains inexplicable. Continuing conflicts over road proposals in Dublin have tended to overshadow the logic and the rationale underlying the draft *Dublin City Development Plan, 1987*. This review is based upon the need to give priority to public transportation in the city centre, which in turn would reduce the number of vehicles on streets, diminish the need for road widening and, thereby, allow for the conservation of buildings, enable the retention of street-scapes, reduce pollution levels and provide a framework within which rejuvenation and community development could take place. For Dublin Corporation's planners the key to this scenario is investment in mass transit and the development of a transportation centre. (Fig. 6.2).[21] But the decision of Government not to fund such infrastructure from the public exchequer endangers the entire scenario and it also demonstrates how limited are the powers of planners or indeed local authorities when it comes to resource allocation. The issue of transportation in Dublin is likely to dominate in the 1988 study of the Greater Dublin Area commissioned to bring forward a strategy for the development of the capital city and to enunciate proposals

Policies in the 1980s 167

for funding as part of Ireland's programme of development with the aid of the E.R.D.F.[22]

Urban Regeneration: The Need for Community Participation?
The process of urban regeneration may be seen in terms of either a 'bottom up' or a 'top down' approach, neither of which need be

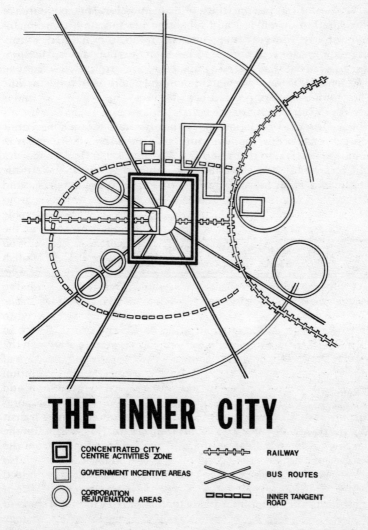

Fig. 6.2 Dublin's Inner City. (Source: Dublin City development Plan [Draft] 1987).

mutually exclusive. In the 1981 National Economic and Social Council Report[23] considerable emphasis was placed upon the need for community based initiatives in job creation, environmental improvement and urban regeneration. This approach has been reinforced throughout the European Community since then.[24]

Within the Irish urban system the approach to urban regeneration has been broadly twofold. Cork Corporation and many smaller urban authorities have placed a priority upon local and community participation in renewal and rehabilitation schemes, even to the point of joint venture arrangements. On the other hand, despite a large number of well organised inner city organisations, Dublin's approach to date has placed a reliance upon Corporation-led initiatives and community participation in the planning or implementation of inner city projects has been limited.

With the enactment of the Urban Renewal Act 1986 the Custom House Docks Development Authority was established as a comprehensive development authority, inclusive of streamlined planning powers, to redevelop the Custom House Docks site. The site is scheduled to accommodate Dublin's Financial Services Centre and Table 6.1 and Fig. 6.3 provide details of the project.

Table 6.1
CUSTOM HOUSE DOCKS DEVELOPMENT AUTHORITY
Gross Built Area of Proposed Scheme ('000 square feet)

Total scheme (excluding car parking)	1,529
Whereof:	
Financial Services	306
Commercial Offices	454
Retail	134
Residential	204
Cultural/	131
Hotel/Conference Area	300
Number of Spaces	
Car parking:	
Unallocated	—
Allocated	1,813
Total spaces	1,813

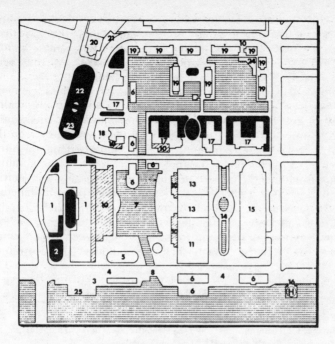

KEY TO THE PLAN

1 International Financial Services Centre.
2 Fountain plaza.
3 Open-air market.
4 Riverside park.
5 Museum of folk art.
6 Restaurants and bars.
7 George's Dock marina.
8 Bridge.
9 Bandstand pavilion.
10 Retail.
11 Museum of modern art; museum of science, flea market & antique shops, lecture theatre.
12 Winter garden.
13 Cinemas and nightclubs.
14 Reflecting pool and sculpture garden.
15 Hotel and conference centre.
16 Heliport.
17 Financial services office buildings.
18 International trade centre / financial services.
19 Residential.
20 Connolly Station.
21 Community centre.
22 Station park.
23 Original stone gateway.
24 Boatclub.
25 Canoe club.

Fig. 6.3 The Custom House Docks Development. (Courtesy of the Custom House Docks Development Authority).

The Custom House Docks Authority is seen as spearheading the rejuvenation of Dublin's derelict inner docks – an area that is also scheduled to accommodate the National Sports Centre and an array of water related developments in the vicinity of the Grand Canal Docks.[25] While the use of a streamlined agency to initiate comprehensive redevelopment may be necessary in the short-term, such an approach raises important questions as to the nature of the planning approach being used, the relationship to the surrounding local authority, Dublin Corporation, and most of all the relationship to the adjacent communities and their participation in or benefit from such an undertaking.

The fundamental importance of community involvement was highlighted at a 1988 Urban Renewal Week organised by the Goethe Institute in Dublin in association with the Irish Planning Institute and University College Dublin. The German and Irish renewal experts drafted the following schedule of principles for future renewal in the context of Dublin and other Irish centres:

Table 6.2
AGENDA FOR URBAN RENEWAL

1. **Community Participation**
a) Involve local communities to identify strengths, weaknesses, character, lifestyle and issues of their area, and to develop local plans.
b) Involve local tradesmen, builders, etc. in the implementation of plans.
c) Create an awareness of the heritage of inner city areas.
d) Provide education and work training in inner city areas.
e) Essential to involve women in the urban renewal process.
f) Take full account of existing mixed uses in inner city areas.
g) Introduce mediators between statutory authorities and local communities.
h) Create a formal structure for major community input into the Development Plans.

2. **Political Progress**
a) Need for a vision of a viable living inner city in all cases.
b) Recognition of the inner city as a national asset.
c) Co-ordination of policies for Dublin City and County and the integration of development agencies.
d) Need for integrated public transport and land use policies.
e) Policies for the young and the homeless.
f) Review legal impediments, incentives and re-examine concept of hope value.
g) Need to co-ordinate efforts of local interest groups.

3. **Other Procedures**
a) Pilot schemes; a step-by-step approach.
b) Creative use of housing demand.
c) Discourage major site assembly in 'target areas'.

There is increasing acceptance need to recognise the role and potential of inner city communities in both revitalising and managing their areas. Local communities need to be viewed as a resource which is receiving increased attention in current community planning approaches.[26] Following on from two decades of rapid and dispersed urbanisation, there is now a considerable emphasis upon urban renewal and upon the need to make existing urban environments more attractive and more satisfying. To a large extent this has taken place in response to advocacy by community groups. Perhaps this change is symbolic of the reality, that not only does the majority of the population now live in towns and cities but, that Irish society has at last come to terms with the values of an urban civilisation.

Strong public pressure, in the context of changing socio-economic circumstances, has led to a significant reappraisal of the model for Dublin's long term development. Whereas the *Eastern Region Settlement Strategy 2011*[27] predicted the continued rapid growth of the capital city region on a highly decentralised and suburbanised model, a 1988 Review of the strategy accepts that growth is likely to be greatly reduced. *The Eastern Region Settlement Strategy 2001*, while still placing emphasis upon taking up the existing infrastructural capacity in the suburbs (Fig. 6.4), subscribes to the 'general consensus that more population is required in the Inner City'[28] and the report advances some interesting suggestions to achieve this objective. The report also advances proposals to accommodate an increased number of households in the existing dwelling stock of inner suburban areas, although the logic of these proposals has not been reflected in the future planned population distribution.

Conclusion

This chapter has examined the recent growth of environmental consciousness and environmental action in Ireland. This awakening is common to both the rural and the urban areas and it has resulted in a new approach to the development of amenities and in greater attention to heritage protection whether of the scientific or the built environment. Above all, there has been a realisation that the quality of urban life in general is governed to a great extent by the quality of the environment at the urban core; the rejuvenation of city and town centres has become a priority task within urban development. The grand master plans for urban expansion have been replaced by programmes of urban renewal and inner area revitalisation. With this has come a realisation 'that housing, of all potential land uses, presently has the greatest potential for making

172 Planning: The Irish Experience

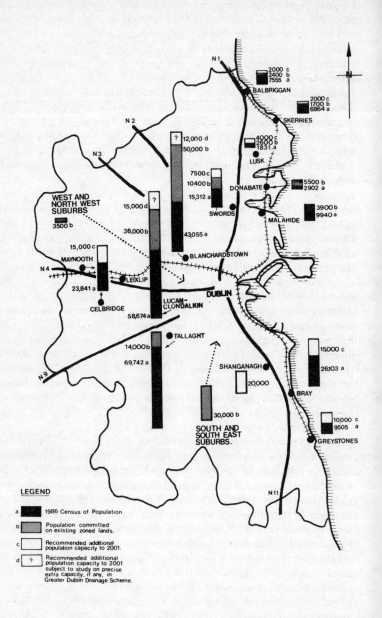

Fig. 6.4 Recommended Settlement Strategy to 2001, Dublin Sub-Region.

a significant impact on the physical and economic rehabilitation of the inner city.'[29]

The growth of a strong environmental movement has been largely a bottom up phenomenon driven by local groups wishing to protect, enhance or develop local amenities, assets or communities. Too often these groups have had to struggle without the assistance of the formal or statutory agencies, if not in the teeth of their opposition. This situation arises to a great extent because of the recurring failure to modernise or reform local government throughout the country. The voluntary and community sectors have demonstrated a dynamic which is not always reciprocated by the statutory authorities.

But the situation is even more serious. Local environmental action requires an overall framework for guidance if it is to be efficient or rational in the long-term. It requires to work within a data, research and policy framework which is enriched by regional and central government investment and action. The abolition of the Regional Development Organisations undermined the minimalist co-ordination frameworks which had been in place up to 1987. The abolition of An Foras Forbartha has deprived local authorities and local groups of a valuable source of independent and comprehensive, scientific advice. The development and implementation of a realistic environmental planning policy for the country as a whole requires a strengthening of the functions and activities of the Department of the Environment together with the re-establishment of an independent centre of environmental research. Proper planning also requires the putting into place of some system of regional co-ordination. In this regard, Dublin remains the benchmark by which Ireland's ability to plan, develop and administer its urban environments will ultimately be judged.

Taking the longer term view, Ireland has made remarkable progress; over the past century many major social and environmental problems have been eliminated or largely ameliorated. However, much remains to be done, especially if Ireland is to abide fully by European Community environmental legislation and if the country is to keep in step with developments in other member states. Looked at in terms of planning and environmental history, the greatest successes have occurred where Ireland drew wisely upon a range of foreign experiences to develop indigenous approaches in public policy and in relation to problem solving. The most serious failures are often attributable to naïve attempts to translate foreign and inappropriate models to Irish conditions. An overview of Irish environmental and planning history demonstrates repeated evidence of substantial achievements. But it also cautions against the superficial attraction of the 'grand plan' when faced with 'the inevitability of gradualness'.

Notes and References

CHAPTER 1

1. *Irish Builder and Engineer* editorial quoted in *Journal* RIBA, Vol. 23 (1916), p.245. Not all were in agreement on this point. Abercrombie did not see the destruction as offering much by way of opportunity since 'the artillery of General Maxwell was not accompanied by a Town Planner,' P. Abercrombie, 'The New Town Plan for the City of Dublin,' *Journal*, TPI, Vol. III (1916), p.49.
2. M. Miller, 'Raymond Unwin and the Planning of Dublin' in M. J. Bannon (ed), *The Emergence of Irish Planning*, (Turoe Press, Dublin, 1985), Ch. 5.
3. Dublin Reconstruction (Emergency Provisions) Act, 6 & 7 Geo 5, (1916).
4. Report of Reconstruction Committee, *Report and Printed Documents of Corporation of Dublin* (RPDCD) Vol II, No. 185 (1922), p.182.
5. RPDCD, Vol I, No. 6 (1917), pp.59-60.
6. See the various official reports of the Corporation's Reconstruction Committee.
7. W. A. Scott, 'Reconstruction of O'Connell Street, Dublin: A Note', *Studies*, Vol. 5 (1916).
8. Correspondence between Professor Abercrombie and City Commissioner, April-May 1925, in Greater Dublin Reconstruction Movement files, Dublin City Archive.
9. See 'Transport and Town Planning,' *Irish Builder and Engineer*, Vol. LXIX (1927), pp.74-8.
10. E. A. Aston, 'The Reconstruction of Greater Dublin,' lecture to Engineering and Scientific Association of Ireland, 11 Dec. 1922.
11. Thanks to information kindly supplied by Dr Michael Cuthbert, the author has had access to a lengthy correspondence between Mears and his father-in-law, Patrick Geddes, relating to Dublin and extending over the years 1911 to 1924.
12. Letter from Mears to Geddes, 5 June 1923. National Library of Scotland (F.14-6).
13. H. de Blacam, 'Greater Dublin', *Illustrated Review*, Vol. 192, p.150.
14. *Greater Dublin Reconstruction Sketch Plan of Proposals for Development of North Eastern and South Eastern, Harbour, Railway and Factory Areas* (Rapid Printing, Dublin, March 1923), 4pp.
15. In 1911 the Dublin Citizens Association had called for one authority as did Aston in evidence to the 1913 Housing Inquiry. For a detailed account of administration proposals for Dublin see A. A. Horner, 'The Dublin Region 1880-1980. An Overview of Its Development and Planning' in M. J. Bannon (ed), *The Emergence of Irish Planning* (Turoe Press, Dublin, 1985), Ch. 1.
16. H. H. Hely, 'Town Planning and Reconstruction', *Freeman's Journal*, (4 January 1923).
17. 'Artifex' (E. A. Aston), 'The Housing Problem II,' *The Irish Times*, (9 March 1923).
18. 'A Great New Dublin', report of interview with E. A. Aston, *Irish Times*, 16 September 1922. The continuing relevance of this suggestion is evident when one looks at the proposals for the disused Harcourt Street line as set out in the Dublin Rail Rapid Transit Study (Voohers & Assoc, 1975).
19. H. de Blacam, *op. cit.*, p.149. In 1922 Lord Justice O'Connor, Chairman of the Railway Inquiry, had discussed this idea of a central station, generating considerable hostility, when he spoke of it being 'impossible to rebuild the Custom

20. Second Report of Joint Committee on Oireachtas Accommodation — See *Dáil Debates*, Vol. VII, 1924, col. 2941.
21. De Blacam *op. cit.*, p.152.
22. Letter from Lady Aberdeen to Frank Mears, 10 May 1922, National Library of Scotland (F.136).
23. *Dáil Debates*, Vol. II, 19 Dec. 1922, col. 384. The reuse of the College Green site for Government offices had featured in a number of the Dublin Town Planning Competition entries, including Abercrombie's.
24. Senator James Moran, 'The Reconstruction of Greater Dublin', Manchester Guardian Commercial, *European Reconstruction Series: Ireland*, Section Two, 10 May 1923, p.43.
25. *Dáil Debates*, Vol. VI, 1924, col. 565 (19 Jan. 1924).
26. Letter from E. A. Aston, in *Irish Builder and Engineer*, Vol. LXIV (1922), p.674.
27. *Dáil Debates*, Vol. VI, 19 March 1924, cols 2139 and following.
28. *Ibid.*, and Vol. VII 1924 cols 2941 and following.
29. J. Meenan and D. Clarke (eds), *The Royal Dublin Society, 1731-1981* (Gill and Macmillan, Dublin, 1981), p.47.
30. Greater Dublin Reconstruction, 1923, *op. cit.*, pp.2 and 3.
31. Minute No. 54, Dublin Corporation, 1923.
32. *Irish Builder and Engineer*, Vol. LXIII (1922), p.642.
33. P. Abercrombie et al., *Dublin of the Future* (Civics Institute of Ireland),58pp.
34. Letter from Lady Aberdeen to Frank Mears, 10 May 1922, National Library of Scotland (F.136).
35. Letter from Frank Mears to Geddes, 5 June 1923, NLS (F.146).
36. See 34 above.
37. 'The Future of Dublin', *Irish Builder and Engineer*, Vol. LXV (1923), p.461.
38. *Ibid.*, quoting letter from President Cosgrave.
39. *Ibid.*
40. Report of Railways Commission on *Irish Railways* (Stationery Office, Dublin, 1922), p.13.
41. R. Unwin, *Town Planning In Practice* (T. Fischer Unwin, London, 1909).
42. See M. J. Bannon, 'The Genesis of Modern Irish Planning' in M. J. Bannon, *op. cit.*
43. Evidence of Patrick Geddes to Departmental Committee *Inquiry into Housing Conditions of the Working Class in The City of Dublin* (cd 7317) (T. Fischer Unwin, London, 1914), Evidence, p.208.
44. Memorandum by J. F. McCabe, *ibid.*, p.30.
45. M. J. Bannon, *op. cit.*
46. *Report of Adjudicator's*, Dublin Town Planning Competition (Civics Institute of Ireland, Dublin, 1916), p.3.
47. J. V. Brady, *Practical Slum Reform* (Dollard, Dublin, 1917), p.26.
48. *The Dublin Civic Survey* (Civics Institute of Ireland, Dublin, 1925), p. XIII.
49. Report in the *Irish Builder and Engineer*, Vol. LXV (1923), p.97.
50. Lord and Lady Aberdeen, *We Twa* (Collins, Sons & Co. London, 1925), Vol. II p.191.
51. *Irish Builder and Engineer*, Vol. LXV (1923), p.845.
52. H. T. O'Rourke, *Dublin Civic Survey: Why You Should Support A Work of National Importance* (Civics Institute, Dublin, 1923), p.4.
53. *Irish Builder and Engineer*, Vol. LXVI (1924), p.226.
54. *The Dublin Civic Survey, op. cit.*, p.5.
55. *Ibid.*, p. XVII.
56. *Ibid.*, p. XIX.
57. *Ibid.*, p. XVI.
58. *Ibid.*, p. XIX.
59. *Ibid.*, p.13.
60. *Ibid.*, p. 16
61. *Ibid.*, p. 38.
62. *Ibid.*, p. 46.
63. H. T. O'Rourke, *op. cit.*, (1923) p.8.

64. *The Dublin Civic Survey, op. cit.*, p. 73.
65. *Ibid.*, p. 82.
66. *Ibid.*, p. 119.
67. *Irish Builder and Engineer*, Vol. LXVII(1925), p. 1049.
68. *The Builder*, Vol. CXXX (1926), p. 275.
69. M. Robertson, 'Town Planning in Dublin,' *Dublin Civic Week, Handbook* (Mansion House, Dublin, 1929), p. 26.
70. R. M. Butler, 'Dublin: Past and Present', *Dublin Civic Week, Handbook* (Mansion House, Dublin 1927), p.33.
71. Cork Town Planning Association, *Cork: A Civic Survey* (The Univ. Press of Liverpool and Hodder and Stoughton, London, 1926), 30 pp.
72. See M. Gough, 'Socio Economic Conditions and The Genesis of Planning in Cork', in M. J. Bannon (ed) *The Emergence of Irish Planning* (Turoe Press, Dublin, 1985), Ch. 6.
73. *Cork: A Civic Survey, op. cit.*, p. 6.
74. *Ibid.*, p. 15.
75. *Ibid.*, p. V.
76. *Irish Builder and Engineer*, Vol. LXVIII (1926), p. 750.
77. Dublin Civic Week, *General Programme*, (17-25 Sept. 1927).
78. M. Daly, 'Housing Conditions and The Genesis of Housing Reform In Dublin, 1880-1920' in M. J. Bannon (ed), *The Emergence of Irish Planning* (Turoe Press, Dublin, 1985), Ch. 2.
79. RPDCD, Vol. III, No. 176 (1903), pp. 383-96.
80. See M. J. Bannon, *op. cit.*
81. RPDCD, Vol. I, No. 78 (1915), pp.722.
82. P. C. Cowan, *Report on Dublin Housing* (Cahill & Co. Ltd., Dublin, 1918), p.10.
83. *Ibid.*, p. 31.
84. RPDCD 1915, *op. cit.*, p.742.
85. *Ibid.*, p.753.
86. T. W. Cosgrave, *New Ireland* (1917).
87. L. McKenna, 'The Housing Problem in Dublin', *Studies*, Vol. 18 (1919), p.293.
88. RPDCD, Vol. I, No. 13 (1918), pp.122.
89. *Ibid.*, Vol. III, No. 210 (1919), pp.51-80.
90. *Ibid.*, Vol. I, No. 13 (1918), pp.119.
91. P. C. Cowan, *op. cit.*, p.14.
92. The problem of urban housing was repeatedly tackled by Civics Institute — see also *Report on Slum Clearance in Dublin* (Citizens' Housing League, 1933), 22 pp.
93. E. P. McCarron, 'The Present Position of Housing', *Irish Builder and Engineer*, LXIX (1927), p.109.
94. *Ibid.*
95. C. T. Ruthen 'Housing and Planning — A National Policy', *The Irish Builder and Engineer*, Vol. XLI (1919), p.265.
96. RPDCD, Vol. III, No. 210 (1919), pp.51-80.
97. Memorandum from City Architect Department on Documents Relating to Croydon Park Housing Scheme.
98. See correspondence between Frank Mears and Patrick Geddes, 13 April 1921, National Library of Scotland (F.101). The Killester Housing Scheme was the largest scheme carried out under the Irish Land (Provision for Sailors and Soldiers) Act, 1919. A total of 465 cottages at 10 locations around Dublin were erected under this Act (82.9 and 10. George V.) For details see:
F. H. Aalen, 'Homes for Irish Heroes', *Town Planning Review*, forthcoming.
99. *Irish Builder and Engineer*, LXVII (1925), p.59.
100. 'The Spoiling of the Dublin Suburbs', *Irish Builder and Engineer*, Vol. LXVII (1925), p.929. For an overview of Irish housing design see:
Seán Rothery, *The Influence of International Design Movements on Irish Architecture in the Early 20th Century*, PhD. Thesis, Trinity College, 1988, (publication forthcoming).
101. *Ibid.*, Vol. LXIX, 1927, p.469.
102. *Ibid.*, p.5.
103. P. L. Dickinson, 'The Spoiling of the Countryside', *ibid.*, p.605.

104. P. L. Dickinson, *The Dublin of Yesterday* (Methuen & Co., London, 1929), p.145.
105. J. F. McCabe, 'Town and Country' *Dublin Magazine*, Vol. 2-3 (1925), p.676.
106. R. M. Butler, 'Dublin Past and Present', *Dublin Civic Week Handbook* (Civic Week Council, Dublin, 1927), p.33.
107. H. T. O'Rourke, 'The Control of Building Design', *The Irish Builder and Engineer*, Vol. LXIX (1927), p.537.
108. P. L. Dickinson, 'Methods of Control of Design', *ibid.*, Vol. LXVIII, (1926), p.591.
109. E. P. McCarron, *op. cit.*, p.109.
110. A draft bill prepared by the Royal Institute of Architects of Ireland in 1923 did not come before the Oireachtas until 1929, see below.
111. P. H. Pearse, writing in *The Sprak*, Vol. III, No. 2 (9 April 1916).
112. *Dáil Debates*, Vol. IV, (1923), col. 1718.
113. *Ibid.*, col. 1719.
114. *State Paper Office*, Courts of Justice Bill, (1923), S3. 195.
115. *Dáil Debates*, Vol. VII, (1924), col. 1606.
116. For an overview of the work of the Industrial Development Associations see E. N. Sommers in *The Irish Yearbook* (Dublin, 1921), pp.91-4.
117. *Reports of Commission of Inquiry into Resources and Industries of Ireland* (Stationery Office, Dublin, 1920-22).
118. J. M. Fay, 'Economic Aspects of The Shannon Power Development', *Transactions of Inst. of Civil Engineers of Ireland*, Vol. LIV (1929), pp.37-85. See also:
M. Manning and Moore McDowell, *Electricity Supply in Ireland: the History of the E.S.B.*, Gill & MacMillan, (1984), 281 pp.
119. A. Horner, 'The Dublin Region 1880-1980; An Overview on Its Development Planning', in M. J. Bannon (ed), *The Emergence of Irish Planning* (Turoe Press, Dublin, 1985), Ch. 1.
120. *Report of Greater Dublin Commission of Inquiry* (Stationery Office, Dublin, 1926), 21 pp.
121. For an overview of the application of the Co. Manager system to Ireland see: J. Collins, 'The Genesis of City and County Management,' *Administration*, Vol. 2 (1955), pp.27-38.
122. *Report, ibid.*, p. 11.
123. *Ibid.*, p.16.
124. 'Planning Greater Dublin; Hesitation! Procrastination! Patchwork,' *Irish Builder and Engineer*, LXXI (1929), pp.1074-77.
125. 'Greater Dublin etc.', *ibid.*, LXXII (1930), pp.274.
126. *Ibid.*, pp.89, and 1118-22.
127. *Ibid.*, LXXI (1929), p.1001.
128. *Ibid.*, Vol. LXVI (1924), p.961.
129. 'The Greater Dublin Bill,' *ibid.*, Vol. LXXII (1930), p.195.
130. 'The Greater Dublin,' *ibid.*, Vol. LXXI, (1929), p.825.
131. *Dáil Debates*, Vol. XXXIII (1930), col. 940.
132. *Ibid.*, col. 1009.
133. *Ibid.*, col. 1010.
134. *Irish Builder and Engineer*, Vol. LXXII (1930), p.180.
135. *Ibid.*, p.243.
136. Reprinted in *ibid.*, Vol. LXXI (1929), pp.86-90.
137. *Ibid.*, p.301.
138. Manning Robertson, 'Old and Future Dublin', *Centenary Conference Handbook* (RIAI, Dublin, 1939), p.69.
139. Town Planning Bill (Long Title), No. 15 of 1929.
140. The Irish Bill had been one of the few to attempt to give statutory effect to the belief of Thomas Adams, 'that a compulsory survey is much more important than a compulsory plan' — see 'Irish Town Planning Bill', *Town Planning Inst. Journal*, Vol. XV (1929), p.226.
141. *Dáil Debates*, Vol. XXXIII (1930), col. 740.
142. *Irish Builder and Engineer*, Vol. LXXI (1929), p.415.
143. *Ibid.*, Vol. LXXII (1930), pp.274-7.

144. Manning Robertson 'Town Planning in Dublin' *Dublin Civic Week, Handbook* (Mansion House, Dublin 1929), p.28.
145. Manning Robertson, 'Ireland's Countryside,' *The Dublin Magazine*, Vol. 4 (New Series) (1930), p.46.
146. Manning Robertson, *op. cit.* (1929), p.28.
147. For an account of these measures see K. A. Mawhinney, 'Environmental Conservation: Concern and Action, 1920-1970' in Ch. 3 below.
148. Quoted from *Irish Builder and Engineer*, Vol. LXXI (1929), p.961.
149. The alternative uses for the £40,000 could include (a); a park, (b) a hall, (c) other form of monument, (d) industry on lines of the German home industries, (e) ship to take tourists around Ireland, (f) a stately home and gardens, e.g. Castletown, (g) a Distress fund, (h) a Lane Picture Gallery, 'say at Parnell Square', (i) an apprenticeship scheme, (j) suburban playgrounds, (k) a housing scheme, and (l) a children's education fund. *Mulcahy Papers*, 2 March 1929, Univ. College, Archives.
150. 'Housing in The Free State', *Irish Builder and Engineer*, Vol. LXXII (1930), p.542.
151. 'The Slum Problem in Dublin,' *ibid.*, Vol. LXXIII (1931), p.99.
152. *Ibid.*, p.1001.
153. F. McGrath, 'Homes for People,' *Studies* (June 1932), p.272.
154. D. A. Levie 'Housing' — lecture to Cork Rotary Club, reported in *Irish Builder and Engineer*, Vol. LXXII (1930), p.371.
155. H. T. O'Rourke, 'Cost per Room for Tenement Flats,' *ibid.*, Vol. LXXIV (1932), p.918.
156. *Ibid.*, Vol. LXXI (1929), p.901.
157. *ibid.*, p.1001.
158. Quoted in *ibid.*
159. 'North Dublin's Seaboard,' *ibid.*, Vol. LXXII (1930), pp.942-5.
160. Along with the Fairview 'sloblands' and Merrion Strand, the Bull Island was considered as a site for a Dublin airport — see *ibid.*, pp.1118-22.
161. *Ibid.*, Vol. LXXIII (1931), p.144.
162. See official plan reproduced in *ibid.*, Vol. XC (1948), pp.538. Also P. G. Kennedy, 'Violation of Sanctuary,' *Studies*, Vol. 38 (1949), pp.37-45.
163. Manning Robertson, 'Town Planning and Slums,' *Irish Builder and Engineer*, Vol. LXXIII, p.445.
164. In a letter dated 7 Nov. 1929, Unwin wrote to Manning Robertson that he 'had a hasty trip to Belfast the other day to talk about town planning, at the University, and to discuss their new Town Planning Act which they propose to introduce. I gave them much the same suggestions as I have already given to you and to General Mulcahy in regard to the Free State Bill.' Robertson papers, MS.24:282, National Library of Ireland. But in 1933 Unwin stated that he had not studied the Irish Bill, nor was he familiar 'with the peculiar conditions and requirements of Dublin or of Ireland', see *Irish Builder and Engineer*, Vol. LXXXV (1933), p.856C.
165. *Dáil Debates*, Vol. 49 (1933), col. 225.
166. *Ibid.*, col. 2282.
167. 'The Town and Country Planning Bill', *ibid.*, p.754.
168. *Ibid.*
169. *Ibid.*, p.842.
170. 'Artifex', 'The Town and Regional Planning Bill: Some Suggested Amendments,' *ibid.*, p.885.
171. Reported in *ibid.*, p.948. The designation of the Dublin Region is the first indication that the army area command regions were being adopted for civil purposes.
172. S. T. O'Kelly opening Architectural Exhibition as reported in *ibid.*, 1075.
173. *Ibid.*, Vol. LXXI (1929), p.1120.
174. *Ibid.*, Vol. LXXVI (1934), p.856C.
175. *Ibid.*, p.1075.

176. *Cautionary Guide to Dublin* (RIAI, Dublin, 1933), p.5.
177. 'Money for Town Planning in Free State,' *Irish Builder and Engineer*, Vol. LXXVI (1934), p.471.
178. *Town and Regional Planning: Model Clauses for Use In The Preparation of Schemes* (Stationery Office, Dublin, 1937), 63 pp.
179. M. Robertson, 'The Irish Free State Town and Regional Planning Act,' *Journal of The T.P.I.*, Vol. XX (1934), p.271.
180. Manning Robertson, *Dun Laoghaire: The History, Scenery and Development of the District* (Dun Laoghaire Corporation, 1936), 77 pp.
181. *Ibid.*, p.75.
182. *Ibid.*, introduction.
183. D. O'Toole, *Borough of Galway Planning Scheme: Report on Sketch Development Plan* (Galway Corporation), 28 pp.
184. Referred to in M. Robertson & R. S. Wilshere, *Town Planning In Ireland* (The Irish Association, Dublin, 1944), pp. 18-19.
185. M. Robertson, *County Borough olf Cork and Neighbourhood Town Planning Report: Sketch Development Plan* Cork Corporation, 1941), 35 pp. See also M. Gough 'Socio Economic Conditions and The Genesis of Planning in Cork', in M. J. Bannon (ed), *The Emergence of Irish Planning* (Turoe Press, Dublin 1985), Ch. 6.
186. M. Robertson, *ibid.*, p.9.
187. F. Gibney, *Co. Borough of Waterford and Environs: Town Planning Scheme* (Preliminary Report) (Waterford Corporation, 1943), 24 pp.
188. P. Abercrombie, S. Kelly and M. Robertson, *Sketch Development Plan for Dublin* (Dublin Corporation, 1941), 62 pp.
189. P. Abercrombie, *Dublin of the Future*, (Civics Institute of Ireland, Dublin, 1922), 58 pp.
190. P. Abercrombie et al., *op. cit.* (1941), p.51.
191. *Ibid.*, p. 43. In fact the evidence for rural migration to Dublin at this time is meagre.
192. *Ibid.*, p.33.
193. Personal memorandum on 'Dublin Municipal Area' by H. T. O'Rourke, reprinted in *Irish Builder and Engineer*, Vol. LXXVIII, p.739.
194. *Ibid.*, p.740.
195. *Report of Inquiry Into The Housing of the Working Classes of The City of Dublin, 1939-43* (Stationery Office, Dublin, 1944), 279 pp.
196. *Report of the Local Government (Dublin) Tribunal* (Stationery Office, Dublin 1938), p.131.
197. P. Abercrombie et al. *op. cit.* (1941), p.55.
198. E. E. Benson, Chairman of Town Planning Committee, Introduction to P. Abercrombie *et al., ibid.*, p.10.
199. Reported in *Irish Builder and Engineer*, Vol. LXXXVIII (1946), p.864.
200. M. O'Brien, 'The Planning of Dublin,' *Journal of TPI*, Vol. 36 (1950), p.208.
201. *Ibid.* Inevitably, discussion of the future shape and arrangement of Dublin generated a number of abstract proposals. Most notable of these was Frank Gibney's Beaux Arts conception with eight community units focused upon a new city centre located in the Phoenix Park — see 'A Plan for The City of Dublin,' *Irish Builder and Engineer*, Vol. LXXXVII (1945), pp.430-3.
202. *Irish Builder & Engineer*, LXXXIII (1941), p.6.
203. P. Abercrombie, 'The Dublin Town Plan,' *Studies*, Vol. 31 (1942), pp.155-70.
204. G. Gavan Duffy, 'Comments on the foregoing Article,' *ibid.*, p.162.
205. C. T. Ruthen, 'Housing and Planning — A National Policy,' *Irish Builder & Engineer*, Vol. LXI (1919), p.265.
206. *National Economic Recovery* (The Talbot Press, Dublin, 1935), 87 pp. The author of this pamphlet was almost certainly P. O'Loghlen who was a member of the Currency Commission.

207. *Ibid.*, p.53.
208. Minority Report No. 1 (by S. P. Campbell, W. O'Brien and A. O'Reilly) *Report of Commission of Inquiry Into Banking, Currency and Credit* (Stationery Office, (p. No. 2628) Dublin, 1938), p.582.
209. Minority Report No. III (by P. O'Loghlen), *ibid.*, p.675.
210. *The Irish Builder and Engineer* frequently dealt with the Irish village which it characterised in 1941 as 'shapeless, ugly and drab' — Vol. LXXXIII (1941), p.78. Perhaps it was this attack on villages which stimulated Michael Scott's provocative proposals for 'The Village Planned,' *The Bell*, Vol. 3 (1941), pp.232-9.
211. 'Artifex', Greater Dublin, 1922-1938 — and After,' *The Irish Yearbook* (Duffy, Gill & Co., Dublin, 1938), p.153.
212. 'Farm and Factory, Building and Employment, Energy and Hard Work.' Report of Survey and Outlook by Sean Lemass, *Irish Builder & Engineer*, Vol. LXXXII (1940), p.78.
213. Report in *Minutes* of Cabinet Meeting, 9 July 1940.
214. Report of sub-Committee on 'Regional and Area Organisation for Carrying Out of Government Functions' — included in memorandum from Dept. of Supplies for Cabinet Meeting of 9 July 1940.
215. The author wishes to thank Commandant Peter Young of the Defence Forces for help in tracing the relationship between the army command areas of the 1920s and 1930s and the Emergency Regions.
216. *Statutory Rules and Orders*, No. 266, 1940, Emergency Powers (No. 48) Order, 1940, (pp. No. 4342), 13.
217. Reported in *Irish Builder & Engineer*, Vol. LXXXII (1940), p.646.
218. *Ibid.*, p.593.
219. *Ibid.*, LXXXIII (1941), p.302.
220. *Ibid.*, p.364.
221. *Ibid.*, Vol. LXXXIV (1942), p.83.
222. M. Robertson, *Journal of The Town Planning Institute*, Vol. XXIV (1941-2), p.101.
223. F. Gibney's plea for an 'Irish National Plan' in *Irish Times*, (17 Feb. 1940) and *Irish Independent*, (1 March 1940).
224. *Irish Builder and Engineer*, Vol. LXXXIV (1943), p.190.
225. *Ibid.*
226. Responses to 'The Village Planned,' *The Bell*, Vol. III (1941), pp.367-8.
227. The fullest account of this inaugural meeting was provided by Aston (Nomad) in *Irish Builder & Engineer*, Vol. LXXXIV (1942), p.225.
228. *Ibid.*, p.258.
229. 'National Planning Conference,' letter from Hon. Sec. in *ibid.*, p.370.
230. *Ibid.*, p.407.
231. Item 6 of memorandum from Dept. of Taoiseach to Dept. of Local Government, 15 July 1942 on S. 12887.
232. Referred to in *Irish Builder & Engineer*, Vol. LXXXIV (1942), p.288.
233. 'Planning Foundations,' *ibid.*, p.400.
234. F. Gibney, *Framework for an Irish National Plan* (Educational Co., Dublin, 1943), 6 pp.
235. *Ibid.*, p.4. Gibney's idea for a national centre near Athlone was welcomed by Arnold Marsh who had proposed a similar idea to A.E. soon after the Treaty to overcome the absurd position of Dublin – letter from A. Marsh to F. Gibney 18th July 1943.
236. F. Gibney, *Suirbhéaracht Éireann* (An Irish national Survey), Provisional Volume, unpublished. This volume, which is now held in the Planning Library in University College, had been presented to An Taoiseach, Eamon De Valera, and through the intervention of John Martin it was donated to UCD following the President's death.
237. *Irish Builder & Engineer*, Vol. LXXXV (1943), p.362.

238. *Report of Commission on Vocational Organisation*, (p. No. 6743) (Stationery Office, Dublin 1943), 539pp.
239. *Ibid.*, p.444.
240. *Ibid.*
241. *The International Labour Office Summary of the Report of the Commission on Vocational Organization in Ireland* (James Duffy & Co. Ltd., Dublin, 1945), 14 pp. (Copy of paper in *International Labour Review*, January 1945.
242. 'Minister's Statement on Report of the Vocational Commission,' *Irish People*, No. 42, 10 March 1945.
243. D. O'Toole, 'Text of Presidential Address,' *The Green Book* (Architectural Association of Ireland, 1944), pp.28-9.
244. Manning Robertson, *Town Planning*, Reconstruction Pamphlet, No. 1 (Duffy & Co., 1944), 10 pp.
245. N. Moffett, *Leisure*, Reconstruction Pamphlet No. 7 (1944).
246. M. Robertson and R. S. Wilshere, *Town Planning In Ireland*, Pamphlet No. 2 on Irish Affairs (Dundalgan Press, 1944), 36 pp.
247. National Planning Exhibition, *Official Guide* (Dublin, 1944), 18 pp.
248. H. Allbery, 'National Planning Exhibition: A Foreword,' *Irish Builder & Engineer*, Vol. LXXXVI (1944), pp.161-4.
249. *Irish Times*, 26 April 1944.
250. *Irish Builder & Engineer*, Vol. LXXXVI (1944;, p.181.
251. 'The Exhibition's Centrepiece,' *ibid.*, pp. 201-04.
252. N. Moffett and R. Malcolmson, 'Irish Planning Exhibition' in Physical Planning Supplement of *Architects' Journal*, Vol. 101 (1945), pp.223-5.
253. See *Irish Times*, April 27 to May 6 1944.
254. *National Planning and Reconstruction*, The Official Handbook of the National Planning Exhibition (Parkside Press, Dublin, 1944), 184 pp.
255. J. M. Hayes, 'Closing Address' to Muintir na Tíre Rural Week, *Rural Week Record* (1944), p.109. Indeed *Rural Ireland* continued to campaign for planning (see 1950, p.49) and one of the few official documents calling for development planning in the 1950s was the report of the *Commission on Emigration and Other Problems* with its cogent arguments in favour of administrative decentralisation, reducing the relative size of Dublin together with the setting up of a 'Land Utilization Body'.
256. 'Town and Regional Planning', memo from Dept. of Local Government to Dept. of finance and Government, 21 April 1944.
257. J. O'Gorman, 'Building and Order,' *Capuchin Annual* (1936), pp. 118-44 and including comments by the Minister for Local Government and Public Health and seven other invited contributors.
258. H. Hill, 'Town Planning in Cork,' *ibid.* (1941), pp.181.
259. M. Scott, *op. cit.* See note 210 above.
260. See for example, 'Presidential Address' by N. O'Dwyer, in *Transactions of the Inst. of Civil Engineers of Ireland*, Vol. LXIII (1935), pp.1-22.
261. E. Murphy, 'The Engineer and Town Planning', *ibid.*, Vol. LXII (1935-6), pp. 89-117.
262. M. O'Brien, 'The Engineers Contribution to Town and County Planning', *ibid.*, Vol. LXIX (1943), p. 137.
263. *Minutes* of Civics Institute of Ireland, meeting of 16 Oct. 1922.
264. E. Murphy, *op. cit.*, p.100.
265. *Irish Builder and Engineer*, Vol. LXXVIII (1936). p.238.
266. *Minutes*, Civics Institute of Ireland, 16 May 1922.
267. The Institute organised a succession of Civic Weeks and Housing Conferences, most notably the 1938 Housing Conference for which Rita Childers acted as organising secretary — see correspondence file in Civic Museum, Dublin.
268. See Minutes 1922-1932. This

socio-physical integration was last seen in the Dublin playgrounds movement which the Civics Institute took over from the Women's National Health Association of Ireland and which it has continued in co-operation with Dublin Corporation.
269. Manning Robertson, 'Town and Regional Planning' in F. C. King, *Public Administration in Ireland* (The Parkside Press, Dublin, 1944), pp. 201-23).
270. Manning Robertson, 'The Town and Regional Planning Act, 1934,' *Irish Builder and Engineer*, Vol. LXXVIII (1936), p.238.
271. *Ibid.*
272. *Journal of Town Planning Institute*, Vol. XXVIII (1941-2), p. 33.
273. *Handbook of National Planning*, *op. cit.*, p. 4.
274. Quoted in *Irish Builder & Engineer*, Vol. LXXXIII (1941), p. 385. The *Public Service Organisation Review Group* (Devlin) Report was to put forward a broadly similar proposal in 1969 which was not implemented.
275. *Irish Builder & Engineer*, Vol. LXXXVII (1945), p. 128.
276. Reported in *Journal TPI*, Vol. XXXIII (1947), p. 160.
277. Records of the work of Manning Robertson have been largely dispersed and his career and work requires careful research. Some of his papers have been left to the National Library and others have come to the Dublin City Archive.
278. *Irish Builder & Engineer*, Vol. LXXVII (1935), pp. 64-5.
279. Details provided by Mr McNamara of Bord na Mona.
280. F. Gibney, 'District Planning Scheme', *The Irish Contractor*, March 1952.
281. *The Irish Times*, April 26 (1944).
282. *Irish Builder & Engineer*, Vol. LXXXV (1943), p. 419.
283. J. Lee & J. D. O'Tuathaigh, *The Age of De Valera* (Ward River Press, Dublin, 1982), p. 159.
284. 'Mr. Sean Lemass as National Planning Minister,' *ibid.*, Vol. LXXXVII (1945), p. 570.
285. D. Cronin, *Town Planning in Ireland* (Sceptor, Dublin, 1965), p. 12.

CHAPTER 2

1. The Local Government (Planning and Development) Act, 1963 (No. 28 of 1963).
2. *Dáil Debates*, Vols. 197 and 199 of 1962.
3. For an overview of the Management system see J. Collins, 'The Genesis of City and Co. Management', *Administration*, Vol. 2 (1955), pp.27-38.
4. Town and Regional Planning Act, 1934, Section 49 and following (No. 22 of 1934).
5. An Bord Pleanála was established to take over the function of planning appeals from the Minister for Local Government. The granting of this power to the Minister had been a constant cause of disquiet during the Dáil Debates in 1962.
6. The Local Government (Planning and Development) Acts of 1976 and 1983 have contributed to rather than reduced this bureaucracy.
7. Town and Regional Planning (Amendment) Act, 1939 (No. 11 of 1939), see also K. I. Nowlan 'The Planning Acts,' *Irish Builder & Engineer*, Vol. C (1958), pp.309-10.
8. *Journal of Town Planning Institute*, Vol. XXXIII (1947), p.160.
9. Betterment can be defined as 'an increment in the value of private property accuring to its owner because of the provision of facilities, roads, open spaces, or other improvements'.
10. The 'Uthwatt' *Report of Committee on Compensation and Betterment* (1941-42), (comd. 6836 HMSO August 1942).
11. *Dáil Debates*, Vol. LXXIII, 1938, cols 45-77 (second stage).
12. Such recommendations had been put forward in the Uthwatt Report (see reference 9) and in the *Barlow*

Notes and References   183

Report (1940) and the *Scott Report* of 1942.
13. The Ministry was established in 1943 (see 6 and 7 George VI. c.29).
14. P. Abercrombie, S. Kelly and M. Robertson, *Dublin: Sketch Development Plan* (Dublin Corporation, 1941), 62 pp.
15. Documents in the Manning Robertson file in the Dublin City Archive give considerable detail regarding the desired growth of populations in the city and in settlements within the green belt.
16. P. Abercrombie and S. and A. Kelly, *Dublin of the Future: The New Town Plan* (Univ of Liverpool Press, Liverpool, 1922), 58 pp. For the background and context to this plan see M. J. Bannon, 'The Genesis of Modern Irish Planning,' Ch. 4 of *The Emergence of Irish Planning*.
17. Robertson's records show that he had been invited to join Abercrombie and Kelly as an equal partner on the Dublin Study in an effort more easily to understand local circumstances.
18. 'Interim (Development) Control' Provisions were operable under Section 4 of the 1934 Act from the date upon which a Resolution to prepare a Planning Scheme had been passed by the Planning Authority.
19. Dublin Corporation, *Planning Scheme*.

CHAPTER 3

1. Henry Wheeler, 'State's Participation' in *Architectural Conservation. An Irish Viewpoint*, (The Architectural Association, Dublin 1975).
2. George Eogan, 'A Forgotten Centenary?' in *Taisce Journal*, Vol. 6, No. 1 (1982), pp. 16-17.
3. R. A. S. Macalister, 'The Debit Account of the Tourist Movement', in *The New Ireland Review*, Vol. VIII (October 1897), p. 91. See also his entertaining observation on the previous page: 'American and English tourists are probably the worst foes an ancient building has ever had to encounter; the former because of their idiotic habits of breaking off fragments, and amassing collections of worthless trophies; the latter because of their equally inane scribbling propensities.'
4. *Records of Eighteenth-Century Domestic Architecture and Decoration in Dublin*, The Georgian Society, Dublin, 1909. Reprinted Shannon (1969). See Introduction to the reprint by Desmond Guinness, and the original Introduction, both in Vol. 1.
5. Speech at Annual Meeting of SPAB, 1889, quoted in Jane Fawcett (Ed.), *The Future of the Past* (Whitney, London, 1976), p. 17.
6. In 'Historical Monuments of Ireland' published in *The Nation*, 28 October 1843.
7. W. Valentine Ball, (Ed.) *Reminiscences and Letters of Sir Robert Ball*, (London, 1915), p. 49.
8. A. W. Stelfox, and M. D. Stelfox, *The National Programme. Rural Science or Nature Study* (Educational Co., Dublin, 1928). See p. 114: 'In every district there are little areas . . . and these it should be our duty to preserve . . . . As is done in many other countries we should jealously guard these natural oases for the generations which come after us. The best we can do is see that they are left in their natural state . . . . But each year more and more quickly and more steadily the natural beauty spots of our country are vanishiong, and it is time we raised our voices in protest and tried to save what is left. Ireland is now probably the only country in Europe in which famous beauty spots are not protected by law and in which nothing has been done to preserve the animal fauna and flora of the country.' I am indebted to Maura Scannell of the National Botanic Gardens for this reference.
9. Rev. P. G. Kennedy, *An Irish Sanctuary* (The Three Candles,

Dublin, 1953), p. 10.
10. Manning Robertson, 'Ireland's Countryside' in *The Dublin Magazine*, 5 (N. S.) (1930), p. 46.
11. *Ibid.*, p. 47.
12. *Ibid.*, p. 47, quoted by Manning Robertson.
13. Sir Shane Leslie, 'National Parks for Éire' in *Studies* (September 1945), pp. 289-99.
14. *An Taisce Association Handbook,* (An Taisce, Dublin, *c.* 1980). A loose-leaf folder with no pagination.
15. Robert Lloyd Praeger, *Our National Trust. An address broadcast by Radio Éireann on 10 October, 1948,* (Dublin, 1949), p. 7.
16. An Taisce, *op. cit.*
17. Brendan Clarke, 'The Environment 1945-1970' in J. J. Lee (Ed.), *Ireland 1945-70,* (Dublin, 1979), p. 100.
18. Desmond Guinness, in his Introduction to the reprinted edition of the Georgian Society's *Records, etc.,* (1969), p. ix.
19. L. P. Cuffe, 'Presidential Address' in *Royal Institute of Architects of Ireland Year Book* (Dublin, 1962), pp. 5-7.
20. An Taisce, *Preliminary Report from the Sub-Committee on Nature Conservation* (1963). Typescript.

CHAPTER 4
1. A. Murie, 'Planning in Northern Ireland: A Survey', *Town Planning Review,* Vol. 44, No. 4 (1973), pp.337-58.
2. J. Forbes, 'Towns and Planning in Ireland' in N. Stephens, and R. E. Glascock, (eds), *Irish Geographical Studies* (Belfast, 1970), p.292.
3. G. Camblin, *The Town In Ulster,* Wm. Mullan & Sons (Belfast 1951), p.17.
4. *Ibid.*, p.18.
5. *Ibid.*, p.80.
6. E. Evans and E. Jones, 'The Growth of Belfast', *Town Planning Review,* Vol. 26, No. 2 (1955), p.97.
7. R. S. Wilshere, 'Town Planning in Northern Ireland' in *Town Planning in Ireland* (The Irish Association, Dublin, 1944), p.33.
8. *Ibid.*, p.34.
9. E. Evans, *op. cit.*, pp.98 and 103.
10. G. Camblin, *op. cit.*, p.106.
11. Ulster Architectural Heritage Society, *What's Left of Ulster?* (Belfast, 1968).
12. For a full account, see J. Hendry, 'Conservation in Northern Ireland', *Town Planning Review,* Vol. 38, No. 4, pp.373-88.
13. Planning Advisory Board, *Housing In Northern Ireland* (Belfast, HMSO, 1944), p.14.
14. R. S. Wilshere, *op. cit.*, p.23.
15. Planning Advisory Board, *op. cit.*, p.7.
16. *Ibid.*, p.30.
17. *Proposals for Dealing with Unfit Houses* (Belfast, HMSO, 1959, cmd. 398).
18. *Housing (No. 2) Act (NI)*, 1946.
19. *Housing Act (NI),* 1945.
20. The history of the Northern Ireland Housing Trust has never been recorded and this is a serious omission, for the quality of its products and the efficiency of its organisation were of the highest order. A brief account of the work of the Trust is given in C. Brett, *Housing a Divided Community,* I.P.A., Dublin 1986, pp. 27-31.
21. C. F. S. Newman, 'A Short History of Planning in Northern Ireland', *Journal of the Town Planning Institute,* Vol. 52, No. 2 (1965), p.48.
22. C. F. S. Newman, *op. cit.*, provides a brief account of the main proposals contained in each of the Board's reports.
23. R. H. Mathew et. al., *Northern Ireland Development Programme 1970-75,* (Belfast, HMSO, 1970).
24. A. Murie, *op. cit.,,* pp.351 and 355.
25. *Location of Industry in Northern Ireland* (Belfast, HMSO, 1944, cmd. 225).
26. *Road Communications in Northern Ireland* (Belfast, HMSO, 1946, cmd. 241).
27. *Planning Proposals for the Belfast Area* (cmd. 227, 1945), and *Second Report on Planning Proposals for the Belfast Area* (cmd. 302, 1952).
28. Building Design Partnership, *Belfast Urban Area Plan,* Vol. 2

Notes and References 185

(1969), p.22.
29. C. F. S. Newman, *op. cit.*, p.51.
30. *Ibid.*, p.51.
31. J. M.. Aitken, 'Regional Planning in Northern Ireland' in *Report of Town and Country Planning Summer School* (1967), p.6.
32. R. Wiener, *The Rape and Plunder of the Shankill* (1975), pp.37-8.
33. J. Forbes, *op. cit.*, p.296.
34. R. H. Mathew, *Belfast Regional Survey and Plan, 1962* (Belfast, HMSO 1964), 326pp + maps.
35. *Economic Development in Northern Ireland* (Belfast, HMSO, 1965), 153pp.
36. J. M. Aitken, *op. cit.*, p.9.
37. A. Murie, *op. cit.*, p.342.
38. J. Forbes, *op. cit.*, p.295.
39. A. Murie, *op. cit.*, p.356..
40. *Ibid.*, p.345.
41. R. Wiener, *op. cit.*, p.33.
42. An account of the evidence is assembled in 'Sandy Row at the Public Enquiry' by the Sandy Row Development Association, Belfast, 1972.
43. J.. M. Aitken, *op. cit.*, pp.12-13.
44. L. A. Allen, 'New Towns and the Troubles', *Town and Country Planning* (November/December 1981), p.284.
45. *Report of the Review Body on Local Government in Northern Ireland* (Belfast, HMSO, cmd. 546, 1970), 337 pp.

CHAPTER 5
1. Among the few unpublished papers on Irish Physical Planning in the years 1946-1960, we may cite M. O'Brien 'The Planning of Dublin', *Journal of T.P.I.*, Vol. 36, (1950), pp. 199-212; R. Hogan and M. O'Brien, 'Ireland' in *Die Stadt und IhR Umland* (Proceedings of Int. Congress for Housing and Town Planning, Vienna, 1956), pp. 186-98, also K. I. Nowlan, 'The Planning Acts', *Irish Builder & Engineer*, Vol. C. (1958), pp. 309-10.
2. See Chapter One above.
3. M. J. Bannon, 'Urban Growth and Urban Land Policy', in P. J. Drudy (ed.) *Ireland: Land, Politics and People* (Cambridge Univ. Press, Cambridge, 1982), pp. 297-323.
4. A. A. Horner and S. Daultrey, 'Recent Population Changes in the Republic of Ireland', *Area*, Vol. 12 (1980), pp. 129-35.
5. As early as 1949 McElligott called for the decentralisation of both industry and government from Dublin — see T. J. McElligott, 'Decentralisation', $_{cv}$*Christus Rex*, Vol. III (1949), pp. 26-35. The continued growth of Dublin was frequently questioned as in M. D. McCarthy, 'Is Dublin Too Big?' *Administration* Vol. II (1954), pp. 35-48.
6. T. K. Whitaker, 'Capital formation, Savings and Economic Progress', *Administration*, Vol. IV (1956), p. 18.
7. For an overview of this phase of Irish Economic policy see M. Daly, *Social and Economic History of Ireland Since 1800* (The Educational Co., Dublin, 1980), Ch. 6.
8. J. A. O'Brien, *The Vanishing Irish* (W. H. Allen, London, 1954), pp. 15-45.
9. G. Fitzgerald, 'Grey, White and Blue', *Administration*, Vol. VI (1958-9), p. 193.
10. G. A. Meagher, 'Planning and National Development', *Christus Rex*, Vol. XVIII (1964), p. 157.
11. R. C. Geary, 'Irish Economic Development since the Treaty', *Studies*, Vol. XL (1951), pp. 399-418.
12. *The European Recovery Programme: Ireland's Long Term Programme, 1949-53*, (Ireland's case for Marshall Aid), p. No. 9198 (Stationery Office, Dublin, 1949), pp. 19-20.
13. For example, foreign trade departments were to be established in Irish Embassies — see *Dáil Debates*, Vol. 110 (1948), cols. 1002-3.
14. J. P. Dunne, 'The I.D.A. — Origins, Structure and Activities', *Administration*, Vol. 20, No. 1 (1972), pp. 17-23.

15. P. Quigley, *A Case Study of Investment Promotion in Ireland - SFADCO*, Paper read to RSA Conference on The Financing of Regional Development in the EEC (Dublin, 1979), (mimeo) 10 pp.
16. F. Rogerson, 'Shannon New Town', *Planning in Ireland* (An Foras Forbartha, Dublin, 1967), pp. 81-85.
17. T. K. Whitaker, *op. cit.* (1956), p. 39.
18. The *first report* of the Capital Advisory Committee (1957) called for a severe cut-back in all areas of non-productive investment.
19. *Economic Development* (Pr. 4803). (Stationery Office, Dublin 1958), 253 pp.
20. *Programme for Economic Expansion*, (Pr. 7239) (Stationery Office, Dublin 1958), 50 pp.
21. See, for example, Pierre Masse 'French Planning', *Administration*, Vol. 10 (1962), 280 pp.
22. *Second Programme for Economic Expansion*, (Pr. 7239), (Stationery Office, Dublin, 1963), Vol. 1, p. 8.
23. *Second Programme, ibid,* and *Third Programme for Economic and Social Development, 1969-72* (Stationery Office, Dublin, 1969), 260 pp.
24. Memo from T. K. Whitaker to Government, 15 December 1958; reprinted in *Economic Development*, p. 228.
25. T. K. Whitaker, 'Merits and Problems of Planning', *Administration*, Vol. 12 (1964), p. 226.
26. S. Lemass, 'The Organisation Behind the Economic Programme', *Administration*, Vol. 9 (1961), p. 8.
27. P. Lynch, 'Economic Planning in Ireland', *Administration*, Vol. 8 (1960), p. 188.
28. Charles Abrams, *Urban Renewal Project in Ireland* (Dublin), U.N. Report TAO/IRE/2 (restricted) April 1961, p. V.
29. *Ibid.*
30. *Ibid.*, p. 25.
31. *Ibid.*, p. 27.
32. *Dáil Debates*, Vol. 196, col. 2187.
33. *Statutory Instrument* No. 211 of 1964.
34. *Dáil Debates*, Vol. 197, 1962, col. 1761.
35. *Ibid.*, col. 1763.
36. *Ibid.*
37. *Ibid.*, col. 1762-3.
38. *Ibid.*, col. 1770.
39. *Ibid.*, Vol. 204, col. 1665.
40. *Dáil Debates*, Vol. 199, 1962, col. 64.
41. *Ibid.*, col. 55.
42. *Ibid.*, col. 122
43. *Ibid.*, Vol. 204, 1963, cols. 1664-5.
44. This section of the Act was directed at solving the persistent problems of urban decay which had prompted the Abrams report. See 'Town Planning from a National Standpoint', *Irish Builder and Eng.*, Vol. CIV (1962), pp. 885-6.
45. *Irish Builder and Engineer*, Vol. C1V (1962), pp. 619-20.
46. *Planning in Ireland* (An Foras Forbartha, Dublin, 1967), 200 pp.
47. P. Delany, 'Town Planning', *Irish Times Annual Review* for 1965 published 3 Jan. 1966, p. 46.
48. 'Can Ireland Avoid England's Planning Mistakes?' *Architect's Journal*, 7 Sept. 1966, p. 595. See also K. I. Nowlan, 'Planning in the Republic of Ireland', *Journal T.P.I.*, Vol. 52, 1965, pp. 54-59.
49. A subsequent report on planning education estimated that an additional 25 planners would be required annually up to 1975. Report of Education and Training Committee on *Education of Planners in Ireland* (An Foras Forbartha 1966), p. 3.
50. Both the approach and the difficulties encountered by Dublin were illustrated in M. Macken, 'City and County Management and Planning Administration', *Journal of T.P.I.*, Vol. 53 (1967), pp. 267-72.
51. P. Delany, 'Planning in Ireland', *Irish Times Annual Review* for 1965, published Jan. 1965, p. 58.
52. B. Clarke, 'The Environment, 1945-1970' in J. Lee, *Ireland 1945-70* (Gill and MacMillan, Dublin,

1979), p. 105.
53. P. O hUiginn, *Address* to Liberty Study Group of ITGWU, 13 March 1966, p. 2.
54. A good idea of the range of work carried out by the Institute in its formative years can be seen in *Planning in Ireland*, and also *Building and Contract Journal*, Vol. 4 nos. 31-32 (Feb. 1968), pp. 25-81.
55. R. Stringer, 'Planning the Towns' in *Planning In Ireland*, p. 68.
56. N. T. Blaney, *Address* at the closing of Seminar, Great Southern Hotel Galway, 17 June 1965, p. 3.
57. J. Eustace and G. Walker, *Galway City Provisional Plan* (Draft) (An Foras Forbartha, Dublin, 1966), 35 pp. + maps.
58. A. Kreditor, 'The Provisional Plan', in *Industrial Development and the Development Plan* (An Foras Forbartha, Dublin, 1967), pp. 27-36.
59. *Address* by N. T. Blaney, opening planning seminar in Malahide 30 Nov. 1965.
60. R. Stringer *op. cit.*, pp. 68-9.
61. R. Stringer, 'The Urban Development Plan: The Next Steps', *Industrial Development and the Development Plan*, p. 41.
62. K. Boland, 'Ireland - the Planning Scene', *Journal. T.P.I.*, Vol. 53 (1967), p. 284.
63. R. Stringer, 'The Importance of Survey for Development Plans', in M. J. Bannon (ed.) *The Application of Geographical Techniques to Physical Planning* (An Foras Forbartha, Dublin, 1971), pp. 34-5.
64. M. O'Brien, 'Planning in Dublin, *Journal T.P.I.*, Vol. 53 (1967), p. 292.
65. Myles Wright, *The Dublin Region: Advisory Regional Plan and Final Report* (Stationery Office, Dublin 1967), 2 vols.
66. M. Macken, 'Dublin and the Future', text of *Address* to Dublin Chamber of Commerce (1971), 9 pp. + maps.
67. N. Lichfield, *City of Dublin: Pilot Scheme for Central Area Redevelopment* (mimeo) 22 pp.
68. *Third Programme*, p. 163.
69. C. O Beolain, 'The Planning Act as it Affects Community and Voluntary Groups', *Rural Ireland* (1967), p. 90.
70. *Address by* An Taoiseach, Mr Lynch, at opening of Dublin Congress of IFHP, 19 May 1969.
71. M. J. Bannon, 'Urbanisation in Ireland: Growth and Regulation', *Promise and Performance: Irish Environmental Policies Analysed* (REPC, Dublin, 1983), p. 281.
72. K. Boland, *Opening Address*, I.F.H.P. Conference, (1969), p. 14.
73. H. S. Perloff and L. Wingo Jr., 'Planning and Development in Metropolitan Affairs', *JAIP*, Vol. 28 (1962), pp. 67-90, deals with the issues involved in establishing an integrated planning system.
74. Paper by C. Rosser, 'From Master Plan to Development Programme: The Case of Calcutta', P. H. G. seminar on *Exporting Planning* (London, March 1980).
75. *The Future of Development Plans* (P.A.G., HMSO, London, 1965), 62 pp.
76. M. J. Bannon *et al.*, *Urbanisation: Problems of Growth and Decay in Dublin*, N.E.S.C. Report No. 55 (Stationery Office Dublin, 1981), 376 pp.
77. See K. I. Nowlan, Ch. 2 above.
78. During the Dáil Debates one of the few consistent objections to the details of the Bill, expressed on both sides of the House, was the proposal to give the Minister for Local Government the power to decide on appeals – see for example: Deputy S. Flanagan, *Dáil Debates*, Vol. 199 (1962), col. 812.
79. As early as 1967 the Opposition unsuccessfully promoted a *Planning Appeals Bill* (No. 19 of 1967) to establish an independent Planning Appeals Board. Two years later the Minister for Local Government introduced the *Local Government (Planning and Development) (No. 2) Bill*, designed to set up

An Bord Achomharc Pleanála, which lapsed with the dissolution of the Dáil. In 1973 the Coalition Government introduced the *Local Government (Planning and Development) Bill*, enacted in 1976, which established An Bord Pleanála, an independent Planning Appeals Tribunal. Under the *Local Government (Planning and Development) Act, 1983*, detailed procedures were established to ensure the appointment of a politically independent Board and a new Board under the Chairmanship of Frank Benson took office in March 1984.

80. P. O'Riagain, 'Planning in the Irish Republic: Rural Planning', *Jour<al T.P.I.*, Vol. 58 (1972), p. 443.
81. *Urban Development Areas Bill*, 1982, (No. 12 of 1982). This bill lapsed with dissolution of the Dáil towards the end of 1982.
82. B. Grist, *Twenty Years of Planning: A Review of the System since 1963* (An Foras Forbartha, Dublin, 1983), 49 pp.
83. See references to S. Lemass and to P. Lynch above.
84. T. J. Barrington, 'National Development and Local Government', *Administration*, Vol. 10 (1962), p. 357.
85. T. K. Whitaker, 'The Civil Servant and Development', *Administration*, Vol. 9 (1961-2), p. 87.
86. *Local Finance and Taxation* (Pr. 2745) (Stationery Office, Dublin, 1972), p. 31.
87. White Paper on *Local Government Re-organisation* (Prl. 1572) (Stationery Office, Dublin, 1971), p. 25.
88. McKinsey & Co., *Strengthening the Local Government Service*(Prl. 2252) (Stationery Office, Dublin, 1972), 75 pp.
89. *Ibid.*, p. 23.
90. *Ibid.*, pp. 38-40.
91. *More Local Government* (Institute of Public Administration, Dublin 1971), 64 pp.
92. *Ibid.*, p. 9.
93. *Local Government Re-organisation*, Discussion document (Department of Local Government, 1973), 9 pp.
94. See, for example, the National Tourist Plans of Bord Fáilte or the various national Industrial Plans of the Industrial Development Authority. The autonomy of such agencies in regard to policy-making was the subject of severe criticism in the *Telesis Report*.
95. T. J. Barrington, 'Social Balance and Social Concern' in *Ireland in the Year 2000* (An Foras Forbartha, Dublin, 1981), p. 6.
96. R. B. Haslam, 'The Local Authority Development Framework – Its Power and Scope', Paper to Irish Planning Institute Conference on the *Role of the Local Authority as a Development Agency*, 1978 (mimeo), p. 6. This issue has been explored at length in Muintir na Tíre's Report *Towards A New Democracy*, (IPA, Dublin, 1985), 87pp.
97. See: *Report of The Committee on The Price of Building Land*, (Pr. 3632) (1973). Various proposals since 1973 have been set out in M. J. Bannon, 'Urban Growth and Urban Land Policy' in P. J. Drudy (ed), *Ireland: Land, Politics and People*, pp. 298-323. See also: F. Convery and A. Schmid, *Policy Aspects of Land Use Planning in Ireland*, Broadsheet No. 22 (ESRI, Dublin, 1983). The 1985 *Report of the Joint Committee on Building Land* (Pl. 3232) did not support the concept of 'designation' as set out in the 1973 report; rather it concentrated on improvements in the supply and pricing of land.
98. *Dáil Debates*, Vol. 197 (1962), col. 1800.
99. M. J. Bannon, 'Urban and Regional Planning in The Republic of Ireland', in M. J. Bannon & J. Hendry, *Planning in Ireland: An Overview*, Occasional Papers in Planning, No. 1 (QUB, 1984), pp. 1-20.
100. C. Abrams, *op. cit.*, p. 25.
101. One of the Deputies to raise the regional issue was Noel Lemass,

Dáil Debates, Vol. 199 (1962), cols. 815-9.
102. In the *Senate Debates* Senator Dooge alluded to the need for public involvement in plan-making at the regional scale – Vol. 56 (1963), col. 1710-1.
103. P. Delany, *op. cit.* (1965), p. 60.
104. Second Programme for Economic Expansion, *op. cit.*, Vol. II, p. 179.
105. *Address* by N. T. Blaney at the opening of National Conference on Regional Planning, Dublin, 19 May 1965, p. 3.
106. These nine regions, whose boundaries were deemed to be provisional, were derived in large measure from the Emergency Regions of 1940 (Statutory Rules & Orders, 1940, No. 266), which in turn was based upon the divisional command structure of the Army during the 1930s.
107. *Address* by N. T. Blaney when introducing Dr N. Lichfield in Limerick, 15 Dec. 1964, p. 3.
108. *Regional Planning*, proceedings of the 1965 National Conference on Regional Planning (An Foras Forbartha, Dublin, 1966), 66 pp.
109. *Ibid.*, p. 12.
110. *Ibid.*, p. 7.
111. D. Herlihy, *ibid.*, p. 40.
112. G. A. Meagher, 'Planning and National Development', *Administration*, Vol. 13 (1965), p. 240.
113. D. Turpin, 'Physical Planning – a Review', *Planning in Ireland, op. cit.*, p. 40.
114. C. H. Murray, 'National and Physical Planning', *Administration*, Vol. 13 (1965), p. 249.
115. *Government Statement*, May 1969.
116. White Paper, *op. cit.*, (note 87 above) p. 29.
117. *Institutional Arrangements for Regional Economic Development* (NESC Report No. 22, 1976), 54 pp.
118. M. V. Cullinane, 'Framework for Regional Development: The Regional Development Organisation Viewpoint', *Administration*, Vol. 24, No. 3 (1976), p. 322.

119. S. Murphy, 'Regional Planning: A Vital Link', R.S.A. 1982 Annual Conference on *Central, Regional and Local Planning: The Case for Integration* (Dublin 1982) (mimeo), p. 8.
120. In *Economic Development* (1958) Whitaker raised the question of selectivity in Industrial location. From the inception of economic expansion in 1958 a vigorous dispute emerged in respect of the optimum pattern of industrial development. The Committee on Industrial Organization, the National Industrial Economic Council and, almost all economists, accepted the essence of Garret FitzGerald's argument for concentration in his paper on 'The Role of Development Centres in the Irish Economy', *Administration*, Vol. 12 (1964), pp. 171-80. Indeed this view was largely accepted in the Government's statement of 31st August 1965. The cause for a wider dispersal of Development opportunities was promoted vigorously by Newman, who argued for a hierarchy of development centres, corresponding to the existing hierarchy of central places. See J. Newman, *New Dimensions in Regional Planning* (An Foras Forbartha, Dublin 1967), 128 pp.
121. C. Buchanan and Partners, *Regional Studies in Ireland* (An Foras Forbartha, Dublin, 1969), Preface, p. 1.
122. N.I.E.C. *Report on Physical Planning* (Stationery Office, Dublin 1969), p. 9.
123. *Government Statement*, 19 May 1969, p. 1.
124. *Government Statement*, 4 May 1972, p. 3.
125. Industrial Development Authority, *Regional Industrial Plans* (Dublin, 1972), 11 vols.
126. With the failure to follow through on either regional planning or the formulation of a national strategy, the planning function within the Department of the Environment

went into decline – a decline symbolized by the virtual absence of a departmental 'Planning and Development' circular during the 1970s.
127. Myles Wright and Partners, *The Dublin Region: Advisory Plan and Final Report*, 2 vols. (Stationery Office, Dublin), 1967.
28. *Transportation in Dublin*, (An Foras Forbartha, Dublin), 1973, 44 pp. Appendices.
129. N. Lichfield and Associates, *Report and Advisory Outline Plan for The Limerick Region*, (Stationery Office, Dublin), 1967, 2 vols.
130. O.E.C.D., *Regional Policies: The Current Outlook*, (O.E.C.D., Paris, 1977).
131. J. Lee *Reflections on Ireland in The EEC*, (I.C.E.M.), Dublin, 1984, p. 22.
132. *Ibid.*, p. 23.
133. M. J. Bannon, 'Urbanisation in Ireland: Growth and Regulation' in Blackwell, J. and F. Convery (eds.), *Promise and Performance: Irish Environmental Policies Analysed*, (R.E.P.C., Dublin, 1983), pp. 261-285.
134. *Eastern Region Settlement Strategy 2011*, (E.R.D.O. 1985), 269 pp. + appendices.
135. The regions covered by these studies include the South East, Midlands, North East, West, East, North West, Donegal (and the South West, unpublished).
136. Such studies include *The Irish Border Areas*, Economic and Social Affairs Committee of the EEC and the *Erne Catchment Study* by Brady-Shipman-Martin, 1980.
137. J. M. Blackwell and H. van der Kamp, *Regional Planning in the 1990s: A Discussion of the Issues*, (An Foras Forbartha, Dublin, 1987, p. ix.
138. B. Grist, *Twenty Years of Planning*, (An Foras Forbartha), Dublin, 1983, p. 17.
139. See for example, Advisory Report on *The Protection of the National Heritage*, (An Foras Forbartha), Dublin, 1969, 92 pp. and the *National Coastline Study*, (An Foras Forbartha), Dublin, 1972, 3 vols.
140. E. McKiernan, *Statutory Requirements and Policies which affect the Planning of Residential Areas*, Discussion Paper No. 5, Planning Division, (An Foras Forbartha), Dublin, 1973, 50 pp.
141. J. M. Blackwell and H. van der Kamp, *op. cit.*, pp. 6-7.
142. J. Lee, *Centralisation and Community in Ireland: Towards a Sense of Place*, (Cork University Press), 1985, p. 95-6.
143. O.E.C.D., *Innovation Policy: Ireland*, (Paris), 1987, pp. 30-35.
144. Hume, J., *Regional Problems of Ireland*, (A Report to the European Parliament), Oct., 1987, 34 pp.
145. T. Boylan, 'Integrated Programmes: A Critical View', in proceedings of Conference on *Integrated Economic Development in Border Areas of the North West*, 1988, (in press).
146. Text of address by Minister for Finance, 26/8/88.
147. For example, see Paul-Henry Gendebien, *Report on A European Regional Planning Scheme*, (European Parliament, 1983), Report No. 1-1026/83.

CHAPTER 6
1. See: *The Europeans and Their Environment in 1986*, (Commission of the EC, Brussels), 1986, 102 pp.
2. Quoted in *The Irish Times*, Nov., 1987.
3. D. Cabot (editor) *The State of the Environment* (An Foras Forbartha, Dublin), 1985, 206 pp.
4. J. Blackwell and F. Convery (eds.) *Promise and Performance: Irish Environmental Policies Analysed*, (Resource and Environmental Policy Centre, Dublin), 1983, 434 pp.
5. F. Convery et. al. (eds), *Managing Dublin Bay* (Resource and Environmental Policy Centre, Dublin), 1987, 191 pp.

6. For outline see: *Your Rights under Community Legislation*, (Brussels), 1988, 28 pp.
7. Brady Shipman Martin, *Grand Canal, Royal Canal, Barrow Navigation: Management and Development Strategy*, (Office of Public Works, Dublin), 1987, 120 pp.
8. Wicklow Mountain Environmental Group, *A Plan for the Wicklow Hills*, (Dublin, 1988), 4 pp.
9. P. Mullally, 'Policy for the Environment: What happened to it?' in J. Blackwell and F. Convery (eds.) *op. cit.*, p. 410.
10. J. Pike, 'The Impact of Policies on Medium Sized Towns' in J. Blackwell and F. Convery, *Managing Our Buildings: Replace or Maintain?* (R.E.P.C., Dublin), 1988, pp. 87-91 in press.
11. *Ibid.*, p. 1.
12. An Taisce, *Urbana – Study of Dublin*, (An Taisce, Dublin), 1982, 32 pp. + appendices.
13. J. Blackwell and F. Convery, (eds.) *Revitalising Dublin: What Works?* Proceedings of the Heritage Trust Millennium Conference Series, (R.E.P.C. and The Heritage Trust, Dublin) 1988. pp. 1-68.
14. For details see: F. H. A. Aalen, 'The Working-Class Housing Movement in Dublin, 1850-1920' in M. J. Bannon (ed.) *The Emergence of Irish Planning, 1880-1920*, Turoe Press, 1985, pp. 131-188.
15. *A Summary of Draft Proposals*, Dublin Metropolitan Streets Commission, 1987, p. 3.
16. M. J. Bannon, et al., *Urbanisation: Problems of Growth and Decay in Dublin*, N.E.S.C. report No. 55 (Stationery Office, Dublin), 1981, 376 pp.
17. Dublin Metropolitan Streets Commission, *op. cit.*, 77 pp. + appendices.
18. J. O'Donnell, 'Transport — The Cork Experience' in J. Blackwell and F. Convery, *Revitalising Dublin*, *op. cit*, pp. 128-133.
19. See P. Kelleghan, 'The Dublin Roads Plan', *ibid.*, pp. 134-145.
20. The conflict between road proposals and the read of existing communities lay behind many of the papers read to the *Dublin Crisis Conference*, Dublin Crisis Conference Committee, (Dublin), 1986, 98 pp. See also 'Developing A Rational Transport Policy' in *Manifesto for The City*, Crisis Conference Committee, 1987, pp. 11-13.
21. *Dublin City Development Plan, Draft*, (Dublin Corporation), 1987, 260 pp.
22. *Consultants' Brief for the Preparation of A National Programme of Community Interest for the Greater Dublin Area*. (Dept. of Finance, Dublin), 1988, 14 pp.
23. M. J. Bannon et al, 1981, *op. cit.*
24. T. Roseingrave, 'The Role of Local Employment Initiatives in assisting Long Term Unemployment in the European Community', paper read to Conference on Local Authorities and Long-Term Unemployment – The European Dimension, (Bradford), 1988, 23 pp.
25. See No. 7 above, especially pp. 69-75.
26. *The Future of the Planning Profession*, Report of Seminar organised by Irish Planning Institute in association with R.T.P.I. (Irish Branch), Dublin, 1988, 56 pp.
27. *Eastern Region Settlement Strategy 2011*, E.R.D.O., Dublin), 1985, 269 pp.
28. *Eastern Region Settlement Strategy 2001* (E.R.D.O. Dublin), 1988, p. 34.
29. *Towards An Inner City Policy for Dublin*, (Society of Chartered Surveyors in The Republic of Ireland, Dublin), 1986, p. 3.

INDEX

A

Aalen, F. H., 148
Abercrombie, Patrick, 14, 15, 26, 57, 103 (p)
   on Belfast, 108
   and Dublin reconstruction, 16, 20, 22, 28
   Dublin Sketch Plan, 51-6, 68, 82
Aberdeen, Lady, 16, 67
Abrams, Charles, 129, 130, 140
Abrams Report, 128-9
Adams, Thomas, 48
advertising, control of, 26, 42
agriculture
   and planning, 137, 152
Allen, L. A., 120
amenity planning, 93-4, 98, 107-8, 160-2
   in Northern Ireland, 108-9
   Special Amenity Areas, 75, 99 100, 136-7
Amiens Street Station, 17
Ancient Monuments Act, 1913, 108
Ancient Monuments Act (NI), 1926, 108
Ancient Monuments Act (NI), 1937, 108-9
Ancient Monuments Protection Act, 1882, 87
Ancient Monuments Protection (Ireland) Act, 1892, 87
AnCO, 164
Anglo-Irish Free Trade Agreement, 126-7
archaeology, 23, 86-8
Architects' Journal, 34, 64, 132
Architectural Association of Ireland, 22, 40, 63
archives protection of, 12
Ardgillan House, Co Dublin, 162
Ards Forest Park, Co Donegal, 160
Areas of Scientific Interest, 101 (p)
Arterial Drainage Act, 1940, 98
Artifex, 47, 67
Ashbee, C. R., and Chettle, G. H., 21
Assessment of the Effects of Certain Public and Private Projects on the Environment, 160
Aston, E. A., 16, 17, 20, 31, 44, 59, 67-8, 122, 103 (p)
Atlas of Ireland (RIA), 62
Australia, 42

B

Ball, Sir Robert, 89
Ballincollig Park, Co Cork, 162
Bangor, Co Down, 117
Bank of Ireland, College Green, 163
Bannon, Michael, 11
Barrington, T. J., 138
Barrow Navigation, 161
Beckett, George F., 22
Belfast, 28, 48, 113-14
   development in, 107-8
   housing in, 110
   Regional Plan, 115-19
Belfast Corporation, 110, 113
Belfast County Borough, 114
Belfast Regional Plan, 113, 115-19
betterment, 137
   under 1934 Act, 46-7, 76-8
birds, protection of, 89, 91, 95
Blaney, Neil T., 129-30
Blue Lagoon, Dublin, 39, 43, 44-5, 67, 94-5
Blythe, Ernest, 16
Board of Works, 20
Booth, Charles, 21
Bord Fáilte, 99, 162
Bord na Mona, 69, 98
Bord Pleanála, An, 73, 137
Bradford, Roy, 115
Brady, J. V., 21-2
Britain, 76, 79
   conservation, 88-9
   New Towns, 53, 117
   planning legislation, 9, 77, 115, 121, 136
   regiional planning, 29
Browne, Dr R. F., 94
Brunker, J. P., 95-6
Buchanan, Colin, and Partners, 144-5
Builder, The, 26, 93
buildings, preservation of, 88-9, 91, 97-8
   in Northern Ireland, 109
Bull Island, 44, 90, 91, 94-5
Burren, Co Clare, 90, 160
Butler, Professor R. M., 34, 91
Butt Bridge, 16

C

Cabra, Dublin, 31, 33
Camblin, G., 106-7

Canavan, Fr J. E., 61
Capital Advisory Committee, 127
Capwell, Cork, 33
Cashel, Rock of, 87
Casino, Marino, 163
Cattle Market, Dublin, 20
Cautionary Guide (Robertson), 48, 68
Childers, Erskine, 59-60, 66
Christchurch Cathedral, 18
circuit courts, 36-7
civic surveys, 13, 20, 21-9, 40, 42, 49
Civics Institute of Ireland, 13, 22, 40, 59, 66, 68, 92
   exhibition 1927, 28-9
   National Planning Conference, 60
Clarke, Brendan, 96
Clontarf, Co Dublin, 31, 69
co-operative housing, 32
Coakley, D. J., 26
Commission of Inquiry into Banking, Currency and Credit, 57
Commission of Inquiry into the Resources and Industries of Ireland, 36
Commission on Vocational Organisation, 62
Committee on Public Works, 1935, 69
community groups, 11, 140, 158
   and road development, 166
   and urban renewal, 167-71, 173
compensation, 83
   under 1934 act, 46-7
   under 1934 Act, 76, 78
   under 1929 Bill, 42, 43
   in Northern Ireland, 114
compulsory acquisition, 74-5
conservation, 11, 86-102
   in Northern Ireland, 108-9
Conservation Areas, Northern Ireland, 109
Conservation Orders, 99, 100
Cork, 164
   Civic Survey of, 26-8
   development plan, 155
   housing, 33, 166
   roads, 166
   town planning report, 50-51
Cork Corporation, 162, 166, 168
Cork County Council, 162
Cork Exhibition, 1907, 67
Cork Region, 26-7, 50 (p)
Corkagh Demesne, Co Dublin, 162
Cosgrave, W. T., 18, 20, 31
County Councils, 36, 60, 75-6

County Councils (NI), 14
County Managers, 38, 71-2, 139
Courts of Justice Bill, 35-6
Cowan, P. C., 31, 32
Craig, Sir James, 117
Craig, William, 120
Craigavon, 117
Cronin, D., 70
Crumlin, Dublin, 31
Cuffe, L. P., 97-8
Cullinane, V., 143
Curtin, V., 141
Custom House, Dublin, 17-18, 163
Custom House Docks Development Authority, 168-70

D

Damer House, Roscrea, 164
Davidge, W. R., 14, 112
Davis, Thomas, 89
de Valera, Eamon, 61, 64, 70
Deane, Thomas Newenham, 87
decentralisation, 35-6, 157
Delany, P., 132, 140
derelict sites, 15, 44
developers, 72, 114-15
   betterment payments, 77-8
development
   under 1963 Act, 137-8, 140, 148-50
   control of, 72
   in Northern Ireland, 119-20
Development, Ministry of (NI), 120
Development Plan, 1980, 83
Development Plans, 72-3, 99-100, 136
   under 1963 Act, 131-2, 132-5
   importance of, 154-5
devolution, 35-6, 157
Dickinson, P. L., 34
Dillon, James, 47, 131
District Planning Schemes, 69
Donadea Forest Park, Co Kildare, 160
Donald, R. B., 48
Doneraile Forest Park, Co Cork, 160
Douglas Street, Cork, 164
Drumcondra, Dublin, 31, 33
Dublin, 9, 11-12, 20, 83, 150
   cathedral proposed, 18, 51
   Civic Survey of, 22-6, 24 (p)
   development plans, 98, 134, 155, 166
   housing, 13-14, 31-4, 165-6
   migration to, 25, 32, 57, 124, 148
   planning scheme, 56, 77, 82-5
   population forecasts, 52-3

redevelopment of, 14-21
rehabilitation, 162-63
satellite development, 54-6
Sketch Plan, 51-7, 68, 81 (p), 82
transport in, 150, 163, 166
Dublin, Co, 38-9, 134, 141
Dublin Bill, 1929, 43
Dublin Castle, 163
Dublin Chamber of Commerce, 60
Dublin Chronicle, 43
Dublin Citizens' Housing League, 67
Dublin City Development Plan, 1987, 166
Dublin Civic Exhibition, 1927, 28-9, 64
Dublin Civic Survey, 22-6, 92
Dublin Civic Weeks, 28, 68
Dublin Corporation, 15-16, 20, 39, 83, 95
  Development Plan, 72-3, 134
  failed county acquisition, 75-6
  housing, 54, 165-6
  Housing Committee, 32
  planning scheme, 83-5
  peripheral expansion, 56 (p)
  Reconstruction, 15-21
Dublin County Council, 151 (p), 162
Dublin Draft Review, 73
Dublin Housing Inquiry, 54, 67
Dublin Metropolitan Corporation proposed, 54-5
Dublin Metropolitan Streets Commission, 166
Dublin Naturalists Field Club, 95
Dublin Reconstruction (Emergency Provisions) Acts, 15
Dublin Rotary Club, 22
Dublin Summer School of Civics, 21
Dublin Town Planning Commission proposed, 21-2
Dublin Town Planning Competition, 21
Duffy, George Gavan, 54, 57
Dun Laoghaire, Co Dublin, 39, 49, 68
Dundrum, Dublin, 55

E

Easter Rising, 1916, 15
Eastern Region Settlement Strategy, 2011, 152, 171
Eastern Region Settlement Strategy to 2001, 171, 172 (p)
ecology, 71, 98
Economic Consultants Ltd., 144-5
economic development, 10, 125-6
  and conservation, 96-7
  and planning, 10, 70, 127-8
Economic Development (Whitaker), 97, 127
Economic Planning Committee, 70
economic war, 83
Edinburgh, 28
education
  in Dublin Civic Survey, 25
Electricity Supply Board, 97-8, 163-4
Emergence of Irish Planning, 1880-1920, The, 11-12, 14
emigration, 123-4, 127
energy crisis, 102
Engineering and Scientific Association of Ireland, 16
engineers
  and town planning, 65-6
Environment Department of (NI), 120
Environment, Department of the, 148, 159
Environment Parks, 160
Environmental Awareness Bureau, 160
environmental conservation, 10, 34, 86-102, 158-62
  before 1920, 86-90
  1920-45, 90-93
  1960-70, 96-102
European Architectural Heritage Year, 102
European Conservation Year, 102
European Economic Community, 102, 127, 157, 158, 160
  Ireland as undeveloped region, 148, 151-2
  planning legislation, 173
  pollution directives, 163
  urban renewal, 168
European Environmental Bureau, 160
European Regional Development Fund, 151-2, 167
European Year of the Environment, 160

F

Faulkner, Brian, 115, 120
Finance, Department of, 152
Fine Arts Commission, 34
Finglas, Co Dublin, 54
First Programme for Economic Expansion, 127
Fitzgerald, Desmond, 66
Fitzwilliam Street, Dublin, 97-8, 164
flora and fauna, conservation of, 89-90, 91

Flora of the County Wicklow (Brunker), 95-6
Foras Forbartha, An, 98, 100, 102, 132-3, 144-5, 159, 173
Foras Tionscail, An, 126
Forbes, Jean, 115
forest parks, 160
Four Courts, 17-18
free trade, 13

G
Galway, 51, 133
  town planning report, 49-50
Game Preservation Act, 91
garden cities, 29, 33, 61
Geddes, Patrick, 13, 14, 21, 23, 31, 64, 67
General Post Office, 18
Georgian Society, 88, 97
Germany, 29
Gibney, Frank, 51, 59, 61-2, 68-9, 103 (p)
Glasnevin, Dublin, 33
Glen River Park, Cork, 162
Glenavy Committee, 35-6
Glenbeigh, Co Donegal, 160
Gloucester Street, Dublin, 45 (p)
Goethe Institute, 170
Gogarty, Oliver St John, 38, 42
Government Buildings, Merrion Street, 20
Government of Ireland Act, 1920, 115
Government Statement, 1972, 145
Grand Canal, Dublin, 98, 161
Greater Dublin Commission of Inquiry, 38
Greater Dublin Council
  proposed, 38, 44
Greater Dublin Reconstruction Movement, 13, 20, 67
  proposals of, 16-21
Greater London Plan, 1944, 53
green belts, 50-51, 53, 55
Green Property Co., 98
Griffith Avenue, Dublin, 33

H
Hackett, Dr Felix, 94
Hayes, Rev J. M., 64
Healy, Tim, 16
Hendry, John, 11
Heritage Council
  proposed, 102
Heritage Trust, 159

Hernon, P. J., 49
Hill, H., 65
Hill, D. A. (Belfast), 107
Hillery, P. J., 159
Hogan, R., 66
Horner, Arnold,, 11
housing
  approved density, 33
  Cork, 28, 166
  Dublin, 25, 54, 165-6
  in Northern Ireland, 109-11
  number of houses built, 32-3, 43, 54, 165-6
  problems, 13-14, 29-35
Housing Acts, 32, 75, 84
Housing and Planning, International Federation of, 132
Housing and Town Planning Association, 21
Housing (Building Facilities) Act, 1924, 32
Housing Conference, 1903, 29, 31
Housing Inquiry, 1913, 21, 31
Housing (Miscellaneous Provisions) Act, 1931, 43-4
Housing (Miscellaneous Provisions) and Rent Restriction (Amendment) Act (NI), 1956, 111
Housing of the Working Classes Act, 1890, 109
Howth, Co Dublin, 39
Hume Street, Dublin, 98
hygiene
  in Dublin Civic Survey, 25

I
ILAC Centre, 84
Industrial Development Association, 36
Industrial Development Authority, 145
Industrial Grants Act, 1956, 126
inner cities, 11, 167 (p)
  and communities, 170-1
  Dublin, 134
  rehabilitation opposed, 31
  see also urban renewal
Institute of Engineers, 65
Institute of Public Administration, 139
Interim Development Act (NI), 1944, 114-15
International Labour Organisation, 63
International Town Planning Conference, 40
Ireland's Long Term Recovery Programme,

1949-53, 126
Irish Architectural Archive, 12
Irish Association, 107
Irish Builder and Engineer, 15, 20, 67
   on 1934 Act, 47
   on 1929 Bill, 42
   on Blue Lagoon, 44
   on Cork Civic Survey, 28
   on Dublin Civic Survey, 22, 26
   and Dublin reconstruction, 20
   on lack of planning, 34, 40
   on local government bill, 38-9, 39
   on regionalism, 58, 59
Irish Church Act, 1869, 87
Irish Georgian Society, 97
Irish Housing Act, 1919, 33
Irish National Survey, 62
Irish Naturalists' Journal, 96
Irish Planning Institute, 170
Irish Proportional Representation Society, 67
Irish Sanctuary, An (Kennedy), 95
Irish Society for the Protection of Birds, 95
Irish Times, The 67-8, 97
Irish Tourist Board, 60, 94, 95, 99, 162
Irish Trades Union Congress, 60
Irish Wildbird Conservancy, 98
Iveagh Trust, 164

J
Johnson, Thomas, 14, 36, 40, 47, 92
   town planning Bill, 40-42
Joint Committee of Architects, Surveyors and Engineers, 65-6, 68

K
Kanturk Castle, Co Cork, 89, 94
Kelly, Sydney A., 26, 68, 82
   Dublin Sketch Plan, 51-6
Kennedy, Fr P. G., 91, 95
Kerry Naturalist, 89
Killarney, Lakes of, 90
Killester, Dublin, 33, 67
Killykeen Forest Park, Co Cavan, 160
Kreditor, A., 133

L
Labour Party, 14, 36, 40
Land Commission, 36
land development, 74-5
   under 1963 Act, 137-8, 140
   lack of planning controls, 77

national parks, 162
urban spread, 29
Land Development Values (Compensation) Act (NI), 1965, 115
Lee, J. 152
legislation
   see planning law
Leinster House, Dublin, 19, 20
Leisure (Moffett), 63
Lemass, Sean, 59, 63, 67, 70, 122, 128, 150
   on town planning, 39
Leslie, Sir Shane, 93-4
Letterfrack, Co Galway, 160
Leydon, John, 58, 127
Lichfield, Nathaniel, 134, 141, 150
Limerick, 50, 51
Limerick, Co, 143
   development study, 141, 142 (p)
local government
   decline of, 138-40
   need for reform, 10, 16, 38-9
   planning powers, 72-3
   white paper on, 139, 143
Local Government, Department of, 75, 129
   and civic surveys, 42
   memo on planning, 64-5
   and planning, 39, 56, 66-7, 145, 148
   planning appeals, 132, 137
   planning inertia, 70, 73-4, 122
   reports of, 82
   town planning legislation, 34-5
Local Government, Minister of, 49, 141
Local Government Bill, 1924, 36
Local Government Board, 21, 31
   housing regulations, 33
   rebuilding loans, 15
Local Government (Dublin) Bill, 38-40
Local Government (Dublin) Tribunal, 54
Local Government (Planning and Development) Act, 1963, 71-3, 79, 85, 122-3, 129-31
   betterment under, 77-8
   conservation under, 92, 99-100
   context of, 136-8
   development plans, 72-3, 84
   implementation of, 132-5
   principal provisions, 131-2
   Section 22, 141
   Section 26, 77
   Section 42, 75

Section 77, 132, 137-8
Local Government (Planning and Development) Act, 1976, 73, 102
Local Government Reorganisation, 139, 143
Local Government (Water Pollution) Act, 1977, 102
Local Loans Fund, 48
London County Council, 29
Longford County Council, 75
Loop Line Bridge, 17
Lucan, Co Dublin, 54
Lynch, Jack, 128, 135
Lyons, F. S. L., 96

M
Macalister, R. A. S., 88
MacBride, Sean, 94
McCabe, J. F., 21, 34
McCarron, E. P., 34-5
McCrory Commission, 120
McKenna, L., 31
Magennis, Prof William, 38
Malahide, Co Dublin, 54, 162
Managing Dublin Bay, 159
Mansion House, Dublin, 16
manufacturing industry, 147 (p)
Marino, Co Dublin, 32-3
Marlay Park, Co Dublin, 162
Marshall Aid, 126
Matthew, Sir Robert, 113, 115-19
Matthew Report, 105, 113
Mawhinney, Ken, 11
Mayo County Council, 75
Mears, Frank, 16, 18,, 33, 67
Meighan, P. J., 44
Merrion Square, Dublin, 163-4
migration, 57, 123
 to Dublin, 25, 32, 124, 148
Miller, Mervyn, 15
Mitchell, G. F., 94
Moffett, Noel, 63
Monnet, Jean, 127
monuments, protection of, 23, 87, 91
 in Northern Ireland, 108-9
Moran, James, 18-19
Morris, William, 88
mortality rates, 28
Muintir na Tíre, 60, 64
Mulcahy, Richard, 40, 43
Mullaly, Philip, 162
municipal reform
 called for, 16-17

Murie, Alan, 105, 113, 119
Murphy, E., 65
Murphy, Sean, 143
Murray, C. H., 143

N
Nagraiguebeg Lough, Co Galway, 90
National Atlas, 62
National Development Strategy, 145-7
National Economic and Social Council, 165, 168
National Economic Development Commission proposed, 57-8
National Industrial Economic Council, 145
National Institute for Physical Planning and Construction Research. *see* Foras Forbartha, An
National Monuments Act, 1930, 91
National Monuments Bill, 43
National Museum, 88
National Parks, 93-4, 160-62
National Planning Conference, 1942, 10, 59-65, 68, 104 (p)
National Planning Exhibition, 1944, 59, 62-4, 122
National Sports Centre, 170
National Trust, 89, 90
National Trust for Ireland. *see* Taisce, An
National Vocational Assembly proposed, 62-3
nature reserves, 90
New Industries Development Acts, 112
New Towns, 53, 117
Newbridge Demesne, Co Dublin, 162
Newgrange, 88
Newtownards, Co Down, 117
Nomad, 67
North Coastal Area, 44
North Earl Street, 15
Northern Ireland
 development proposals, 116 (p)
 planning authorities, 114
 planning in, 9, 11, 14, 105-21
  background, 106-8
  1960s, 115-20
  1940s-50s, 111-15
  white paper on, 119-20
 planning legislation, 44
Northern Ireland Housing Executive, 111

Northern Ireland Housing Trust, 111
Nowlan, Kevin, 11, 47, 56
Nugent, Sir Roland, 109

O
O'Brien, Michael, 65, 66
O'Connell Street, 15, 17, 26, 44
O'Dalaigh, Cearbhall, 94
O'Gorman, J., 65
Oireachtas, buildings for, 18-19, 20
O'Neill, Captain Terence, 115, 120
O'Neill, William Purcell, 16
open space provision, 25, 28, 32, 162
Organisation for Economic Cooperation and Development, 157
O'Rourke, Horace, 14, 15-16, 54
   Dublin Civic Survey, 22-5
   on zoning control, 34
O'Ruadhain, Michael, 96
O'Toole, D., 49-50
Outline Advisory Plans (NI), 114

P
parks, 93-4
Parliament House, College Green, 18
Pearse, P. H., 35
pedestrianisation, 166
Pembroke Ward, Dublin, 39
Phoenix Park, Dublin, 23, 25
planning. *see also* town planning
   community involvement, 158
   and economic development, 127-8
   government policy, 126-7, 144-5, 148
   government role, 41-3, 46-7, 64-5
   lack of regional dimension, 140-44
   national policy develops, 57-65
   pioneers of, 67-9
   in 1980s, 158-73
   socio-economic context of, 123-6
   status of, 65-7
   underachievement, 135-6
Planning Advisory Board (NI), 109-10, 110-11, 112-14, 119, 120
Planning and Development Officers, 139
Planning and Housing Act (NI), 1931, 109, 112
Planning and Public Works, Department of proposed, 66
planning appeals, 131, 132, 137
Planning Authorities, 80 (p)
   under 1934 Act, 72
   under 1963 Act, 72-3, 136-8
Planning commission (NI), 112-14
Planning districts
   under 1934 act, 46-7
Planning for Amenity and Tourism, 100
Planning History Group, 136
Planning in Ireland, 132
Planning Institute, 60
planning law, 9-10, 41-3. *see also* individual Acts
Planning (NI) Order, 1972, 121
Planning Order (NI), 1972, 109
planning profession, 10
planning regions, 37 (p), 156 (p)
planning schemes, 69, 73-4, 74-5
   and betterment, 76-7
   Dublin, 82-5
   and the environment, 92
pollution, fears of, 96
population, patterns of, 123-4, 126 (t), 139, 144 (t)
Powerscourt House, Co Wicklow, 94
Praeger, Robert Lloyd, 91, 94
Preliminary Report on Reconstruction and Planning, 112
preservation orders, 91
Problems of Water and Sewerage, 112-13
Promise and Performance, 159
Protection of the National Heritage, The, 100, 102
protectionism, 13, 125, 126
public utility societies, 32
Public Works, Commissioners of, 87, 108
Public Works, Office of, 91, 161

R
Railway Commission, 20-1
railway system, Dublin, 17, 20-1
Rathgar, Dublin, 39
Rathmines, Dublin, 39
recreation
   in Dublin Civic Survey, 23, 25
Regional Commissioners, 58-9
Regional Development, Ministry of proposed, 148, 149
Regional Development Organisations, 143, 145, 150, 173
regional planning, 35-40
   under 1934 Act, 75-6
   decline of, 150-54
   need for national policy, 58-9
   neglect of, 136-57

Regional Strategies, 153 (p)
rehabilitation, 11
   grants scheme, 164
Relief Works Bill, 1940, 59
Resource and Environmental Policy Centre, UCD, 159-60
Road Communications in Northern Ireland, 113
road plans, 83, 166
   in Northern Ireland, 117-18
Roantree, 21
Robertson, Manning, 14, 29, 40, 46, 66, 69, 91, 122, 103 (p)
   on 1934 Act, 48-9
   and 1929 Bill, 42
   career of, 68
   Cork planning report, 50-51
   on Dublin Civic Survey, 26
   Dublin Sketch Plan, 51-6
   National Planning Conference, 61, 62-3
   need for national survey, 59
   Town Planning Advisor, 49
Roscrea Heritage Centre, 164
Rosse, Earl of, 94
Rosser, C., 136
Rossmore Forest Park, Co Monaghan, 160
Rostow, W. W., 96
Royal Canal, 161
Royal Dublin Society, 19, 48
Royal Hospital, Kilmainham, 18-19, 163
Royal Institute of the Architects of Ireland, 40, 48, 65, 68, 92, 97-8
Royal Irish Academy, 15, 23, 62, 87-8, 94
Royal Society for the Protection of Birds, 89
Royal Society of Antiquaries of Ireland, 23, 87-8
Royal Town Planning Institute, 114
Royal Zoological Society of Ireland, 89
Ruthen, C. T., 33, 57
Ruttledge, P. J., 59

S
Sandymount Strand, 98
Scott, Michael, 59, 65
Scott, Professor W. A., 15
Sean MacDermott Street, Dublin, 15
Second Programme for Economic Expansion, 145

'Set Aside Directive', 160
Shankill, Co Dublin, 55
Shanley, J. M., 64
Shannon Free Airport Development Company, 127, 130
Shannon Scheme, 28, 36
Sherlock, Mr, 47-8
Simms, H. G., 66
Single European Market, 157
Slieve Bloom mountains, 160
slum clearance, 43-4
   in Northern Ireland, 109-10, 111
Smyllie, R. M., 67-8
social employment schemes, 164
Society for the Preservation of Nature Reserves, 89-90
Society for the Protection of Ancient Buildings, 88-9, 90
spatial planning, 154, 155-6
Special Amenity Areas, 75, 99, 100, 136-7
State of the Environment (Foras Forbartha), 159
Stelfox, A. W., 91
street widening, 15
Strengthening the Local Government Service, 139
Stringer, R., 133-4
Study of Amenity Planning Issues in Dublin and Dun Laoghaire (An Taisce), 98
suburbanisation, 25, 54, 163
   in Belfast, 113
   in Dublin Sketch Plan, 51
   problems of, 29-32
Suirbhearacht Eireann, 62, 69
Sunday Times, 44
Sutton, Co Dublin, 39, 43
Swords, Co Dublin, 54

T
Tailors' Guild Hall, Dublin, 164
Taisce, An, 91, 94, 98, 99, 163
Tallaght, Co Dublin, 54
Temple Hill, Dun Laoghaire, 68
Tourism, 95, 99, 162
Town and Country Planning, Ministry of (UK), 79
Town and Country Planning Acts (UK), 109, 115, 131, 136
Town and Regional Planning Act, 1934, 11, 44-9, 61, 65, 68, 71-78, 128
   advisory reports, 49-51
   conservation under, 91-3

Dublin region suggestion, 46, 47-8
implementation of, 74-5, 79, 83
repealed, 85
Section 20, 76
Section 21, 75-6
Section 72, 77
Town and Regional Planning Act, 1939, 11, 61, 128
changes under, 78-9
implementation of, 79, 83
repealed, 85
Town in Ulster, The 106-7
town planning, 9
under acts, 71-5
Bill 1928, 40-44
complaints of lack of, 36, 38-40.
government role, 57-8, 79
lack of legislation, 33-5
professional training, 65-6
see also civic surveys
Town Planning Bill, 1929, 40-44
Town Planning in Ireland (Robertson and Wilshere), 63
Town Planning in Practice (Unwin), 21
Town Planning Institute, 85, 112, 132
Irish branch, 66, 68, 128
Town Planning Review, 105
Town Planning (Robertson), 63
traffic. *see* transport
Tralee Urban District Council, 75
tramway system, 17, 25, 29
transport, 166
in Cork, 28
in Dublin, 26, 83, 150, 163
in Northern Ireland, 113, 117-18
urban, 166
Tree Preservation Orders, 99, 100
Trinity College, Dublin, 66
Turf Development Act, 1946, 98
Turners Cross, Cork, 33
Turpin, D., 141-2
Tymon Demesne, Co Dublin, 162

U
Ulster Architectural Heritage Society, 109
Undeveloped Areas Act, 1952, 126
unemployment, 13, 58, 124
United nations, 128-9, 132-3, 144

Special Fund, 100
United States of America, 34, 48, 130, 136
University College, Dublin, 28, 66, 159, 170
Unwin, Raymond, 14, 15, 21, 48
and 1934 act, 46
on suburbanisation, 31
Urban Development Commissions proposed, 138
Urban Renaissance Year, 102
urban renewal, 11, 158, 162-71
Dublin, 134
report on, 128-9
Urban Renewal Act, 1986, 168
Urban Renewal Week, 170
Urban Structure, 153 (p)
Urbana – City of Dublin (An Taisce), 163
urbanisation, 35, 124, 152, 158
problems, 29-35, 165-6
see also urban renewal
Urbanisation: Problems of Growth and Decay in Dublin (NESC), 165
Uthwatt Report, 76

V
valuation, 77
voluntary groups, 140

W
Walters, Tudor, 33
water pollution, 96, 163
Waterford, 51, 68-9, 164, 166
Welwyn Garden City, 29
Western Development Board proposed, 143
Wexford, Co, 90
Whitaker, T. K., 97, 127, 128, 139
Wicklow, Co, 90
Wicklow Way, 161
Wiener, R, 115
Wild Birds Protection Act, 1930, 91
Wildlife Act, 1976, 102
wildlife protection, 43
Wilshere, R. S., 63, 107-8, 109, 110
Wilson, Prof Tom, 115
Wood Quay, Dublin, 98
Wright, Myles, 134, 141, 148, 150